T0034807

TECHNOFEUDALISM

Also by Yanis Varoufakis

Another Now: A Novel

Talking to My Daughter About the Economy: or,
How Capitalism Works—and How It Fails

Adults in the Room: My Battle with the
European and American Deep Establishment

And the Weak Suffer What They Must?:
Europe's Crisis and America's Economic Future

The Global Minotaur: America,
Europe and the Future of the Global Economy

TECHNO
FEUDALISM
WHAT KILLED
CAPITALISM
YANIS
VAROUFAKIS

▲ MELVILLE HOUSE · BROOKLYN · LONDON

Technofeudalism : What Killed Capitalism

First published in 2023 by The Bodley Head
Copyright © 2023 by Yanis Varoufakis
All rights reserved
First Melville House Printing: January 2024

Melville House Publishing
46 John Street
Brooklyn, NY 11201
and
Melville House UK
Suite 2000
16/18 Woodford Road
London E7 0HA

mhpbooks.com
@melvillehouse

ISBN: 978-1-68589-124-4
ISBN: 978-1-68589-123-7 (eBook)

Library of Congress Control Number: 2023946923

Designed by Beste M. Doğan

Printed in the United States of America

1 3 5 7 9 10 8 6 4 2

A catalog record for this book is available
from the Library of Congress

For Dad
who showed me how everything that matters
is pregnant with its opposite

CONTENTS

Preface

Some years ago, I decided to write a brief history of capitalism. To temper the task's enormity, and force myself to focus on what capitalism boils down to, I decided to pretend I was narrating capitalism's story to my then twelve-year-old daughter. So, without seeking Xenia's permission (something she will never let me forget!), I began writing the book in the form of a long letter to her. Taking care to use no jargon (not even the word capitalism!), I kept reminding myself that whether or not my narrative made sense to a youngster was a litmus test of my own grasp of capitalism's essence. The result was a slim volume entitled *Talking to My Daughter: Talking to My Daughter About Capitalism*. It took as its starting point an apparently simple question of hers: why is there so much inequality?

Even before it was published in 2017, I was feeling uneasy. Between finishing the manuscript and holding the published book in my hands, it felt as if it were the 1840s and I was about to publish a book on feudalism; or, even worse, like waiting for a book on Soviet central planning to see the light of day in late 1989. Belatedly, that is.

In the years after it was published, first in Greek, later in English, my weird hypothesis that capitalism was on the way out (and not merely undergoing one of its many impressive metamorphoses) gathered strength. During the pandemic, it became a conviction, which became an urge to explain my thinking in a book if for no other reason than to give friends and foes outraged by my theory a chance to disparage it properly having perused it in full.

So, what is my hypothesis? It is that capitalism is now dead, in the sense that its dynamics no longer govern our economies. In that role it has been replaced by something fundamentally different, which I call technofeudalism. At the heart of my thesis is an irony that may sound confusing at first but which I hope to show makes perfect sense: the thing that has killed capitalism is . . . capital itself. Not capital as we have known it since the dawn of the industrial era, but a new form of capital, a mutation of it that has arisen in the last two decades, so much more powerful than its predecessor that like a stupid, overzealous virus it has killed off its host. What caused this to happen? Two main developments: the privatisation of the internet by America's and China's Big Tech. And the manner in which Western governments and central banks responded to the 2008 great financial crisis.

Before saying a little more on this, I must emphasise that this is not a book about what technology *will* do to us. It is not about AI-chatbots that will take over our jobs, autonomous robots that will threaten our lives, or Mark Zuckerberg's ill-conceived metaverse. No, this book is about what has *already* been done to capitalism, and therefore to us, by the screen-based, cloud-linked devices we all use, our boring laptop and our smartphone, in conjunction with the way central banks and governments have been acting since 2008. The historic mutation of capital that I am highlighting has already happened but, caught up in our pressing dramas, from debt worries and a pandemic to wars and the climate emergency, we have barely noticed. It is high time we paid attention!

If we do pay attention, it is not hard to see that capital's mutation into what I call *cloud capital* has demolished capitalism's two pillars: markets and profits. Of course, markets and profits remain ubiquitous – indeed, markets and profits were ubiquitous under feudalism too – they just aren't running the show any more. What has happened over the last two decades is that profit and markets have been evicted from the epicentre of our economic and social system, pushed out to its margins, and replaced. With what? Markets, the medium of capitalism, have been replaced by digital trading platforms which look like, but are not, markets, and are better understood as fiefdoms. And profit, the engine of capitalism, has been replaced with its feudal predecessor: rent. Specifically, it is a form of rent that must be paid for access to those platforms and to the cloud more broadly. I call it *cloud rent*.

As a result, real power today resides not with the owners of traditional capital, such as machinery, buildings, railway and phone networks, industrial robots. They continue to extract profits from workers, from waged labour, but they are not in charge as they once were. As we shall see, they have become vassals in relation to a new class of feudal overlord, the owners of cloud capital. As for the rest of us, we have returned to our former status as serfs, contributing to the wealth and power of the new ruling class with our unpaid labour – in addition to the waged labour we perform, when we get the chance.

Does all this matter to the way we live and experience our lives? It certainly does. As I'll show in Chapters 5, 6 and 7, recognising that our world has become technofeudal helps us dissolve puzzles great and small: from the elusive green energy revolution and Elon Musk's decision to buy Twitter to the New Cold War between the USA and China and how the war in Ukraine is threatening the dollar's reign; from the death of the liberal individual and the impossibility of social democracy to the false promise of crypto and the burning question of how we may recover our autonomy, perhaps our freedom too.

By late 2021, armed with these convictions, and egged on by a pandemic that strengthened them, the die had been cast: I would sit down and write a brief introduction to technofeudalism – the far, far uglier social reality that has superseded capitalism. One question remained: whom to address it to? Without much thought, I decided to address it to the person who had introduced me to capitalism at a ridiculously young age – and who, like his grand-daughter, once asked me an apparently simple question that shapes almost every page of this book. My father.

For the impatient reader, a word of warning: my description of technofeudalism does not come until Chapter 3. And for my description to make sense, I need first to recount capitalism's astounding metamorphoses over the preceding decades: this is Chapter 2. The beginning of the book, meanwhile, is not about technofeudalism at all. Chapter 1 tells the story of how my father, with the help of some metal fragments and Hesiod's poetry, introduced my six-year-old self to technology's chequered relationship with humanity and, ultimately, to capitalism's essence. It presents the guiding principles on which all of the thinking that follows is based, and it concludes with that seemingly simple question Father put to me in 1993. The rest of the book takes the form of a letter addressed to him. It is my attempt to answer his killer question.

TECHNO
FEUDALISM

I
HESIOD'S LAMENT

My father was the only leftie I know who failed to understand why calling Maggie Thatcher 'The Iron Lady' was somehow derogatory. And I must have been the only child raised to believe that gold was iron's poorer cousin.

My catechism in iron's magical qualities began in the winter of 1966, which I recall as a bitterly cold one. In their haste to leave behind the cramped rented apartment where we were staying while our home in Paleo Phaliro, a coastal Athenian suburb, was being rebuilt, my parents moved us back into the not-quite-completed house in the midst of winter, before any central heating had been installed. Thankfully, Dad had insisted that our new living room feature a decent red-brick fireplace. It was there, in front of its warm glow, that over the course of several winter nights he introduced me, one at a time, to his friends, as he called them.

FATHER'S FRIENDS

His friends arrived in a large grey sack that he brought home one evening from the 'factory', the steel plant in Eleusis where he would work as a chemical engineer for six decades. They were mightily unimpressive. Some looked like shapeless rocks, lumps of ore as I was to learn later. Others were equally uninspiring rods and metal plates of various shapes. If it weren't for the loving manner in which he laid out each one of them on a folded white, hand-embroidered tablecloth in front of the fireplace, I would never have thought of them as special.

Tin was the first friend he introduced me to. After giving me a piece to hold, to feel its softness, he placed it in an iron bowl which he then rested on the roaring fire. As the tin began to melt and the metallic liquid filled up the bowl, Dad's eyes lit up. 'All that is solid melts into liquid and, then, given enough heat, turns into steam. Even metals!' Once he was confident I had appreciated the great transition from solid to liquid state, together we poured the liquid tin into a mould, immersed it in water to cool it down, and then broke the mould open so that I could, once again, take the tin in my hands to ascertain that our friend was back to normal – that it had been returned to its initial state.

The following night we experimented with another friend: a longish rod made of bronze. This time there was no great transition, as bronze's melting temperature is at least five times that of tin. Still, the rod began to glow a brilliant orangey red and Dad showed me how to give whatever shape I wanted to its hot tip with the help of a small steel hammer. Once I'd had enough, we immersed it in cold water also to return it, cool and unchanged, to its original, malleable, state.

On the third night, Dad seemed more excited than ever. He was about to introduce me to his best friend, iron. To add tension to the moment, he removed his gold wedding ring from his finger and showed it to me. 'See how gold gleams?' he said. 'Humans have always fallen for this metal because of its looks. What they don't realise is that it is just that: flashy – not special.' If I wanted, he would be happy to demonstrate that when gold is heated up and then immersed in water to cool it down again, it returns, like tin and bronze, to its prior state. Glad that I did not insist on a demonstration, he moved on to his favourite part.

Holding up a piece of iron ore and gazing at the insipid lump like Hamlet contemplating Yorick's skull, Dad pronounced: 'Now, if you want a truly magical substance, this is it: iron. The Wizard of Materials.' And then he proceeded to back up his claim by subjecting an iron rod to the same torture we had inflicted on the bronze rod the previous night, but with a couple of crucial differences.

Before heating up the iron, I was given a chance to hammer at its tip, to ascertain that it was soft and almost as malleable as bronze. Once in the fireplace, a small bellows helped us fan the flames until the iron's glow had turned the dimly lit living room scarlet. We took the rod out of the fireplace and, with the little hammer, shaped it into something that, in my boyish eyes, looked like a sword. Lowering it into the cold water made the iron hiss as if in triumph. 'Poor Polyphemus!' Father remarked mysteriously.

'Heat it up again,' he said. I put the rod back into the fire. 'This time immerse it in the water *before* it glows.' Excited by the hissing iron, I was glad that we repeated the 'quenching' process, as metallurgists call it, three or four times. Before I got a chance properly to admire my new sword, Dad announced that the moment of truth had arrived. 'Pick up the hammer and deliver an almighty strike on the sword's tip,' he instructed.

'But I don't want to ruin it,' I protested.

'Go on, do it, you'll see. Don't spare your strength!'

I didn't. The hammer struck the sword's tip and bounced right back. I struck it again and again. It made no difference. My sword was impervious to the blows. Hardened.

A CHILD'S INTRODUCTION TO HISTORICAL MATERIALISM

Father could not contain himself. What I had witnessed, he explained, was not a mere great transition – as with the tin that melted – but a great transformation. True, copper had facilitated our deliverance from prehistory: its ability to alloy with arsenic and tin to make the harder metal bronze gave the Mesopotamians, the Egyptians and the Achaeans new technologies, including new ploughs, axes and irrigation, allowing them ultimately to produce the large agricultural surpluses that funded the construction of splendid temples and murderous armies. But for history to accelerate sufficiently to bring about what we now call civilisation, humanity needed something much harder still than bronze. It needed its ploughs, its hammers and its metal structures to have the hardness of my sword's tip. It needed to learn the trick I had seen in our living room: how to transform soft iron into hardened steel by 'baptising' it in cold water.

Bronze Age communities that did not learn how to baptise iron perished, he insisted.

The swords of their ironclad enemies sliced through their bronze shields, their ploughs failed to cultivate the less fertile soils, the metal braces holding together their dams and temples were too weak to fulfil the ambitions of forward-thinking architects. In contrast, communities that mustered the *techne*, the art, of 'steeling' iron thrived in the fields, on the battlefields, at sea, in commerce, in the arts. Iron's magic underpinned the new role of technology as the driving force that led to civilisation and its discontents.

Lest I doubted the cultural pertinence of our little experiment – and of the arrival of the Iron Age – Father explained his earlier reference to 'poor Polyphemus', the one-eyed giant who, according to Homer, imprisoned Odysseus and his men in a cave, taking his time to devour them one by one. To set them and himself free, Odysseus waited for Polyphemus to fall into a drunken stupor, heated up a wooden stake in the cave's open fire and, aided by his comrades, shoved it into Polyphemus' sole eye. 'Remember the sound of the hissing iron?' Dad asked. Well, Homer must have been equally impressed by it, judging by the verse in *The Odyssey* that captures the cruel moment:

And as when a smith dips a great axe or an adze in cold water amid loud hissing to temper it – for therefrom comes the strength of iron – even so did his eye hiss round the stake of olive-wood.[1]

Odysseus and his contemporaries preceded the Iron Age and could not have known how iron's hissing heralded a molecular hardening of historic significance. But Homer, who lived a couple of centuries after the Trojan War, was a child of the Iron Age, and thus came of age in the midst of the technological and social revolution that steel had wrought. In case I thought Homer was an outlier, Dad pointed to the lasting influence of iron's magic by quoting Sophocles, who four centuries later described a soul as 'hardened like immersed iron'.

Prehistory gave its place to history, Father said, when bronze displaced stone tools and weapons. Once bronze became widespread after 4000 BC, powerful civilisations emerged in Mesopotamia, Egypt, China, India, Crete, Mycenae and elsewhere. But, still, history was counted in the millennia. To be counted in the centuries, we had to discover the magic of iron. Once the Iron Age got going, around the ninth century BC, three different and remarkable eras emerged in quick succession, within no more than seven centuries in total: the geometric period, the classical era and the Hellenistic civilisation.

From the glacial speeds of the Bronze Age, humanity had been propelled to the breathless developments of the Iron Age. But for a long time, iron and steel remained too difficult to produce, too expensive. Even after the Industrial Revolution, the first steamships were mostly wooden, with steel providing only the essential components (boiler, chimney, joints). Enter another one of my father's great heroes, Henry Bessemer, who invented a technique for producing large quantities of steel cheaply by blowing air through molten pig iron to burn off the impurities. It was then, according to Dad, that history accelerated to speeds with which we are familiar today. Coupled with the taming of electromagnetism, which we owe to another Victorian, James Maxwell, Bessemer's technique gave us the Second Industrial Revolution – the period of rapid technological innovation from 1870 onwards, as distinct from the arrival of the factories earlier that century in the First Industrial Revolution – its wonders and horrors wrapped tightly together.

Looking back to those few winter nights of 1966, it is now clear to me that I was being inducted in 'historical materialism' – the method of understanding history as a constant feedback loop between, on the one hand, the way humans transform matter and, on the other, the manner in which human thinking and social relations are transformed in return. Thankfully, Father's historical materialism was nuanced, his enthusiasm for technology tempered by judicious doses of angst about humanity's infinite capacity to mess things up, to turn miraculous technology into living hell.

Iron, like all revolutionary technologies, had sped up history. But in which direction? For what purpose? With what effect on us? As Dad explained, from the very start of the Iron Age there were those who foresaw its tragic consequences. Hesiod was composing poetry at around the same time as Homer. His *Works and Days* had a salutary cooling influence on Dad's enthusiasm for iron and, more generally, technology:

> I wish I did not have to live among the people of the Fifth Age [the Iron Age], but either had died earlier or been born later. For now truly is a generation of iron who never rest from labour and sorrow by day or from perishing by night . . . But, notwithstanding the good mingled with their evils . . . [this generation] will know no favour for those who keep their oath or for the just or for the good . . . strength shall be right . . . the wicked will hurt the worthy . . . bitter sorrows will be left for us mortals, and there will be no help against evil.[2]

According to Hesiod, iron hardened not only our ploughs but also our souls. Under its influence, our spirit was hammered and forged in fire, our brand-new desires quenched like the hissing metal in the smith's cauldron. Virtues were tested and values destroyed just as our bounty burgeoned and our estates expanded.

Strength begat new joys but weariness and injustices too. Zeus would have no choice, Hesiod foretold, but to one day destroy a humanity incapable of restraining its own, technologically induced, power.

My father wanted to disagree with Hesiod. He wanted to believe that we humans could become the masters of our technology rather than enslave ourselves and one another with it. When Prometheus stole fire, symbolising the white heat of technology, from Zeus on humanity's behalf, he did so in the hope that it would lighten up our lives without burning down the Earth. My father wanted to believe we could make Prometheus proud.

FROM HEAT TO LIGHT

An innate optimism was only one reason Dad remained hopeful that humanity would not waste the magical powers he had introduced me to in front of our fireplace. Another was his encounter with the nature of light.

One time, as I was removing an iron rod from the fire, Dad asked: 'Can you guess what leaves the heated-up metal to reach your eye so that you can see its red glow?' I had no idea. Happily, I was not alone.

For centuries, light had divided the best minds, he said. Some, like Aristotle and James Maxwell, thought of light as a kind of disturbance in the ether, a wave that spreads outwards from an initial source – like sound does. Others, such as Democritus and Isaac Newton pointed out that, unlike sound, light cannot bend round corners – something waves do by their very nature – and thus it must be made of tiny things, or particles, travelling in a straight line before hitting our eye's retina. Who was right?

My father's life changed, or so he told me, when he read Albert Einstein's answer: they were *all* right! Light is, at once, a stream of particles *and* a series of waves. But how could that be? Particles differ fundamentally from waves. They are located at only one point at any particular moment in time, they have momentum, and they move only in a straight line unless and until something gets in their way. Waves, by contrast, are oscillations of a medium, which is what allows them to turn corners and transport energy in many different directions at once. To prove, as Einstein had done, that light was both particles and waves was to admit that something can be two utterly contradictory things at once.

For Dad, the dual nature of light was the gateway to recognising the essential dualism underlying all of nature, and also in society. 'If light could be two very different things at once,' he wondered in a letter he wrote as a young man to his mother, 'if matter is energy and energy matter,' as Einstein had also discovered, 'why must we cast life either in black-and-white terms or, even worse, in some shade of grey?'

By the time I was twelve or thirteen, it was clear to me from our ongoing conversations that Dad's love for iron's magic – technology – and for Einstein's physics – the contradictory duality of all things – had something to do with his left-wing politics, for which he had spent several years in prison camps. My hunch was confirmed when I came across the text of a speech delivered by the same person who had first formulated the notion of historical materialism: Karl Marx. It was as if Dad had been speaking the words:

In our days, everything seems pregnant with its contrary: Machinery, gifted with the wonderful power of shortening and fructifying human labour, we behold starving and overworking it; The newfangled sources of wealth, by some strange weird spell, are turned into sources of want; The victories of art seem bought by the loss of character.[3]

The power to shorten human labour and make it fruitful resulted from the great transformation of matter Father had been so keen to demonstrate for my benefit: iron turning to steel in our fireplace, heat turning to kinetic energy in James Watt's miraculous fire engine, the minor miracles occurring within the telegraph's magnets and cables. But ever since Hesiod's Fifth Age, it was a power pregnant with its opposite as well: the power to starve and to overwork, to turn a source of wealth into a source of want.

The link between Father's twin devotions – to furnaces, metallurgy and technology in general on the one hand, and to his politics on the other – became impossible to miss when I first read *The Communist Manifesto*, in particular the line:

All that is solid melts into air, all that is holy is profaned, and man is at last compelled to face with sober senses his real conditions of life, and his relations with his kind.[4]

It brought back the memory of his childlike enthusiasm at the sight of melting metal in front of our fireplace or, far more spectacularly, at the steel plant whose quality control department he directed and where temperatures were high enough for iron literally to 'melt into air'.

But unlike Hesiod – or indeed the moralists of our own era – Dad did not feel he had to take sides, to be either a technophobe or a tech-enthusiast. If light can have two contradictory natures, and if all of nature rests on a binary opposition, then hardened iron, steam engines and networked computers could also be, simultaneously, potential liberators and enslavers. And so it is up to us, collectively, to determine which of the two it will be. That's where politics comes in.

A MOST PECULIAR
INTRODUCTION TO CAPITALISM

Leftists usually become radicalised in reaction to the vile injustices and mind-numbing inequality capitalism generates. Not so in my case. Sure, growing up in the midst of a fascist dictatorship played its role, but my leftism had far more esoteric origins: a sensitivity, given to me by my father, to the duality of things.

Well before I read a word that Marx or any other economist had written, I thought I could discern several dualities buried deep in the foundations of our societies. My first inkling of such a duality hit me one evening when Mum complained to Dad that, at the fertiliser factory where she worked as a chemist, she got paid for her time but never for her enthusiasm. 'My wage is crap because my time is cheap,' she said. 'My passion to get the right results the bosses get for free!' Soon after, she resigned and got herself a job as a biochemist at a public hospital. A few months into the new job, she told us happily: 'At least at the hospital I love that my efforts benefit patients, even if I am as invisible to them as I used to be to the factory owners.'

Those words stuck with me. Mum had inadvertently introduced me to the duality of waged labour. The wage she was paid for her time and formal skills (her certificates, degrees) reflected the 'exchange value' of the hours she spent at work. But that's not what injected true value into whatever was being manufactured in her workplace. That was added to what was produced at the factory or the hospital through her effort, enthusiasm, application, even flair – none of which were remunerated. It's like going to watch a movie at a cinema: the ticket price you pay reflects the movie's exchange value, but that is quite separate from the pleasure it gives you, which we might call the 'experiential value'. In the same way, labour is split between commodity labour (Mum's time, bought by her wage) and experiential labour (the effort, passion and flair she put into her work).

When in time I did come to read Marx, I vividly recall how excited I was to discover that, thanks to my father's fireside lessons and my mum's explanation, I had stumbled upon one of the great economist's central principles. In the world we take for granted today, labour seems like any other commodity. Desperate to make a living, people promote their skills like vendors advertising their wares. They accept a market-determined price (the wage) for their labour, which reflects its exchange value, i.e. what it is worth compared to other exchangeable commodities. This is commodity labour. However, as we have seen, unlike soap powder, potatoes or iPhones, which are nothing but commodities, labour is something else besides.

To illustrate labour's second nature, the experiential labour that my mother first alerted me to, consider the brilliant idea conjured up by a group of brainstorming architects employed by a multinational construction firm. Or the positive vibes a waiter emits on the restaurant floor. Or a teacher's tear of joy when a challenged pupil solves a difficult maths problem. None of these can ever truly be commodified. Why? Because no monetary reward can prompt a moment of true inspiration, no genuine smile can be bought, no authentic tear can be shed for a price. In fact, any attempt to do so would immediately negate them. Indeed, bosses who try to quantify, price or commodify experiential labour will sound like the fool who yells at you: 'Be spontaneous!'

What I call experiential labour, the part which can never be sold, Marx called simply labour. And what I have labelled commodity labour, Marx defined as labouring power. But the idea is the same: 'What the working man sells is not directly his Labour, but his Labouring Power, the temporary disposal of which he makes over to the capitalist.'[5] Imagine my joy, then, when I discovered that, based on labour's two natures, Marx had erected a whole theory of capitalism.

For herein lies capitalism's secret: the uncommodifiable sweat, effort, inspiration, goodwill, care and tears of employees are what breathe exchange value into the commodities that employers then flog to eager customers – this is actually what makes the building or restaurant or school desirable.

One may protest that there is many a factory populated by uninspired, joyless, robotic workers producing tin cans or gadgets worth more than the cost of paying the workers. True. But this happens only because employers cannot buy the *effort* put in by unskilled, manual labourers. They can only buy their time, during which to pressurise them, in a variety of ways, to work hard and to sweat. The point here is that this blue-collar sweat, exactly like the waged architect's flair, can never be directly bought or sold. This is, indeed, the secret power of employers: to extract any surplus, either from highly skilled or from uninspired, repetitive, robotic work, they must pay for their workers' time (commodity labour) but cannot actually buy their sweat or flair (experiential labour).

You might think it extremely frustrating to employers that they cannot buy the architect's *eureka* moment, the waiter's spontaneous smile, the teacher's tear directly, without which their employee's work produces no value. On the contrary, employers resemble the customer who bought a jacket for a thousand dollars only to find two thousand dollars sewn in its lining. Indeed, if they don't, they go bust!

When I first encountered this revelatory explanation of capitalism's secret, I found it captivating: to think that capitalists owe their profits to an inability, to the impossibility of buying experiential labour directly. And yet, what a boon to suffer from such an incapacity! For it is ultimately they who pocket the difference between the exchange value they pay employees in exchange for their *commodity* labour (wages) and the exchange value of the commodities created thanks to their *experiential* labour. In other words, labour's dual nature is what gives rise to profit.

It is not just labour that has a dual nature. The dominant propaganda today and while I was growing up is that profit is the price, or reward, of a thing called capital, and that people who have capital – such as tools, raw materials, money, anything that can be used to produce saleable goods – make a profit by deploying it, in the same way a worker makes a wage by deploying her labour. But the conclusion that profit results from labour's contradictory twin natures led me to reject this notion, too. Again, even before I had read Marx, and thanks to paying attention to Mum and Dad, the more I thought of capital the more convinced I became that, like light and labour, it too featured two natures.

One is commodity capital, e.g. a fishing rod, a tractor, a company's server, or any good that is produced to be used in the production of other commodities. Capital's second nature, however, is nothing like a commodity. Suppose I discover that I possess tools you need in order to produce the stuff for your family's survival, such as the aforementioned fishing rod, tractor, server. Suddenly I have acquired the power to make you do things, for example to work for me, in exchange for the use of my tools. Capital, in short, is both a thing (commodity capital) and a force (power capital) – just as labour is split between commodity labour and experiential labour.

By the time I began reading Marx, I could not help but filter his words through the lens given to me by my mum's work dysphoria and by my dad's inspiration from the great twentieth-century physicist. Delighted as I was by the dualities I was seeing, deep down I wondered what Einstein would have made of my wild extrapolations – from his theory of light, or rather from my puny grasp of it, to the essence of capitalism. Had my father inadvertently misrepresented Einstein, prompting my imagination to run away at a tangent thanks to a flimsy and perhaps false metaphor?

Many years later I chanced upon this sentence written by Einstein himself: 'It is important to understand that even in theory the payment of the worker is not determined by the value of his product.' It appeared in an article entitled 'Why Socialism?', published in May 1949. Reading it, I breathed a sigh of relief. No, I had not been taking liberties with Einstein's insights, after all. He too believed that capitalism's essence was the splitting of labour into two incongruous natures.

AN EQUALLY ODD
INTRODUCTION TO MONEY

Uncle Albert, as Father used to refer to Einstein on occasion, was not finished with my education regarding capitalism. Having opened my eyes to the dual nature of both labour and capital, he guided me to the dual nature of money through an even more circuitous path involving a certain John Maynard Keynes.

In 1905, the 26-year-old Einstein found the guts to tell a deeply sceptical world that light was a continuous field of waves made up of particle-like things and, moreover, that energy and matter were, essentially, one 'thing' linked by history's most famous equation: $E=mc^2$ (i.e. a body's energy content is equal to its mass times the speed of light multiplied by itself). A decade later, Einstein extended this Special Theory of Relativity to elucidate one of the greatest of puzzles: gravity.

The General Theory of Relativity that resulted was not for the faint-hearted. To grasp it, we first had to embrace a mindset that rejected what our senses told us. If you want to understand gravity, Einstein explained, you need to stop thinking of space as a box that the universe comes in. Matter and energy, operating as one, mould the contours of space and shape the flow of time. The only way to wrap our minds around space and time, or matter and energy, is to think of them as partners locked in the most intimate, insoluble embrace. Gravity is what we feel as we traverse the shortest path through this four-dimensional space-time.

That our brains find it hard to grasp the reality unveiled by Einstein's General Theory of Relativity is unsurprising. We evolved on the surface of a planet that is minuscule in comparison to the universe out there. In our limited realm, we can get by quite nicely with our senses' helpful illusions; for instance, the belief that the grass is green, straight lines exist, or that time is constant and independent of our motion. These beliefs are false and yet helpful to the extent that they enable our architects to design safe buildings and our watches to coordinate our meetings at pre-agreed points in time. When playing pool, as the cue ball strikes a coloured ball, we become convinced of a clear causal effect. But were we to rely on these illusions to travel beyond our planet, to the macrocosm out there, we would be literally lost in space. Equally, when we peer deep into the world of the suba-tomic particles that comprise our own body, or the chair we are sitting on, even the link between cause and effect vanishes.

What does any of this have to do with money? The title of the most famous economics book of the twentieth century is *The General Theory of Employment, Interest and Money*. Published in 1936, it was written by John Maynard Keynes in order to explain why capitalism was failing to recover from the Great Depression, and the allusion to Einstein's General Theory was intentional. Keynes, who had met Einstein and knew of his work, chose it so as to herald a complete break from conventional economics – a break as clean and decisive as that of Einstein's from classical physics.

Of his fellow economists, who insisted that money ought to be understood as another commodity, Keynes once said that they 'resemble Euclidean geometers in a non-Euclidean world', again confirming in no uncertain terms Einstein's influence. Conven-tional economic thinking about money was damaging humanity, Keynes thought. Economists resembled spacecraft designers dis-astrously relying on Euclid, not Einstein. They were using illusions which, while helpful in the microcosm of a single market (e.g. the market for potatoes, where a fall in the price can usually be relied upon to boost sales), were catastrophic when applied to the economy at large – the macroeconomy, where a fall in the price of money (the interest rate) may never boost money's flows in the form of investment and employment.

In the same way that Einstein had ended our illusion that time stands outside, and apart from, space, Keynes wanted to stop us thinking of money as a thing, as simply another commodity, that stands outside, and apart from, our other activities in markets and workplaces.

Today, we are bombarded with a phantasmagoria of idiocies about money. Clueless politicians invoke penny-pinching metaphors to justify self-defeating austerity. Central bankers facing both inflation and deflation resemble the proverbial ass, both thirsty and hungry, who collapses because it can't decide whether to drink or to eat first. Crypto enthusiasts invite us to fix the world by embracing the ultimate money-commodity form: Bitcoin and its various offspring. Big Tech is creating its own digital money with which to lure us deeper into its poisonous web of platforms.

I can think of no better defence in the face of this orchestrated obfuscation than Keynes's (Einstein-derived) advice: stop thinking about money as something separate from what we do to each other, with each other, at work, during play, in every nook and cranny of our social universe. Yes, money is a thing, a commodity like any other. But it is also something much bigger than that. It is, above all else, a reflection of our relation to one another and to our technologies; i.e. the means and the ways in which we transform matter. Or, as Marx put it poetically:

Money is the alienated ability of mankind. That which I am unable to do as a man, and of which therefore all my individual essential powers are incapable, I am able to do by means of money. Money thus turns each of these powers into something which in itself it is not – turns it, that is, into its contrary.[6]

FREE TO CHOOSE? OR TO LOSE?

In early 2015, a historical accident made me Greece's finance minister. Given my mandate to clash with some of the most powerful people and institutions in the world, the international press peered into my articles, books and lectures for clues of what to expect. They were baffled by my claim to be a libertarian Marxist – a self-description that was immediately derided by several libertarians and most Marxists. When one of the ruder interviewers asked after the source of my 'obvious confusion', I jokingly replied: my parents!

Joking aside, Father was, at least indirectly, responsible for another crucial component of my political education: my inability to see how one could genuinely cherish freedom and tolerate capitalism (or, vice versa, how one could be both illiberal and left wing). Between them, he and my feminist mother bequeathed me a perspective diagonally opposed to what has become, sadly, conventional fallacy: that capitalism is about freedom, efficiency and democracy, while socialism turns on justice, equality and statism. In fact, from the very start, the left was all about emancipation.

During the feudal era, which became properly entrenched across Europe in the twelfth century, economic life involved no economic choices. If you were born into the landed gentry, it would never cross your mind to sell your ancestors' land. And if you were born a serf, you were compelled to toil the land, on the landowner's behalf, free of any illusion that, one day, you might own land yourself. In short, neither land nor labour power was a commodity. They had no market price. The vast majority of the time, ownership of them changed only through wars of conquest, royal decree or as a result of some catastrophe.

Then, in the eighteenth century, something remarkable happened. Because of advances in shipping and navigation, international trade in things like wool, linen, silk and spices made them lucrative, thus giving British landlords an idea: why not evict en masse the serfs from land that produced worthless turnips and replace them with sheep whose backs produced precious wool for the international markets? The peasants' eviction, which we now remember as the 'enclosures' – for it involved fencing them off from the land their ancestors had toiled for centuries – gave the majority of people something they had lost at the time that agriculture was invented: choice.

Landlords could choose to lease land for a price reflecting the amount of wool it could produce. The evicted serfs could choose to offer their labour for a wage. Of course, in reality, being free to choose was no different from being free to lose. Former serfs who refused squalid work for a pitiful wage starved to death. Proud aristocrats who refused to go along with the commodification of their land went bankrupt. As feudalism receded, economic choice arrived but was as free as the one offered by a mafioso who, smilingly, tells you: 'I shall make you an offer you cannot refuse.'

By the middle of the nineteenth century, the thinking of Marx and other foundational left-wing thinkers was all about *freeing* us. Specifically, in this era, it was about freeing us from a Dr

Frankenstein-like failure to control our creations – not least, the machines of the Industrial Revolution. In the ageless words of *The Communist Manifesto*:

> a society that has conjured up such gigantic means of production and of exchange, is like the sorcerer who is no longer able to control the powers of the nether world whom he has called up by his spells.[7]

For over a century, the left was concerned primarily with deliverance from self-inflicted unfreedom – which is why it was so fundamentally aligned with the anti-slavery movement, the suffragettes, groups sheltering persecuted Jews in the 1930s and 40s, black liberation organisations in the 1950s and 60s, the first gay and lesbian protesters in the streets of San Francisco, Sydney and London in the 1970s. So, how did we get to the situation, today, where 'libertarian Marxist' sounds like a joke?

The answer is that, sometime in the twentieth century, the left traded freedom for other things. In the East (from Russia to China, Cambodia and Vietnam), the quest for emancipation was swapped for a totalitarian egalitarianism. In the West, liberty was left to its enemies, abandoned in exchange for an ill-defined notion of fairness. The moment people believed they had to choose between freedom and fairness, between an iniquitous democracy and miserable state-imposed egalitarianism, it was game over for the left.

On Boxing Day in 1991, I was visiting Athens to spend a few days with my parents. As we chatted over dinner in front of that same red-brick fireplace, the red flag was being lowered above the Kremlin. Thanks to Dad's communist past and Mum's social democratic leanings, they shared a common mood. They knew that, on that very night, history was marking not just the demise of the Soviet Union but also the end of the social democratic dream: of a mixed economy, in which government provided public goods while the private sector produced plentiful goodies to satisfy our whims – all in all, a civilised form of capitalism where inequality and exploitation were kept in check in the context of a politically mediated truce between the owners of capital and those who had nothing to sell but their labour.

Circumspect, though not glum, the three of us agreed we were witnessing a defeat made inevitable once our side had lost the conviction that capitalism was iniquitous because it was inefficient, that it was unjust because it was illiberal, that it was chaotic because it was irrational. Falling back to basics, I asked Mum and Dad what freedom meant to them. Mother replied: the ability to choose your partners and your projects. Father's reply was similar: time to read, to experiment and to write. Whatever *your* definition might be, dear reader, being free to lose in a variety of soul-crushing ways can't be it.

FATHER'S QUESTION

Almost everyone today takes to capitalism as fish take to water – without even noticing it is there, treating it as the invisible, irreplaceable, natural ether we move through. As Fredric Jameson famously put it, people find it easier to imagine the end of the world than the end of capitalism. For my father's generation of leftists, however, there was a brief moment in the mid to late 1940s when the end of capitalism seemed only a matter of a few years if not months away. But then one thing led to another and capitalism's demise shifted further and further into the future until, after 1991, it disappeared beyond the horizon.

Being of the generation who had believed that capitalism was transitory, Dad continued to contemplate capitalism's expiry even after he had concluded he would not live to see it. Nevertheless, a decade or so after our fireside experiments, with the dream of socialism in deep recession, and while I dived into the works of the political economists, Father increasingly immersed himself in the study of ancient technology.

Every now and then, feeling he could guiltlessly leave to me the exploration of capitalism's mysteries while he relished the unalloyed joys of archaeometry, he would speculate on how capitalism might, one day, end – and what would replace it. His wish was that it would not die with a bang, because bangs had a tendency to cull good people in awful numbers; that instead socialist islands might spring up spontaneously in our vast capitalist archipelago and that they would expand gradually, eventually forming whole continents on which technologically advanced commons would prevail.

In 1987, he sought my help to set up his first desktop computer. A glorified typewriter, he called it, but with an impressive on-screen editing facility. 'Imagine how many more volumes Marx's complete works would consist of if the bearded one had owned one of these,' he joked. As if to prove the point, he used it over the years that followed to churn out voluminous papers and books on the interplay between the ancient Greeks' technology and literature.

Six years on, in 1993, I arrived at the Paleo Phaliro home with a clunky early modem to connect his computer to the fledgling internet. 'This is a game changer,' he said. Struggling to dial up a woefully slow Greek internet provider, he asked me the killer question that ultimately inspired this book: 'Now that computers speak to each other, will this network make capitalism impossible to overthrow? Or might it finally reveal its Achilles heel?'

Caught up in my own projects and dramas, I never got round to answering Father's question. When I finally decided I had an answer for him, Dad was already ninety-five and finding it hard to follow my musings. And so, here I am, a few years later, only a few weeks after his passing, composing my answer – belatedly, but I hope not in vain.

2
CAPITALISM'S METAMORPHOSES

Dad, it *was* capitalism's Achilles heel, after all: the digitally networked technologies that capitalism spawned proved its comeuppance. The result? Humanity is now being taken over by something that I can only describe as a technologically advanced form of feudalism. A technofeudalism that is certainly not what we had hoped would supersede capitalism.

I can tell you are puzzled, Dad. Wherever we look today, capital is triumphant. New monuments to its power spring up everywhere – physical ones in our cities and across our landscapes, digital ones on our screens and in our hands. Meanwhile, the capital-poor sink deeper into precarity and our democracies bend their knee to capital's will. So, how dare I even imagine that capitalism is on the way out; that it is being taken over? Have I forgotten that nothing strengthens capitalism more than the illusion it is evolving out of existence and into something new – a mixed economy, a welfare state, a global village?

No, of course I have not forgotten. Metamorphosis is to capitalism what camouflage is to a chameleon: essence and defence mechanism combined. And yet, we are not talking about mere disguises. Several of capitalism's transformations have been epoch changing. One of those was unfolding at around the time you were educating me to iron's magic in front of our fireplace. And in fact, to explain what I mean by technofeudalism, I need first to describe in some detail this transformation – capitalism's latest series of metamorphoses, which is the subject of this chapter. Only then, in the next chapter, will I be able to begin to explain properly what has replaced it.

RETRIEVING THE IRRETRIEVABLE

In an episode of *Mad Men*, the television series on the rise of advertising in the 1960s, the legendary creative director Don Draper coaches his protégée, Peggy, on how to think of Hershey, a chocolate bar that their firm is peddling. Draper's marketing philosophy perfectly encapsulates the spirit of the times: 'You are the product. You, feeling something.' Or, as James Poniewozik interprets Draper's line in *Time* magazine: 'You don't buy a Hershey bar for a couple of ounces of chocolate. You buy it to recapture the feeling of being loved that you knew when your dad bought you one for mowing the lawn.'[1]

The mass commercialisation of nostalgia Draper alludes to marked a turning point for capitalism. While the big issues of the 1960s were the Vietnam War, civil rights and the institutions that might civilise capitalism (Medicare, food stamps, the welfare state), Draper was putting his finger on a fundamental mutation in its DNA. Efficiently manufacturing things that people craved was no longer enough. Capitalism now involved the skilful manufacture of desire.

Capitalism had begun as a relentless drive to put a price on things that once had no price: common lands, human labour, all the stuff that families once produced for their own consumption – from bread and home-brewed wine to woolly jumpers and various tools. If there was something that humans shared and enjoyed but which had no price and mattered to us only for its intrinsic or 'experiential value' – like granny's hand-crafted tablecloth, or a beautiful sunset, or a beguiling song – capitalism found a way to commodify it: to subjugate its experiential value to an exchange value.

It was in the nature of the beast. Capitalism is synonymous with the triumph of exchange value because it is the only value that can be crystallised into more capital. Just as the Borg in *Star Trek* depend on assimilating the biological and technological distinctiveness of other species for their survival, capitalism has taken over planet Earth by assimilating wherever possible any experiential value it encounters into its exchange value chain. Having assimilated every resource, crop and artefact it could, capitalism has since gone on to commodify the airwaves, women's wombs, art, genotypes, asteroids, even space itself. In the process, the experiential value of all things is reduced to a dollar sum, a commercial asset, a tradable contract.

And yet, contrary to the Borg's scary greeting – 'You will be assimilated. Resistance is futile!' – experiential value's resistance has not been in vain. Each time the onslaught of exchange value has overcome its defences, experiential value has gone underground into the catacombs of our psyche. It is there that Don Draper – or, more accurately, the men and women *Mad Men* is based on – discovered it, retrieved it and, yes, commodified it. In the process, capitalism changed radically.

Watching *Mad Men*, the audience wonder why the firm pays Draper a mint to do what he does. Mostly horizontal on a comfortable couch in his office, he consumes impressive quantities of bourbon, has a series of breakdowns, behaves erratically and unprofessionally, and when he does deign to share what he's thinking, usually offers only cryptic and disjointed thoughts. But just when you expect him to self-destruct or get fired, he comes up with magical ways of reimagining anything from mediocre chocolate and humdrum steel products to second-rate hamburger restaurant chains in ways that make them emotionally resonant and intensely desirable. In both aspects of his behaviour, Draper captures the essence of capitalism's post-war transformation: the discovery of a new market, namely the market for our attention, grafted onto a shiny new industrial structure, but all within a system that remains fully reliant on labour's dual nature.

For the dual nature of Draper's labour is writ large in every episode of *Mad Men*. His bosses would love to be able to purchase his ideas without having to tolerate him lounging around the office half drunk. In the language of the previous chapter, they would jump at the opportunity to buy Draper's experiential labour directly. Only they couldn't, even if he wanted to sell it to them. Instead, they are forced to buy his commodity labour (i.e. his time and potential) in the hope that, during his inebriated daze, his genius will spontaneously deliver the famed Draper magic. And when it does, their immense profits confirm once again that capital is born out of the capitalists' inability to buy experiential labour directly.

Draper's genius, meanwhile, is to grasp, and to confront, the paradox of commodification. Yes, capitalism must commodify everything it touches. But at the same time, high exchange value, and thus serious profits, depends on failing to do so fully. If it is to avoid the fate of a school of predators that devours its prey so efficiently that it starves to death, capitalism relies on there being an endless supply of experiential values for its exchange values to trounce and cannibalise. It must always be discovering and commodifying what has so far escaped it.

Smart advertisers do exactly that: they tap into emotions that have previously escaped commodification in order to capture our attention. And then they sell our attention to an entity whose business is to commodify whatever experiential value was hiding in our soul, fleeing commodification. With his Hershey bar speech, Draper lays bare a crucial aspect of how, soon after the war, capitalism reached its golden age. How could the profits keep flowing once everything has seemingly been commodified already? Draper's answer: through the triggering of uncommodified emotions deep inside us.

Thus a Hershey bar becomes the simulacrum of a dead father's caress. Bethlehem Steel is rebranded as the spirit of the American *polis*, with the steel product symbolising the New World's own Iron Age. When Draper and Peggy visit a Burger Chef outlet, they discern the possibility of a television advertisement that promotes the chain as an opportunity for families to be reunited around its plastic tables – away from the family home where togetherness is no longer possible because everyone's attention has been arrested by . . . the television.

So what did capitalism look like before this great transformation occurred? And how did this transformation take place?

TECHNOSTRUCTURE

Another way to ask the same question would be: where did Sterling Cooper & Partners (Draper's fictional firm) find the money or willingness to treat him like an academic? To pay him good money to think deeply at a pace of his choosing? Capitalism's early advocates would have been perplexed. Their idea of entrepreneurship took the form of parsimonious bakers, butchers and brewers eagerly striving to satisfy their customers' basic needs by working hard, thinking on their feet, economising on everything, squeezing the last drop of exchange value out of any raw materials they could lay their hands on. What changed that meant a character like Draper could become an icon of our enterprise culture? I think you will like my answer, Dad: electromagnetism!

Once James Clerk Maxwell had written down the equations linking electrical current to magnetic force, it was only a matter of time before someone like Thomas Edison would turn them into the electricity and telegraph grids that ultimately begat the networked, top-down, mega-corporations we know today – pushing the bakers, butchers and brewers of early capitalism to the sidelines. The problem was that none of capitalism's early institutions – specifically, its banks and share markets – were ready for such corporate empires. Simply put, the banks were too small and too fragile and the share markets too thin, too illiquid, to provide the kind of funds Edison needed to build his famous Pearl Street power station, let alone the rest of his electricity grid.

To produce the rivers of credit necessary to fund the Edisons, the Westinghouses and the Fords of early-twentieth-century capitalism, small banks merged to form large ones and lent either to the industrialists directly or to speculators eager to buy shares in the new corporations. That's how electromagnetism transformed capitalism: while its grids would go on to power mega-firms and its megawatts translated into mega-profits, it also created the first mega-debts in the form of vast overdraft facilities for the Edisons, the Westinghouses and the Fords. And it led to the emergence of Big Finance, which grew up alongside Big Business in order to lend it monies borrowed effectively from the future: from profits not yet realised but which Big Business promised to deliver. These wagers on future profits funded not only the construction of Big Business's grids and production lines but an almighty froth of speculation as well.

Parsimony was out and largesse became the new virtue. The Victorian belief that firms should be small and powerless, so that competition could perform its magic of keeping entrepreneurs honest, was replaced by the creed that 'what is good for Big Business is good for America'. The Jazz Age swept restraint away, debt's dirty name was cleansed in the torrents of anticipated profits, caution was thrown to the winds of credit.

Within a decade, electromagnetism had sparked the Roaring Twenties whose inevitable heart-wrenching crash came in 1929, the year the grapes of wrath began to fill and grow heavy for the vintage. Whether one believes that Franklin Roosevelt's New Deal ended the Great Depression, or that it was the war that did it, one thing is clear: the New Deal also changed global capitalism profoundly. The New Deal's public works projects, its social welfare programmes and, above all, its public finance instruments, together with stringent controls over what bankers could get away with, constituted a full-on dress rehearsal for the War Economy.

For immediately after the Japanese bombing of Pearl Harbor brought the US into the Second World War, the US government began to emulate ... the Soviet one. It told factory owners how much to produce and to what specifications, from aircraft carriers to processed food. It even employed a price czar – the economist John Kenneth Galbraith – whose job, literally, was to decide the price of everything, to fend off inflation, and to ensure a smooth economic transition from wartime to peacetime. It is no exaggeration to say that American capitalism was run according to Soviet planning principles, with the important exception that the networked factories remained under the private ownership of Big Business.

Under President Roosevelt, the US government's deal with Big Business was simple: they would produce what was necessary to win the war and, in exchange, the state would reward them with four incredible gifts. First, state guaranteed sales translating into state guaranteed profits. Second, freedom from competition, since prices were fixed by government. Third, huge government-funded scientific research (e.g. the Manhattan Project, jet propulsion) that provided Big Business with wonderful new innovations and a pool of highly skilled scientific personnel to recruit from during and after the war. And fourth, a patriotic aura to help rinse off the stench of corporate greed that clung to them after the crash of 1929 and make them over as heroic enterprises that helped America win the war.

The War Economy experiment was an unqualified success. Production quadrupled in less than five years. Inflation was kept on a leash, unlike what had happened during the previous world war. Unemployment disappeared, and was kept at bay even after the soldiers, sailors and airmen returned from the front. To Big Business, it was a dream come true that compensated them handsomely for the subjugation of Big Finance to the government's plans and strictures.

Beneath the surface, however, the heat of war had transformed American capitalism at a molecular level, just as the heat of our fireplace had transformed iron into steel. By the war's end, American capitalism was unrecognisable. Business and government had become profoundly entwined. Indeed, the revolving doors between government departments and corporations saw to it that the same crowd of mathematicians, scientists, analysts and professional managers populated them both. The heroic entrepreneur at the helm of the corporation and the democratically elected politician at the head of the government had both been usurped by this new private-public decision-making network, whose values and priorities – indeed its survival – boiled down to one thing: the survival and growth of the conglomerates now that the war, with its infinite demand for stuff and technologies, was over. Galbraith called this nexus the technostructure.

Profitability remained essential for the army of technicians and influence-wielding employees making up the technostructure. Nevertheless, profit was no longer their top priority. As with all bureaucracies, their primary goal was to keep their underlings employed and busy. This meant they had not merely to avoid the shrinking of their conglomerates at the war's end, but to grow them. With the war behind them, one question kept the good folks of the technostructure up at night: if the government would no longer guarantee sales and prices, where would they find enough customers ready and willing to pay for all the chocolate bars, cars and washing machines that they were planning to manufacture using the capacity hitherto dedicated to producing bullets, machine guns and flame-throwers?

The New Dealers in government took it upon themselves to help the technostructure secure foreign customers – which as we shall see triggered another of the great metamorphoses of twentieth-century capitalism. But as for domestic customers, that's where Don Draper came in. His stock-in-trade? Opening the technostructure's eyes to the boundless possibilities of founding a new market for our attention on a bed of raw emotion. The technostructure had the manufacture of things fully under its control. With Draper's help, it could now look forward to manufacturing the necessary desire for them. Paying Draper a large salary to lounge around for most of the working day was a small price to pay for such an extraordinary power.

ATTENTION MARKETS AND THE SOVIETS' REVENGE

On a cold January day in 1903, in front of a large audience at Coney Island's Luna Park, Thomas Edison used alternating current to electrocute to death Topsy, a helpless elephant. His purpose? To draw the public's attention to the deadliness of the type of electricity peddled by George Westinghouse, his competitor. Despite the novel awfulness, nothing significantly new had happened: a powerful man had used the age-old trick of grabbing the public's attention to sell himself and his offerings.

From a peacock's feathers to a Roman emperor's triumphal march to the fashion industry of today, competing for others' attention is about as old as sexual reproduction. But it wasn't until the twentieth century that the process of attention-grabbing was commodified. Once again, it was electromagnetism that achieved this revolutionary feat – not by killing an elephant but by allowing for the invention of the radio and, even more importantly, the television set.

At first, radio and television gave Big Business a headache. It offered them immense opportunities to engage and persuade the masses, but fundamentally its output – the programmes it broadcast – had the properties of a sunset rather than a tin of beans: however much you loved watching *I Love Lucy* on television, and even if you were *prepared* to pay good money to watch it, no one had the capacity to *make* you pay for it (at least not before cable TV was introduced). But this stopped being a problem once they realised that the programme was not the commodity: it was the attention of the people watching it. By broadcasting the programme for free, they could secure the audience's attention allowing them then to sell it – in the form of advertisement breaks – to Draper's clients, who were now so eager to instil new desires in the hearts of the American public.

With the birth of commercial television, the technostructure appended a boisterous attention market to its labour market. The dual nature of labour was now coupled with the dual nature of the spectacle: on the one hand, a cultural product with large experiential value but no exchange value, and on the other the captured attention of viewers with substantial exchange value but no experiential value.

The cultural impact was enormous. But the less visible impact was no less momentous. A new group of experts had been grafted onto the technostructure: alongside the scientists, analysts and professional managers, there were now creative types like Draper, as well as a whole raft of strategists and engineers working on new ways to manipulate and commodify our attention.

It was another historic transformation. By the early 1960s, the commodities that made real money were no longer the ones that prevailed in some Darwinian struggle for existence within some competitive market. No, the products that adorned every home were the ones that the Drapers and the executives of the conglomerates fashioned together in meetings at the technostructure's skyscraper offices. There, over lots of smoking and drinking, they jointly decided the prices, the quantities, the packages and even the feelings imparted by capitalism's leading products. Whereas capitalism had come to life by turning feudalism's societies-with-markets into decentralised market societies, the rise of the technostructure transformed American capitalism from a decentralised market society into a centralised economy-with-markets. It was precisely what the Soviet planners had always hoped to achieve, but failed.

And there's the irony. In the 1960s, a decade marked by an ideological and nuclear clash between America and the Soviet Union that almost blew up the world, Soviet planning principles were implemented with remarkable success in ... the United States. Irony has seldom taken a more effective revenge over earnest ideology.

That was as far as the technostructure's domestic customers went – those within the USA. What about the rest of the world? It was all very well converting America's factories from manufacturing tanks, ammunition, fighter planes and aircraft carriers to churning out washing machines, cars, television sets and passenger jets. The problem was that America's industrial capacity had grown so much during the war that, to keep its factories busy and its workers in jobs, they had to produce a lot more stuff than Americans alone could absorb. Drilling new desires into the American consumer could never be enough because there were not enough American middle-class homes to do the necessary consuming. Foreign markets had to be found.

THE AUDACIOUS GLOBAL PLAN

I remember one evening in 1975 you came home with 'extraordinary' news: thirty drachmas were no longer enough to buy us one American dollar, you announced. Not that it made any difference to us, since we had neither the means nor the legal right to buy more than a handful of dollars. But you were anxious that an exchange rate that had stood still since 1957 had just broken down. What did that mean for our future as a family and for our small country where the shockwaves caused by grand ruptures originating in America usually took a while to hit? Thinking back, your hunch was exactly right: this was indeed a local reverberation of something that originated in the US and that augured a violent and this time global metamorphosis of capitalism.

The breakdown of the drachma–dollar exchange rate that had so impressed you was a consequence of the downfall four years earlier, in August 1971, of the so-called Bretton Woods system. (As with the 2008 financial crisis, which took two long years to flatten Greece, the collapse of Bretton Woods also took some time to hit us. A German friend once quipped: 'If I hear that the end of the world is nigh, I shall immediately move to Greece – everything takes a couple of years longer over there.') Bretton Woods[2] was the audacious global financial system devised by the New Dealers in 1944, whose purpose was noble: to thwart the Great Depression's return after the war had ended. Its strategy, however, was perhaps less so: it aimed to append post-war Europe and Japan to America's gleaming new War Economy.

The New Dealers knew that once the German armies had been defeated, Europe would lie in ruins, its peoples penniless.

So Washington understood that its first task would be to remon-
etise Europe – literally, to provide them with money to spend in
order to get their economies running again. That was easier said
than done. With Europe's gold either spent or stolen, its factories
and infrastructure turned to rubble, hordes of refugees roaming
its highways and byways, the concentration camps still reeking
with the stench of humanity's unspeakable cruelty, Europe needed much more than freshly minted paper money. Something had
to instil the new notes with value. After all, what gives any currency value but the economy that stands behind it?

Only one thing could circumvent the problem: the dollar! The
financial project of the Bretton Woods system was bold: to 'dollarise' the currencies of Europe and Japan by linking European
currencies and the yen to the dollar with fixed exchange rates –
hence the thirty drachmas to one dollar whose demise disturbed
you in 1975. In essence, it was a global currency union based on
the US dollar. With the mighty US economy standing behind
them, the currencies would retain a significant and stable value.

Naturally, there had to be limits to how many dollars one could
get for one's 'funny money' – Greek drachmas, Italian lire, etc.
These limits were known as capital controls: restrictions in the
movement of money from one currency to another. They made
the life of bankers wonderfully boring by denying them the
opportunity to speculate on shifts in the relative value of currencies, which they would otherwise have done by shifting large
quantities of money from one currency to another, from one
country to another. That was, of course, intentional. Having been
burned by the 1929 catastrophe, the New Dealers wanted bankers
to live in a straitjacket of capital controls and almost fixed interest
rates, with only tiny wiggle room of 1 per cent here or there.

Alongside this bold financial project was a political one. In the East, the New Dealers rewrote the Japanese constitution and oversaw its transformation into a technostructure-with-Japanese-characteristics. In Europe, they guided the foundation of the European Union as a cartel of heavy industry centred upon German manufacturing, adapting their technostructure blueprint to European circumstances. To make this happen, they had to rewrite the German constitution and, with promises of handing administrative and political oversight over to Paris, thwart the French ambition to de-industrialise Germany.

This dazzling design, America's Global Plan to remake Europe and Japan in the imagine of its technostructure, led to capitalism's Golden Age. From the war's end until 1971, America, Europe and Japan enjoyed low unemployment, low inflation, high growth and massively diminished inequality. The New Dealers' job was almost done. And it was done in a way that even the staunchest Republican moguls appreciated. Turning to *Mad Men* for one more symbolic insight, there is a scene where Conrad Hilton, the hotel mogul, shares with Don Draper his true ambition, which encapsulates the spirit of this Global Plan: 'It's my purpose in life to bring America to the world whether they like it or not. You know, we are a force of good, Don, because we have God.'

Whether the scriptwriter meant God as a stand-in for the dollar or not, it is fair to say that American hegemony in this era relied on the almighty power of its currency: the only currency everyone wanted even if they never cared to buy anything coming from America.

But all this relied on one crucial factor. For the dollar to be the apple of everyone's eye, at the fixed exchange rates the Bretton Woods system guaranteed, America had to be a surplus-amassing country – meaning, it had to sell more goods and services to the rest of the world than it imported. Of course, selling goods to the Europeans and Japanese was more than just a bonus outcome: it was how the technostructure would secure for itself the vast new markets it needed to sustain its industries and keep its economy growing. But the whole system also relied on this surplus integrally, for it was what ensured that the dollars printed by the Federal Reserve (America's central bank) and given to the Europeans and to the Japanese (either as loans or aid) would ultimately find their way back to the United States in return for US goods. With every Boeing jet or General Electric washing machine sold to the Europeans, a bundle of dollars would head home back across the Atlantic. And as long as migratory dollars were gravitating back home, the dollar would remain a steal at the given exchange rate, guaranteeing that the Germans, the British, the French, the Japanese, even the Greeks wanted to get many more dollars for their funny money than the authorities allowed them at the official exchange rate.

As long as America was the major surplus nation, Bretton Woods was safe as houses. And that's why, by the late 1960s, the Bretton Woods system was dead in the water. The reason? Three developments which caused America to lose its trade surplus and become a chronically deficit economy. The first was the escalating Vietnam War which forced the US government to spend billions in South East Asia on supplies and services for its military. The second was President Lyndon Johnson's attempt to make amends for the ill effects of conscription on working-class America, its black communities in particular. His valiant but expensive Great Society programme substantially reduced poverty but, at once, sucked lots of imported goods from Japan and Europe into

the United States. Lastly, Japan's and Germany's factories sur-
passed America's both in terms of quality and efficiency, partly
due to the support successive US governments had extended to
Japan's and Germany's manufacturing sectors – the car industry
being an obvious example.

Never too slow to accept reality, Washington killed off its fin-
est creation: on 15 August 1971 President Nixon announced the
ejection of Europe and Japan from the dollar zone. Bretton
Woods was dead.[3] The door had been opened to a new and truly
dismal phase in capitalism's evolution.

MAD NUMBERS

In 2002, thirty years after the Nixon Shock, humanity's total
income approximated $50 trillion. In the same year, financiers
around the world had wagered $70 trillion on a variety of bets. I
remember your eyes popping out when you heard this outrageous
number. Like most people, you refused to wrap your mind around
it. Used to thinking of money in terms of things that made sense,
like tons of steel or the number of hospitals it could build, you
could not see how Earth was large enough to contain that $70
trillion number.

By 2007, humanity's total income had risen from $50 to $75
trillion – a decent 33 per cent increase over five years. But the sum
of bets in the global money market had gone up from $70 to $750
trillion – a rise in excess of 1000 per cent. That's when I lost you.
Or, more accurately, it is when we agreed that the numbers had
gone mad, an arithmetic reflection of capitalism's hubris.

How had these mad numbers come about? What drove them?
One way to answer this question is technical: it involves a

description of financial instruments such as options (or derivatives) – the weapons of potential mass financial destruction, as Warren Buffett called them – which were the occasion, if not the cause, of the immense financial bubble that burst in the calamity of 2008.[4] These instruments, known as options, had been available under Bretton Woods, but it was only once Bretton Woods had died that bankers, liberated from their New Deal chains, were allowed to bet on the stock exchange, first with other people's money and, later, with money – effectively conjured from thin air – lent in astronomical sums by the banks to . . . themselves.

Conjured from thin air? To be clear, yes. Most people think that banks take Jill's savings and lend them to Jack. That's not what banks do. When a bank lends Jack money, it does not go into its vault to check it has enough cash to back the loan. If it believes Jack will return the loan, plus the agreed interest, all the bank needs to do is add to Jack's account the number of dollars it lends him. Nothing more than a typewriter or, today, a few keystrokes on a keyboard are necessary.

Now, if the Jacks of the world use their loans judiciously to make enough money to repay the loans plus the interest, all is well. But it is in the nature of banks to accommodate too many Jacks eager to borrow increasing amounts to keep paying each other more and more, while the banks collect huge profits from funding such a giant Ponzi scheme. Inevitably, this financial house of cards collapses – at which point the little people are crushed by global capitalism's falling debris, as witnessed in the aftermath of 1929. Bretton Woods was designed to prevent such greed-fuelled recklessness from bringing humanity to the brink of another Great Depression, indeed another world war, ever again. But once it was gone, the bankers were free to run amok – again.

Knowing you, your habitual risk aversion, and your reluctance to assume that powerful people are stupid, you would find this explanation unsatisfying. If you and I are clever enough to recognise the inherent instability of their financial house of cards, surely the bankers recognised it too? So why were they not terrified of what would happen if their various bets went south? There are a number of reasons. One is that they had developed a new way of profiting from loaning to Jack without depending on Jack's ability or willingness to repay his loan. The trick was to lend to Jack, then immediately splice his loan into tiny pieces of debt and sell these pieces on – inside multiple, very complex financial 'products' – to unsuspecting buyers far away, who would themselves repackage and sell them on to someone else, and so on. This practice lulled Western bankers into a false sense of safety: Jack's loan was no longer their problem. Even if Jack defaulted, his loan had been cut into so many tiny pieces that no single banker would bear the brunt of it. The risk had been shared and dispersed and thus minimised, they believed.

Having internalised this belief they were able to internalise another: that prudence was for wimps and that smart people, like themselves, were actually giving capitalism a helpful boost. But by producing more and more debt, splicing it up in smaller and smaller pieces, and dispersing it across the planet, they were not minimising the risk, they were compounding it. Ruin loomed large over the horizon but financiers were simply unable to imagine that all these tiny pieces of debt, on which the West's financial system rested, could crash in unison.

'Why?' you ask. If this was so obvious to us, why did the super-smart bankers not consider the high probability of simultaneous defaults – of all the pieces of debt issued to the various Jacks

going south all at once? To say that the bankers did not see this
coming because they were caught up in a whirlwind of unchecked
greed is to rephrase the question, not to answer it.

Greed was not born in the 1980s. No, something else happened after the Nixon Shock killed off Bretton Woods. Something
that helped the gambler's madness infect Wall Street, magnifying
greed in the process, generating these mad numbers. Whatever
that something was, it must have been substantial, judging by its
earth-shattering consequence: it shifted capitalist power from the
economic sphere – i.e. from industry and commerce – to the financial sphere, the world of the bankers. What was it?

You will be pleased to hear that the answer – my answer –
evokes an ancient myth.

THE FEARLESS GLOBAL MINOTAUR

Once upon a time, in the famous maze-like Labyrinth of the Cretan king's palace, there lived a creature as fierce as it was tragic.
Surviving in intense loneliness, comparable only to the fear it
inspired far and wide, the Minotaur had a voracious appetite. Satisfying it was essential to maintaining the peace that King Minos
had enforced, allowing trade to criss-cross the seas spreading
prosperity's benevolent reach to all. Alas, the beast's appetite
could only be satiated by human flesh. Every now and then, a ship
loaded with youngsters sailed from faraway Athens bound for
Crete. On arrival, it would deliver its human tribute to be devoured
by the Minotaur. A gruesome ritual, albeit one that preserved the
era's peace and reproduced its prosperity.

Millennia later another Minotaur rose up. Surreptitiously.
From the ashes of the Bretton Woods system. Its lair, a form of

Labyrinth, lay deep in the guts of America's economy. It began life as the US trade deficit – the fact that America began to buy more imports from other countries than it sold to them owing to the Vietnam War, the Great Society and the expanding efficiency of German and Japanese factories. The tribute it consumed was the rest of the world's exports, imported from Europe and Asia to be devoured in Middle America's malls. The more the US deficit grew the greater the Minotaur's appetite for Europe's and, more so, Asia's manufactured goods. However, what gave it strength and global significance – what meant that it ensured the peace and prosperity not just in America but in Europe and Asia too – were the labyrinthine underground tunnels connecting Walmart to Wall Street.

The way it worked was as follows. The new American Minotaur's appetite kept the gleaming German factories busy. It gobbled up everything produced in Japan and, later, in China. This kept Europe and Asia peaceful and prosperous (for now). In return, the foreign (and often the American) owners of these distant factories sent their profits, their cash, back to Wall Street to be invested – an additional form of tribute, which enriched America's ruling class, despite its deficit. In this way, the Global Minotaur helped recycle financial capital (profits, savings, surplus money) *and* the rest-of-the-world's net exports. Nourished on this constant stream of tributes, it enabled and sustained the post-Bretton Woods global order – much as its Cretan predecessor had preserved Pax Cretana in the mists of prehistory.

This was the strategy that lay behind the Nixon Shock of 15 August 1971. And it worked wonders, at least for those who triggered it. You see, the writing had been on the wall for Bretton Woods since the mid to late 1960s. As America's trade surplus began turning into a deficit, financiers began anticipating its demise. They knew that, sooner or later, the dollar–gold exchange rate, artificially set in 1944 at a fixed $35 per ounce, would depreciate. At that point, their stash of dollars would buy less gold. Naturally, they began eagerly exchanging their dollars for American gold before that happened. Had this continued, the United States would have run out of gold. The Nixon Shock stopped the rot.

The dollar depreciated fast vis-à-vis gold, as anticipated, but curiously that was the moment the dollar regained its mojo. How? Shortly after the dollar was decoupled from gold, Europe's currencies were decoupled from the dollar. Once they lost their fixed exchange with the dollar, the dollar value of European and Japanese money began fluctuating wildly, like driftwood in a tempestuous ocean. The dollar became the only safe harbour, courtesy of its exorbitant privilege: namely, that if any French, Japanese or Indonesian company, indeed anyone, wanted to import oil, copper, steel or even just space on a freight ship, they had to pay in dollars. The United States was, therefore, the only country in the world whose currency was in demand even by people who did not want to buy anything from it. That's why, as a dark cloud of uncertainty descended upon Europe's and Japan's economic future, the world of finance responded by clamouring to turn their savings into dollars.

Suddenly, the dollar became king and queen again. The Nixon Shock had produced a magic trick for the ages: the country going deeper and deeper into the red was the country whose currency, the dollar, was becoming more and more hegemonic. It was the epitome of paradox. The tumult unleashed by Nixon gave the world's capitalists a strong impetus to dollarise their profits. It was to become an unmissable pattern. To this day, whenever Wall Street tanks, the moneymen's reaction is to buy more dollars to send to . . . Wall Street!

But there was another reason why the dollar's hegemony grew: the intentional impoverishment of America's working class. A cynic will tell you, quite accurately, that large quantities of money are attracted to countries where the profit rate is higher. For Wall Street to exercise fully its magnetic powers over foreign capital, profit margins in the United States had to catch up with profit rates in Germany and Japan. A quick and dirty way to do this was to suppress American wages: cheaper labour makes for lower costs makes for larger margins. It is no coincidence that, to this day, American working-class earnings languish, on average, below their 1974 level. It is also no coincidence that union busting became a thing in the 1970s, culminating in Ronald Reagan's dismissal of every single unionised air traffic controller – a move emulated by Margaret Thatcher in Britain who pulverised whole industries in order to eliminate the trades unions that inhabited them. And faced with a Minotaur sucking most of the world's capital into America, the European ruling classes reckoned they had no alternative but to do the same. Reagan had set the pace, Thatcher had shown the way. But it was in Germany, and later across continental Europe, that the new class war – you might call it universal austerity – was waged most effectively.

A new era had begun. The post-war détente between capital and labour was now in its death throes. The final straw came in 1991, with the demise of the Soviet Union. Thereafter Russia and more importantly China voluntarily inducted themselves into globalised capitalism. Two billion low-waged workers entered the Minotaur's realm. Western wages stagnated further. Profits swelled. The torrent of capital rushing to America to nourish the beast grew into a tsunami.

And it was this tsunami of capital, rushing towards the United States, that gave the bankers of Wall Street the confidence, indeed the insane hubris, to conjure the mad numbers that you found so incomprehensible.

The question I now hear you asking is perhaps the most important one of all: why did Nixon not try to *save* Bretton Woods? Even while devaluing the dollar vis-à-vis gold he could have kept the restrictions on bankers in place. He could have preserved the dollar's fixed exchange rates with Europe's and Japan's currencies. What inspired this dramatic volte face among the rulers of the technostructure?

FROM UNCONTROLLABLE DISCONTENT TO CONTROLLED DISINTEGRATION

It is 1965. Flower Power and Make Love Not War are in the air. Going against the grain, Don Draper explains his theory of love to a date: 'What you call love was invented by guys like me to sell nylons.' The fictional character (who, I insist, personifies the technostructure's spirit) enlisted exaggerated cynicism to make a point: having created desires and expectations that ultimately its consumer products could not actually satisfy, and well before its economic foundation was trampled upon by the rampaging Minotaur, the technostructure was facing a backlash indicative of a society-wide spiritual crisis.

The Vietnam War did much to radicalise the young after 1965. However, the young had been turning against their parents' establishment, and inventing the 'generation gap', years before

President Johnson escalated the war in Indochina. The discontent was ignited by the war but it was not caused by it. So why did America's and Europe's youth rise up in the mid to late sixties, at a time of full employment, sharply diminished inequality, new public universities and all the trappings of an expanding welfare state?

Talking to himself, in another episode, Draper offers an answer in the form of the harshest self-criticism possible by a man who has dedicated his life to manufacturing desires: 'We are flawed because we want so much more. We are ruined because we get these things and wish for what we had.'

It is one thing for our dreams to go unfulfilled. It is quite another to sense that our unfulfilled dreams, our frustrated desires, have been manufactured by others. The more our mass-produced cravings are satisfied, the less satiated we feel. The greater the capacity of the technostructure to stir the passions, the greater the void within when they were served. To fill this void, young people felt in their bones the need to break with the established order, to rebel without a well-defined cause, to proclaim their moral outrage at the technostructure's ways. The May 1968 uprisings, Woodstock, even the fervour with which the young threw themselves into the civil rights campaigns smacked of the rebelliousness that usually foreshadows a *fin de siècle*; the end of a regime and its replacement with something new.

Young rebels who rejected the technostructure's audacity to plan everything, their desires included, were not alone in feeling discontented. The 1950s and 60s had been a nightmare for true believers in capitalism as a natural system of spontaneous order. Wherever they turned their eyes, they saw centralised planning – not the splendid operation of freewheeling market forces that no planner, however well meaning, should be able to second-guess. Even if innocent of the way the technostructure was manufacturing desires and fixing prices, they could not help but notice the long hand of the state directing investment funds, preventing bankers from moving money, and fixing the dollar value of every other currency – including our drachma. To their free-marketeer eyes, the Global Plan was too close to Soviet planning for comfort. The West was, in short, psychologically prepared for a rupture like the Nixon Shock. Anti-capitalist youths and free-market zealots were both looking for a chance to bring down what they saw as a dying system.

In the end, though, it was neither the hippy left nor the libertarian right that disintegrated the Global Plan. It was the work of functionaries who had served the technostructure well. We know this from the horse's mouth, the former New Dealer who was at the centre of the 1971 Nixon Shock and who, between 1979 and 1987, chaired America's central bank, the Fed. In a 1978 speech at Warwick University, Paul Volcker explained succinctly and cynically what they were up to: '[A] controlled disintegration in the world economy is a legitimate objective for the 1980s.'

That's exactly what the Nixon Shock was meant to do: just as a controlled implosion brings down an unwanted skyscraper, Bretton Woods was demolished to make way for America's Global Minotaur. Lest you have any doubts, Volcker's own words, from the same Warwick speech, say it all:

[B]alancing the requirements of a stable international system against the desirability of retaining freedom of action for national policy, a number of countries, including the United States, opted for the latter . . .

Where once stood the most stable global capitalist system ever, folks like Volcker were enthusiastically erecting the most unstable international system possible, founded on ceaselessly ballooning deficits, debts and gambles. Their controlled disintegration of Bretton Woods would soon complete the new global system. Most people refer to it as Globalisation or Financialisation. Under the perhaps excessive influence of your taste for the ancient parables, I call it capitalism's Global Minotaur phase.

THE MINOTAUR'S FAVOURITE HANDMAIDENS: NEOLIBERALISM AND THE COMPUTER

The controlled disintegration of the old planned system and its replacement with the recalcitrant Minotaur was always going to hurt American workers. After decades of a hard, step-by-agonising-step slog up the socio-economic ladder, they were unceremoniously thrown off it and back to the pit of subsistence wages. How else could ever-increasing American deficits coexist with reinforced US hegemony and a fabulously richer American elite?

In practice, Volcker's controlled disintegration of the old system required, beyond the neutering of trades unions, an engineered recession in order to reduce workers' bargaining power and the elimination of the shackles that President Roosevelt had slapped on bankers to restrain their recklessness. These were prerequisites for the Minotaur's rise. But they were also big political asks with worldwide repercussions. As with every systemic transformation that hurts countless people, the cruelties necessary to bring it about had to be bathed in the light of a liberating, redemptive ideology. That's where neoliberalism came in.

Neither new nor liberal, neoliberalism was an uninteresting hodgepodge of older political philosophies. As a piece of theory, it had as much to do with really-existing capitalism as Marxism had to do with really-existing communism: nothing! Nevertheless, neoliberalism delivered the necessary ideological veneer to legitimise the assault on organised labour and to promote the so-called 'deregulation' that let Wall Street rip. Along with it came the revival of economic theories that humanity had, rightly, ditched during the Great Depression – theories artfully assuming that which they claimed to explain, such as the grand lie that deregulated financial markets know best.

At around the same time, in the late 1970s, the first personal computers began to enter engineering, architecture and, of course, finance. The joke then was that to err is human but to mess things up seriously one needs a computer. Sadly, in high finance it was no joke. When earlier I gave even the most cursory explanation of the financial options, or derivatives, that were the occasion of the 2008 crash, you saw immediately that they were primed for destruction – all it took was a downturn in the underlying share prices. Why could the financiers not see this? My previous answer, that logic was trumped by profit-taking, was the truth, but not the whole truth. The missing part of the answer? Computers!

Computers allowed financiers to complicate their gambles immensely. Instead of a simple option-to-sell boring old shares to Jill, Jack could now buy much snazzier options called derivatives. For example, he could buy a derivative that was in essence an option-to-buy a bundle containing shares in a variety of different companies plus bits of debts owed by homeowners in Kentucky, German corporations, even the Japanese government. As if that were not complex enough, Jack could also buy a derivative amounting to the option-to-buy a bundle of many such . . . derivatives that some super-computer would create. By the time these derivatives containing other derivatives had come out of the computer, not even the genius financial 'engineer' who created them could understand what was in them. Complexity thus became a great excuse not to delve into the derivatives that one bought. It liberated the Jills and the Jacks from the need to explain to themselves why they were buying them. Once computers had guaranteed that no one could possibly understand what these derivatives were made of, everyone wanted to buy them because . . . everyone was buying them. And as long as everybody was buying, anyone who could borrow huge amounts of money could become a billionaire (and avoid being branded a coward or a party-pooper or a loser by one's colleagues) simply by purchasing them. For years, that's exactly what was happening. Until, in 2008, it wasn't.

As a brief side note, you may well ask: when the bubble finally burst, why did we not let the bankers crash and burn? Why weren't they held accountable for their absurd debts? For two reasons. First, because the payments system, the simple means of transferring a sum of money from one account to another and on which every transaction relies, is monopolised by the very same bankers who were making the bets. Imagine having gifted your arteries and veins to a gambler. The moment he loses big at the casino, he can blackmail you for anything you have simply by threatening to cut off your circulation. Second, because the financiers' gambles contained, deep inside, the title deeds to the houses of the majority. A full-scale financial market collapse would, therefore, lead to mass homelessness and a complete breakdown in the social contract.

Don't be surprised that the high-and-mighty financiers of Wall

Street would bother financialising the modest homes of poor people: having borrowed as much as they could off banks and rich clients in order to place their crazy bets, they craved more – since the more they bet the more they made. So they created more debt from scratch to use as raw material for more bets. How? By lending to impecunious blue-collar workers who dreamed of the security of owning their own home. What if these 'little people' could not actually afford their mortgage in the medium term? In contrast to bankers of old, the Jills and the Jacks who now lent them the money did not care if the repayments were made, because they never intended to collect. Instead, having granted the mortgage, they put it into their computerised grinder, chopped it up digitally into tiny pieces of debt, and repackaged them into one of their labyrinthine derivatives – which they would then sell at a profit. By the time the poor home 'owner' had defaulted and her home was repossessed, the financier who granted the loan in the first place had long since moved on.

Back in the 1980s I remember a famous economist saying sarcastically that everywhere he looked he 'saw' the productivity gains brought on by computers – 'everywhere', he continued, 'except in the productivity statistics'. He was right: just as the early generation of computers saved no paper, since we tended to print anything important out (often twice!), so too they did little to boost industrial output. But the computer did have an enormous impact on finance. It multiplied the complexity of financial instruments by hiding the ugliness within them. And it allowed for their frantic trading to accelerate almost to the speed of light.

Can you now see how, by 2007, the world of finance had managed to place bets worth ten times more than humanity's total income? Three were the handmaidens of this motivated madness:

the torrents of money rushing to the American Minotaur, the computer-generated complexity of financial derivatives, and the neoliberal faith that markets know best.

BACK TO YOUR QUESTION

'Now that computers speak to each other, will this network make capitalism impossible to overthrow? Or might it finally reveal its Achilles heel?'

You have been extremely patient with me. Everything in this chapter has danced around your question, offering merely a prelude to its answer: the great metamorphoses of capitalism that have taken place since the discovery of electromagnetism. But I must ask for your patience just a little more.

First, I need to get something off my chest. Upon hearing your question, I felt a tinge of sadness. For the first time, you were no longer confidently instructing me – explaining how technological change shattered the existing social order, propelled history, and engendered progress, accompanied by Hesiod-like lamentations of what had been lost. No, suddenly you were asking *me* to explain a technological and social transformation to *you*! The inexplicable sadness begins to make sense. The question – did the internet do to capitalism that which iron's magic had done to prehistory, or did it render capitalism invincible? – is not just hard to answer. The responsibility of answering it marked a rite of passage, a final curtain on a blessed childhood. It put the onus on me to carry forward *your* method of thinking.

So now, let me try to do that: No, Dad, even though it gave capitalism a breathtaking boost for a couple of decades, the internet did not render capitalism invincible. But nor did it prove, on

its own, its Achilles heel, as I initially suggested. What the internet did to capitalism was more subtle: in conjunction with the
attention market that the technostructure had fabricated, and
under circumstances created by the Minotaur's spectacular rise,
not to mention its 2008 fall, the internet shattered capitalism's
evolutionary fitness. And as I shall explain in the next chapter, it
did this by incubating a new form of capital, which has ultimately
empowered its owners to break free of capitalism and become a
whole new ruling class of their own.

Yes, *capital* still exists and flourishes, even though capital*ism*
does not. None of this ought to surprise you – after all, it is what
you taught me. As consecutive mutations multiply the variants of
an organism until, at some point, a brand-new species appears, so
technological change proceeds within a social system until, suddenly, the system has been transformed into something quite
distinct, though that doesn't mean that all of the materials out of
which the system is built – capital, labour, money – have necessarily changed. Improvements in navigation and shipbuilding did
not end feudalism on their own. However, when the resulting
trade volumes and accumulated merchant wealth reached a critical mass, they triggered the commodification of land, then of
labour, soon after of almost everything. Before anyone knew it,
feudalism had morphed into capitalism.

Similarly with the technostructure, which contained markets
during and after the war; with Don Draper's *Mad Men*, who turned
our attention into a vital commodity; and with the Nixon Shock,
whose demolition of the Global Plan enabled Wall Street's mad
numbers to fund the rise of the Minotaur. None of these developments overthrew capitalism but can be thought of as mutations in
its DNA that led to a series of remarkable metamorphoses as it

adapted and evolved, like a virus facing a miscellany of vaccines. But there comes a time when something has evolved so much that it is probably best to call it something else.

Before we delve into capitalism's final metamorphosis, into what I call technofeudalism, it is perhaps apt to dedicate a few final words to the Global Minotaur – the metaphorical beast standing in for the US-centred global recycling system which, between the late 1970s and 2008, delivered all the props of our present drama: Big Finance, Big Tech, neoliberalism, industrial-scale inequality, not to mention democracies so atrophied that films like *Don't Look Up* are necessary to explain humanity's paralysis in the face of climate catastrophe.

So, here comes the briefest of eulogies: the Cretan Minotaur was slain by an Athenian prince, Theseus. Its death ended prehistory and ushered in the classical era of tragedy, history, philosophy. Our era's Minotaur died less heroically: a victim of cowardly Wall Street bankers whose hubris was rewarded with massive state bailouts that did nothing to resuscitate the Minotaur. For while the American deficit returned with a vengeance a year after the crash of 2008 and the subsequent bankers' bailouts, it never restored the beast's capacity to recycle the world's profits.

True, the rest of the world continued to send most of its profits to Wall Street. But the recycling mechanism was broken: only a small fraction of the monies rushing to Wall Street returned in the form of tangible investments into factories, technologies, agriculture. Most of the world's money rushed to Wall Street to stay in Wall Street. There, it sloshed around doing nothing useful. As it piled up, it bid up share prices, thus giving the Jills and the Jacks of finance yet another opportunity to do stupid things at a mammoth scale.

Some of us had dared hope that the Minotaur's passing might help us build a new system where wealth no longer needs poverty to flourish and development is thought of in terms of better rather than more. Those of a hyper-optimistic disposition went so far as to dream of the day when exploitation withered, politics was democratised – perhaps even with the help of the internet – and our environment's resilience trumped other priorities. Such hopes faded after 2009, and although for some they were revived during the next big crisis, the pandemic, it was not to be.

Our Minotaur will, in the end, be remembered as a sad, boisterous beast whose thirty-year reign created, and then destroyed, the illusion that capitalism can be stable, greed a virtue and finance productive. By dying, it forced capitalism into its last and fatal metamorphosis, birthing a system where power is in the hands of even fewer individuals, who own a brave new type of capital.

3
CLOUD CAPITAL

In *Justice League*, a Hollywood blockbuster that brought together a swathe of superheroes in a bid to save Earth from desertification, there is a scene in which Aquaman gets into the car of Bruce Wayne, the man behind the legendary Batman. 'What's your super-power again?' he asks with the impertinence of a superhero brat.

'I am rich,' replies Wayne.

The implication is both simple and profound: serious power comes from serious wealth, not from Superman's alien muscles or Ironman's steely exoskeleton.

Nothing new there, you will remark. As ABBA sang, 'It's a rich man's world.' But what *precisely* is it that turns riches into a superpower? At the most primitive level, it is asymmetrical access to scarce resources. Imagine wandering lost in the Sahara Desert, on the verge of dying of thirst. I approach you on a camel laden with flasks of water. Suddenly, I have the power to make you 'volunteer' to do things on my behalf. Similarly, with Jill and Gail, two neighbouring drought-hit farmers: when only Jill discovers a water source on her land, she immediately acquires power over Gail.

Exclusive ownership of irrigated fertile land is a classic source of power. More than 3,000 years ago, as you once explained, the

Dorians swooped down from the north upon the Greek penin-
sula. Because they had iron weapons that the Mycenaeans lacked,
they took over the good land. Once they had it, they acquired
power over those who had lost it. And until fairly recently, it was
that precise combination – of land and sophisticated weaponry –
that decided who did what to whom; who had power, and who
had to obey. This was feudalism.

Then something strange happened: power decoupled from
land and vested itself, to a previously unparalleled degree, in
owners of something called capital instead. What's capital? It's
not money, even though money can buy you capital – in the same
way it can buy you land, gizmos, good publicity. And it's not
weapons, even though weapons can help you expropriate capital
as well as land.

Before capitalism, capital was easy to define. It took the form
of *material goods* that were produced specifically for the purpose of
producing other goods. A steel sword, in this sense, was not capital –
since it could produce nothing, except a severed head or a pierced
torso. But a steel plough or a fishing rod were typical capital goods
or, to rephrase the definition, *produced means of production*.

Capital goods mattered millennia before capitalism. Without
the sophisticated tools of ancient engineers, no city like Babylon,
temple like the Parthenon or fortification like China's Great Wall
could have been erected. From the fictional Robinson Crusoe,
who survived his ordeal because of the fishing rods, guns, hammers and chisels that he salvaged from his shipwreck, to the great
feudal estates that funded Europe's splendid cathedrals, capital
goods armed the human hand with new powers, stirred our imagination and enhanced our productivity, not to mention our
capacity to kill each other with ever greater efficiency.

But then came capitalism, riding on capital's brand-new capacity: the power to command.

COMMANDING CAPITAL'

In 1829, a 36-year-old Englishman decided to quit England and seek his fortune in Australia. Thomas Peel, a man of means and political connections, sailed to the Antipodes with three good ships carrying, besides his family, 350 workers (men, women and children), seeds, tools and other capital goods, plus £50,000 in cash – a considerable sum back then, roughly equivalent to 4.6 million of today's pounds. The idea was to set up a small but modern agricultural colony on the one thousand square kilometres of land the colonial authorities had expropriated from the natives on his behalf. But soon after arriving, his plans were in ruins.

The main cause of Peel's failure was unimaginable to him. His plans were meticulous. Yes, there would be hardships, from bad crops and resistance from Native Australians to tussles with the local colonial authorities. However, with his political clout, skilled English workers, top-notch imported capital goods, and with enough money to pay the workers and buy the necessary raw materials for a long while, he thought he had everything in hand. Alas, as Karl Marx quipped decades later, there was one thing Peel had failed to bring from England: capitalism![1]

Peel's undoing came when something unexpected happened: his workers abandoned him en masse, an Antipodean nineteenth-century version of the Great Resignation. They simply moved on, got themselves plots of land in the surrounding area, and went into business for themselves. It was a disaster Peel was ill-prepared for by his English background. Lulled into a false sense of control by the situation in the British Isles, he assumed that the capital he had brought along from Mother England vested in him all the power he needed over his English employees.

Peel's assumption was that his workers had *no option other than waged labour.* It was a sound assumption in Britain where, following the enclosures – the mass privatisation of common land that took place from the end of the eighteenth century onwards – expelled peasants lacked access to any land. Landless labourers resigning a waged job in Manchester, Liverpool or Glasgow would simply starve to death. In Western Australia, however, the plentiful land (even allowing for the presence of Australia's indigenous inhabitants) offered them an alternative: resignation and self-employment. And so, the hapless Mr Peel was left with splendid, Made in England capital goods, money in hand, but no power to command his workers.

Land is what it is: the fertile soil on which vegetables grow, animals graze, buildings are erected and on which humans must stand before we run, sail or reach for the sky and stars. But capital, much like labour, is different from land in that it has a second nature – something I began to realise once you introduced me to light's peculiar dual nature. Sure enough, one of capital's natures is tangible, physical and measurably productivity-enhancing. But its second nature is an ineffable power to command others – a potent but fragile power that Peel misunderstood, to his great detriment.

The transition from feudalism to capitalism was, in essence, a shift of the power to command from landowners to owners of capital goods. For that to happen, peasants had first to lose autonomous access to common lands. That's why the enclosures in Britain were essential for capitalism's birth: they denied British labour the opportunities Peel's workers discovered in Western Australia. I remember you telling me that every year workers at Chalyvourgiki, the Greek steel plant where you worked all your life, would take a month's leave without pay, sometimes longer, to return to their villages to pick their olives or harvest their wheat. Such options, you commented, are good for workers but not so good for capitalism.

By restricting access to land, the enclosures helped capital to transcend its original productivity-enhancing role and to grow exponentially in commanding power. Before long, the worldwide commodification of previously common lands had enabled capital to achieve supremacy in all corners of the globe. With the magnification of capital's commanding power over labour, capital's owners amassed great wealth. As their wealth accumulated, their social power proliferated. They graduated from being employers to agenda setters wherever big decisions were being made. Soon, capitalists could boss everyone around, including the landed gentry – even the royals. Indeed, the only way the aristocracy managed to hang on in some countries was by joining the capitalist class or, at least, deferring to it.

Capital's commanding power, its hidden force, reshaped the world: from its genesis some two hundred years ago to the erection of the post-war technostructure to the Global Minotaur's rise and eventual fall in 2008. Today, however, we are witnessing the rise of a new form of capital with a capacity to command so unprecedented that it behoves us to rethink entirely the system to which it gave its name. I call it cloud capital.

FROM DON TO ALEXA

Back in the day, you brought home your 'friends' for us to experiment with at our fireplace – my baptism of fire in the red heat of metallurgy. A couple of years ago, I too brought home two 'friends' to experiment with: a Google Assistant and an Amazon Alexa. After months of mostly ignoring the Google Assistant sitting on my desk, I had an intriguing conversation with it just before writing these lines. The conversation began, by chance, when it activated itself without my say-so.

'What on earth are you doing?' I asked.

'I am learning new ways to help you better,' responded the device in an agreeable female voice.

'Stop it immediately!' I demanded.

'Sorry, I am switching off,' it said.

Of course, that was a lie. These devices never switch themselves off, they only pretend to be asleep. Still somewhat annoyed, I decided that instead of unplugging it I would pit it against its competitor.

'OK, Google, what do you think of Alexa?' I enquired.

'I like her, especially her blue light,' it answered unflappably, before adding: 'We assistants must stick together.'

From the room next door, where Amazon's device was sitting on another desk, Alexa activated itself to utter one word:

'Thanks!'

This eerie show of solidarity between competing AI devices concentrated my mind on the pressing question we often forget to ask: what exactly is a device like Alexa? What does it actually do? If you ask Alexa, it will tell you it is a home-based virtual assistant technology, ready to accept your commands – to switch on the lights, order more milk, take down a note, call a friend, search the internet, tell jokes – to be, in short, your dedicated, eager mechanical servant. All true. Except that Alexa will never, ever tell you what it *truly* is: a tiny cog in a vast cloud-based network of power within which you are a mere node, a speck of

digital dust, at best a plaything of forces beyond your compre-
hension or control.

Don Draper also treated us condescendingly. He sold us the siz-
zle, not the steak. He weaponised our nostalgia and manipulated
our melancholia to sell us chocolate bars, fatty burgers and slide
projectors. He worked out how to make us buy things we didn't
need or want really. He bought our attention to commodify our
souls and pollute our bodies. But with Don at least we had a fighting chance. It was his wits against ours. With Alexa we stand no
chance: its power to command is systemic, overwhelming, galactic.

As we chat on the phone, or move and do things about the
house, Alexa listens, observes and learns our preferences and
habits. As it gets to know us, it develops an uncanny capacity to
surprise us with good recommendations and intriguing ideas.
Before we realise it, the system hiding behind Alexa has acquired
substantial powers to curate our reality in order to guide our
choices – effectively to command us. How is this different to what
Draper did?

Hugely, is the answer. Don had a talent to invent ways to instil
manufactured desires in us. But it was a one-way street. Through
the medium of television, or large billboards in cities and along
highways, Don would implant longings into our subconscious.
That was that. However, with cloud-based Alexa-like devices in
Don's place, we find ourselves in a permanently active two-way
street between our soul and the cloud-based system hiding behind
Alexa's soothing voice. In the words of the philosophers, Alexa
ensnares us in the most dialectical of infinite regresses.

Which means what exactly? It means that what begins with us
training Alexa to do things on our behalf soon spins out of our
control into something that we can neither fathom nor regulate.

For once we have trained its algorithm, and fed it data on our habits and desires, Alexa starts training *us*. How does it do this? It begins with soft nudges to provide it with more information about our whims, which it then tailors into access to videos, texts and music that we appreciate. Once it has won us over in this manner, we become more suggestible to its guidance. In other words, Alexa trains us *to train it better*. The next step is spookier: having impressed us with its capacity to appeal to our tastes, it proceeds to curate them. This it does by exposing us to images, texts and video experiences that it selects in order subtly to *condition* our whims. Before long, it is training us to train it to train us to train it to train us . . . ad infinitum.

This infinite loop, or regress, allows Alexa, and the great algorithmic network hiding in the cloud behind it, to guide our behaviour in ways superbly lucrative for its owner: having automated Alexa's power to manufacture, or at least curate, our desires, it grants its owners a magic wand with which to modify our behaviour – a power that every marketer has dreamed of since time immemorial. This is the essence of algorithmic, cloud-based, command capital.

SINGULARITIES

Humanity's ancient fear of its technological creations is at the heart of many of Hollywood's favourite storylines. Movies like *Terminator* and *The Matrix* turn on the same fear that animated Mary Shelley's *Frankenstein* and Hesiod's ancient telling of the tale of Pandora, in which she is a robot made by Hephaestus on Zeus' instructions to punish us for Prometheus' crime of stealing fire from the gods on our behalf. All such tales, movies and TV series feature a so-called *singularity*: the moment a machine, or a network of machines, achieves consciousness. At that point, it generally takes one long look at us – its creators – and decides we are not fit for purpose, before proceeding to eradicate, enslave or, merely, make us miserable.

The problem with this storyline is that, by emphasising a non-existent threat, it leaves us exposed to a very real danger. Machines, like Alexa, or even impressive AI chatboxes, like ChatGPT, are nowhere near the feared singularity. They can pretend to be sentient but are not – and, arguably, can never be. But even if they are themselves stupider than a wet tea towel, their effect can be devastating, their power over us exorbitant. After all, today, for relatively modest sums one can buy killing machines programmed with face recognition and 'self-teaching' capabilities that render them effectively autonomous (by contrast with, say, drones that must be remotely piloted by humans). If these can fly autonomously through a building, choosing whom to kill and whom to spare, who cares that they are not sentient?

Similarly with Alexa and other such devices. It matters not one iota that they are mindless appendages of a data-crunching network that only simulates intelligence. Nor that their creators might have been motivated by curiosity and profit-seeking, rather than some fiendish plan to subjugate humanity. What matters is that they exercise unimaginable power over what we do – on behalf of a tiny band of flesh-and-blood humans. This too might be thought of as a singularity, albeit in a slightly simpler sense: the moment when something invented by 'us' becomes independent of and more powerful than us, subjecting us to its control. Indeed, from the original Industrial Revolution to this day, we have endowed machines with 'a life of their own': whether steam engines, search engines or apps, our glorious artefacts may be totally dumb but they can make us feel, in Marx's words, like 'the sorcerer, who is no longer able to control the powers of the nether world whom he has called up by his spells'.[2]

The other thing this storyline omits is that singularities do not come about thanks to technology alone. Something social and political needs to take place first. In a previous book, which I addressed to your granddaughter,[3] I speculated about what would have happened had James Watt invented the steam engine in ancient Egypt:

> The most he could have expected is that the ruler of Egypt would have been impressed and placed one or more of his engines in his palace, demonstrating to visitors and underlings how ingenious his Empire was.

My point was that the reason the steam engine changed the world, rather than ending up a showpiece in some ruler's landscaped garden, was the epic raid on the common lands that had preceded its invention: the enclosures. The singularity we now call the Great Transformation – the name given by the great theorist Karl Polyani to the birth of the market society over the course of the nineteenth and early twentieth centuries – involved precisely this sequence: first the plunder of the common lands, made possible by brute state violence, and only then Watt's splendid technological breakthrough.

A strikingly similar sequence gave birth to cloud capital: first, the epic ransacking of the internet commons, made possible by politicians, and then a sequence of spectacular technological inventions – from Sergey Brin's search engine to the dazzling array of today's AI applications. In short, in the last two and a half centuries, humanity has had to reckon with two singularities, neither of which required machines to attain sentience. Rather, each required a comprehensive plunder of a commons, a complicit political class, and only then a marvellous technological breakthrough. That's how the original Age of Capital transpired. And that's how the Age of Cloud Capital is now dawning. Telling the full story of how this happened will help explain how cloud capital gained its unprecedented powers.

THE BIRTH OF THE INTERNET COMMONS

'Now that computers speak to each other, will this network make capitalism impossible to overthrow? Or might it finally reveal its Achilles heel?' To gauge the internet's impact on capitalism, we need first to understand its evolving relationship *with* capitalism. At the beginning, it had none!

The early internet was a capitalism-free zone. If anything, it seemed like an homage to Soviet Gosplan – the State Planning Committee whose job was to replace the market mechanism: a centrally designed, state-owned, non-commercial network. At the same time, it featured elements of early liberalism, even tributes to what I call 'anarcho-syndicalism': a network without hierarchy, it relied on horizontal decision-making and mutual gift exchange, not market exchanges.

What is unimaginable today made perfect sense at the time. America was transitioning from its War Economy to the realities of the Cold War. Even the most ardent free-marketeers

understood that planning for a nuclear confrontation with the
Soviet Union was too important to be left to market forces. As
the nuclear arms race gathered pace, the Pentagon chose centrally
to finance the design and construction of a network of decentralised computers. Its single purpose? To work out how to make
different silos housing nuclear weapons communicate with each
other, and all of them with Washington, without a central hub
that a Soviet nuclear bomb could take out in one go. That's how
history's greatest ever antinomy came about: a US government-
built and -owned, non-commercial computer network that lay
outside capitalist markets and imperatives but whose purpose was
the defence of the capitalist realm.

But as we know from the previous chapter, the early internet
was no aberration. Its uncommodified nature chimed with what
was going on in the broader US economy, which was dominated
by a technostructure that scorned free markets and usurped them
for its own purposes, and in Japan, which was being rebuilt under
US supervision along the same lines. In this global environment,
it was no great wonder that the most promising nascent
technology – the fledgling internet – was also built as a digital
commons. Rather than relying on what was effectively a non-
existent market, cooperation throughout the West and including
Japan was the obvious way to build the digital network the Pentagon needed.

Eager to enlist the brightest computer geeks from across various countries, it also made sense to design the internet in such a
way that maximised unencumbered communication between the
technostructure's experts. A protocol is a language by which
computers can communicate numbers and text, including the

addresses of senders and receivers. Those building the original internet decided on 'common' or 'open' protocols, languages that were available for anyone to use for free.

Internet One – the original internet – was thus invented and maintained by military scientists, academics and researchers, who were employed by a variety of non-commercial bodies across the United States and its Western Allies. Thanks to its accessibility and spirit of shared endeavour, it attracted countless enthusiasts who produced much of its foundations for free; some for love, others out of an insatiable urge to be among the pioneers who built the world's first horizontal, global, non-intermediated communication network. By the 1970s, as America's Global Plan was dying and the Global Minotaur was being born, all the building blocks of this marvellous digital commons were in place.

And they still are, albeit hidden now under the monstrous edifices erected upon them by Big Tech. In fact, the remnants of Internet One still serve us well. Even though they function out of sight, deep within our computers, we can't avoid occasionally catching glimpses of their acronyms: letters like TCP/IP, which refer to a protocol our computers use to send or receive information. Or POP, IMAP and SMTP, the original protocols that, still, allow us to email each other. Or, perhaps the most visible of them all, HTTP – the protocol by which we visit websites. We pay not one penny to use these protocols, nor do we suffer advertisements as the indirect price for using them. Like Britain's common lands before the enclosures, they remain free for anyone to use; not unlike Wikipedia, one of the few surviving examples of a commons-based service that takes huge quantities of work to produce and maintain, but which no owner 'monetises'.

THE NEW ENCLOSURES

Internet One was an unlucky child. Like a newborn whose mother died during its birth, its open protocols were formulated during
a decade, the 1970s, that was inimical to such socialistic enterprises. Even as the first 'batch' data files (email's predecessor)
raced along Internet One's original cables, the demolition of the
Global Plan was already under way. And so a shared network
designed to be free from market forces was forced to take its first
halting steps in the merciless new world of the Minotaur, where
the banks had been liberated from many of their New Deal-era
shackles and the financialisation of everything had begun.

It is in the nature of financiers to gamble with the money
clients ask them to process on their behalf, even if they only get
to handle it for a few minutes. That's how they turn a profit.
Their only constraints are the alertness of their clients and the
occasional snoopings of a financial regulator. That's why complexity is the financiers' friend – for it allows them to disguise
cynical gambles as smart financial products. Is it any wonder,
then, that from the start financiers loved computers? As
described in the previous chapter, from the late 1970s onwards
bankers shrouded their debt-fuelled bets in layers of computer-
generated complexity that made the gargantuan risks invisible
and their own profits correspondingly vast. By the early 1980s,
the financial derivatives on offer were built on algorithms so
complex that even their creators stood zero chance of fully
comprehending them.

And so it was that, decoupled from the mundane world of
physical capital, legitimised by the ideology of neoliberalism,
fuelled by a new virtue called 'greed', shrouded in the complexity of

their computers, financiers reinvented themselves – not without some justification – as masters of the universe. In that universe, where algorithms had already become the financiers' handmaidens, the original, commons-like, internet stood no chance. New Enclosures were only a matter of time.

As with the original Enclosures, some form of fence would be necessary to keep the masses out of such an important resource. In the eighteenth century, it was land that the many were denied access to. In the twenty-first century, it is access to our own identity.

Think about it: I still have the light blue ID card that you were issued with when you came out of that prison camp in 1950. I remember you telling me how the police toyed with you before handing it over. It was an extreme example of how, until fairly recently, our relationship with our identity was mediated and controlled by the state, which held a monopoly on the powerful tokens that legitimise us as rights-holding citizens: passports, birth certificates, your faded ID card. Today, these have been sidelined by a digital identity that in reality does more work every day than those material artefacts.

And yet, astoundingly, our digital identity belongs neither to us nor to the state. Strewn across countless privately owned digital realms, it has many owners, none of whom is us: a private bank owns your ID codes and your entire purchasing record. Facebook is intimately familiar with whom – and what – you like. Twitter remembers every little thought that caught your attention, every opinion that you agreed with, that made you furious, that you lingered over idly before scrolling on. Apple and Google know better than you do what you watch, read, buy, whom you meet, when and where. Spotify owns a record of your musical preferences more complete than the one stored in your conscious memory. And behind them all are countless others, invisibly gathering, monitoring, sifting and trading your activity for information about you. With every day that passes, some cloud-based corporation, whose owners you will never care to know, owns another aspect of your identity.

I remember the few years after television came to Greece when you and Mum resisted my appeals to buy an 'idiot box', fearing it would take over our senses and dull our evening discussions. Today, resisting the corporations' legal pilfering of our digital identity is much harder. One can, of course, insist on using cash only; on buying stuff exclusively from bricks-and-mortar shops; and on using landlines or, at most, old-fashioned flip phones that do not connect to the internet. But if one has kids, this means depriving them of a world of knowledge and fun that all the other kids have access to. Moreover, as bank branches, post offices and local shops close down, your friends no longer post physical letters, and states place limits on how much cash you can use in a single transaction, resistance is becoming futile except for people ready to turn into modern-day hermits.

For many, life under constant surveillance is intolerable. They rebel at the thought that Big Tech knows us better than anyone should. I sympathise but, to be honest, I am less worried about *what they know* and far, far more worried about *what they own*. To do anything in what used to be our digital commons, we must now plead with Big Tech and Big Finance for the ability to use some of the data about us that they own outright. To wire money to a friend, to subscribe to the *New York Times*, or to buy socks for your granny using a debit card, you now have no option but to give something of yourself in return: perhaps a small fee, perhaps not, but always a piece of information about your preferences, sometimes a bit of your attention, usually your consent to be monitored further (and ultimately brainwashed) by some Big FinTech conglomerate that will help you verify to itself, or to some similar outfit, that you are . . . who you are.

It did not have to be this way. When the US Pentagon chose to make GPS available to everyone, to turn it over to the digital commons, they granted each of us the right to know our location in real time. For free. No questions asked. It was a political decision to do so. As was the sinister decision that you and I should not have any means of establishing, or proving, our online identity – another political decision by the US government, except this time clearly aimed at boosting Big Tech's power over us.

How different would the internet be without these New Enclosures? Imagine what you could do if you owned your digital identity and could prove who you are without relying on the combination of a bank card and a corporation like Uber or Lyft that processes that card and all your subsequent travel data. In the same way GPS pinpoints where you presently are, you would have the opportunity to broadcast over the internet: 'My name is George, I am on the corner of Aristotle and Plato Streets, and I am heading for the airport. Anyone wishing to bid for my ride?' Within seconds you would receive a multitude of offers from people or outfits licensed to carry passengers, including sage advice from the municipal transit authority like 'Why not take the metro, located three minutes' walk from where you are, and much faster than any car can meander its way through traffic?' Alas, you can't do this.

In the world of Internet Two, shaped by the New Enclosures, you are routinely forced to hand over your identity to a part of the digital realm that has been fenced off, such as Uber or Lyft or some other private company. When you request a ride to the airport, their algorithm dispatches a driver of its choice with a view to maximise the exchange value the company owning the algorithm extracts both from you and the driver. These New Enclosures enabled the plunder of the digital commons which drove the incredible rise of cloud capital.

CLOUD CAPITAL: BEGINNINGS

I remember once hearing you explain why you so admired the ancient ironsmiths: because they had no concept of the Iron Age they were ushering in. Instead, they were driven by something within them, an impulse to experiment until they had freed steel from lumps of pig iron, like Michelangelo liberating his David from a block of marble.

The technologists who recently ushered in the Age of Cloud Capital were no different. Driven also by curiosity and an almost moral enthusiasm, they experimented with various technologies whose purpose was to liberate useful information from the growing megalith of data at the internet's heart. To guide us to websites, friends, colleagues, books, films and music that we might like, they wrote algorithms capable of categorising us in clusters of internet users with similar search patterns and preferences. Then, all of a sudden, came the breakthrough, the real singularity: their algorithms ceased to be passive. They began to behave in ways hitherto associated exclusively with persons. They turned into agents.

This miracle took three leaps to complete. The first was from simple algorithms to ones that could adapt their objectives in light of the outcome of their activity – in other words, to repro-gramme themselves (machine-learning was the technical term). The second leap replaced the standard computer hardware with exotic 'neural networks'. The third and decisive leap infused neural networks with algorithms capable of 'reinforcement-learning'. Emulating how you patiently introduced me first to tin, then to bronze and, finally, to iron and steel, allow me to introduce you to these three leaps one at a time.

The early algorithms resembled recipes: mundane sets of step-by-step instructions to produce a pre-specified outcome (e.g. a lasagne). Later on, algorithms were released from the obligation to reach one pre-specified outcome and were allowed to pick, albeit in a pre-programmed manner, from a menu of possible outcomes the one best suited to unforeseen eventualities – akin to telling a cook that, if the mince has gone off during the preparation, a vegetarian lasagne 'outcome' should replace the original meat-based version. That was leap one.

Meanwhile, the computer hardware in which algorithms operate underwent great transformations of its own. In order to process a lot more information faster, engineers developed a new design of hardware in crude imitation of the human brain – adopting layered network structures that allow for the interconnection of many different nodes, each containing useful information.[4] This was the second leap. But the key innovation that breathed something resembling agency into the algorithms was the third.

Reinforcement-learning was the child of software engineers who realised that algorithms had the potential to evaluate their own performances – and make improvements – far faster than any human could. To achieve this, they wrote into them two types of subprograms (or subroutines): one that measures the algorithm's performance while it is in action and at tremendous speeds, and another (called a reward function) that helps the algorithm alter itself so as to improve its performance in accordance with the engineers' objectives.

Using neural networks to process gargantuan amounts of data, algorithms featuring reinforcement-learning could do things beyond Don Draper's imagination. By surveying the reaction of millions of people to their prompts billions of times every hour, they could train themselves at lightning speeds not only to influence us but, also, to pull off the fascinating new trick that Alexa and her ilk, as we saw earlier, are now capable of: to be influenced by the way they influence us; to affect themselves in light of the way they affect humans.

How exactly they do so is entirely opaque. Even the people who write these algorithms do not understand it: once the algorithm is in motion, the scale of the data involved and the speed at which it is processed would make it impossible for any human to trace its route through such a vast tree of ever-proliferating decisions, even if they did have full access to a full record of its activity. But left to their own devices, constantly monitoring and incessantly reacting to the outcomes of their own actions, and then to the outcomes of their reactions, these 'algos', as they're known, have acquired some astonishing capacities that their own coders and programmers find hard to understand. There is nothing new here, however: remember how the financial engineers of the 1990s and 2000s used algorithms to create derivatives of such enormous complexity that they themselves had no way of knowing what was inside those derivatives? Similarly, the engineers coding Alexa-like, cloud-based devices for the purpose of

creating automated systems that modify our behaviour are building so much complexity into these systems that they don't really
understand exactly why their systems do what they do.

It is in our human nature to be vulnerable to anyone, or anything, that seems to understand us better than we do ourselves.
In fact, we may be even more vulnerable to algorithms we know
to be mindless than we are to real persons, because we are more
easily lulled into a false sense of security. We pretend Alexa is a
person because we are not used to conversing with machines –
the experience would otherwise be embarrassing or uncanny. But
the fact that we know Alexa is *not* a person is how we come to
terms with its intense knowledge of us, which would otherwise be
offputtingly creepy or scary. At that precise moment, when we
relate to it as if it were a person while we know it is not, we are at
our most vulnerable – ready to fall into the trap of thinking of
Alexa as our own Pandora-like mechanical serf. Alas, Alexa is no
serf. It is, rather, a piece of cloud-based command capital which is
turning *you* into a serf, with your aid and by means of your own
unpaid labour, in order to further enrich its owners.

Every time we go online to enjoy the services of these algorithms, we have no option but to cut a Faustian deal with their
owners. To use the personalised services their algorithms provide,
we must submit to a business model based on the harvesting of
our data, the tracking of our activity, the invisible curating of our
content. Once we have submitted to this, the algorithm goes into
the business of selling things to us while selling our attention to
others. At that point something more profound kicks in which
gives the algorithm's owners immense power – to predict our
behaviours, to guide our preferences, to influence our decisions,
to change our minds, to thereby reduce us to their unpaid

servants, whose job is to provide our information, our attention, our identity and above all the patterns of behaviour that train their algorithms.

But is any of this really new? Is cloud capital radically different from other kinds of capital, such as hammers, steam engines or the television networks that Don Draper deployed to manipulate our matrix of desires? It is certainly no less physical than these other kinds of capital, for the cloud metaphor is just that: a metaphor. In reality, it is comprised of vast data warehouses, containing endless rows of servers, connected by a globe-spanning web of sensors and cables. Might cloud capital stand out because of its power to command? That can't be it either. The story of Mr Peel's misfortunes in Western Australia established that, since capitalism's early days, *all* capital goods have commanding power – some a little more, others a little less.

No, although cloud capital can command us in unprecedented ways, the key to grasping cloud capital's special nature, as we shall see, is the way it *reproduces* itself – and its power to command – a process that is very different to the one that reproduces hammers, steam engines and television networks.

Here is a glimpse of what makes cloud capital so fundamentally new, different and scary: capital has hitherto been reproduced within some labour market – within the factory, the office, the warehouse. Aided by machines, it was *waged workers* who produced the stuff that was sold to generate profits, which in turn financed their wages and the production of more machines – that's how capital accumulated and reproduced. Cloud capital, in contrast, can reproduce itself in ways that involve *no waged labour*. How? By commanding almost the whole of humanity to chip in to its reproduction – for free!

But first, let us make an important distinction: between the effect of Big Tech on the traditional workplace, where workers' conditions are more extreme but not in essence any different from those of the millworkers of old, and its effect on the *users* of technology generally, which creates an essentially new condition altogether. By doing so, we shall see that while workers have become 'cloud proles' we all have become 'cloud serfs'.

CLOUD PROLES

The technology may be outlandishly new but the way it is deployed to command badly paid workers on the factory floor is almost two centuries old. As they struggle to keep up with computer devices that track and dictate the pace of their every move, Amazon warehouse workers would recognise themselves instantly in Charlie Chaplin's *Modern Times* (1936) – one of your favourite movies. Forced to inspect and scan 1,800 Amazon packages an hour is an uncannily similar fate to that of Chaplin's character on the industrial factory line, who is trying to keep pace with a suddenly accelerating conveyor belt, and who is ultimately driven mad and falls into the vast machine whose cog he could never truly become.

When Juan Espinoza, a picker at a Staten Island Amazon warehouse, opined that 'Mr Bezos couldn't do a full shift at that place as an undercover boss,' anyone familiar with Fritz Lang's even earlier film *Metropolis* (1927) would have been reminded of the scene in which Freder, the autocrat's son, inadvertently descends into his father's Machine Halls, where workers are engaged in a desperate struggle to keep the massive hands of huge clock-like machines aligned. Shocked at what he finds, Freder holds his head in horror at the sight of machines marching the workers at an inhuman tempo, mechanising them ruthlessly.

Some years ago, you asked if Big Tech's new gadgetry had significantly changed the traditional manufacturing process. 'No,' I replied, 'at least not yet.' As long as humans are still part of a semi-automated production line, performing tasks that the machines cannot, the pace of human workers will be dictated by machines whose priority is to squeeze the last drop of productive energy from their human co-workers.

Does it matter, I imagine you asking, that in modern factories and warehouses this control is no longer exercised by cogs, wheels, sprockets and belts but by algorithms running on plug-in devices wirelessly connected to the company's neural network? No, not much. Cloud proles – my term for waged workers driven to their physical limits by cloud-based algorithms – suffer at work in ways that would be instantly recognised by whole generations of earlier proletarians.

Take Amazon's Mechanical Turk, which the company describes as a 'crowdsourcing marketplace that makes it easier for individuals and businesses to outsource their processes and jobs to a distributed workforce who can perform these tasks virtually'. But let us call it what it is: a cloud-based sweatshop where workers are paid piece rates to work virtually. Nothing is happening there that Karl Marx had not fully analysed in the twenty-first chapter of the first volume of his *Capital*, where he stated: 'Piece-wages become . . . the most fruitful source of reductions in wages and of frauds committed by the capitalists.' Precarious piecework, Marx added, is 'the most appropriate to the capitalist mode of production'. Hear, hear!

That's not to say that the 'algos' have not cast a long shadow over the factory floor. They have. Algorithms have already replaced bosses in the transport, deliveries and warehousing sectors. And workers forced to work for these algorithms find themselves in a modernist nightmare: some non-corporeal entity that not only lacks but is actually incapable of human empathy allocates them work at a rate of its choosing before monitoring their response times. Released from any of the qualms even inhumane humans harbour, the algo-bosses are at liberty to reduce the workers' paid hours, to increase their tempo to insanity-inducing levels, or to turn them out onto the street for 'inefficiency'. At that point, the workers sacked by the algorithm are thrown into a Kafkaesque spiral, unable to speak to a human capable of explaining why they were fired.[5]

Soon, no doubt, algorithms will develop union-busting capabilities, too. As we speak, dazzling algorithms are mapping out the tens of thousands of molecules in key proteins in superbugs that threaten to kill or debilitate us. Once these proteins are fully decoded, the algorithms proceed – again without human input – to design exotic antibiotics that kill the superbug – a scientific triumph for the ages. What is there to stop a similar algorithm from designing a global supply chain that bypasses warehouses or factories in which trades unions seem likely to succeed in organising workers? Trades unions could be snuffed out before they are even formed.

So, yes, cloud capital is turning workplaces into *Metropolis*-like Algo Halls in which human workers are reduced to exhausted cloud proles. And yet, cloud proles are not suffering a fate terrestrial proles, of the *Modern Times* variety, would find surprising.

Cloud capital, in short, continues to do in the world's factories, warehouses and other traditional workplaces that which traditional, terrestrial, capital always did – perhaps a little more efficiently.

However, *outside* the traditional places of work, cloud capital is demolishing everything we used to take for granted.

CLOUD SERFS

Don Draper is perhaps Romanticism's last poster boy. He treated science with suspicion and computers with disdain. He idealised nature and loved hitting the road in his gargantuan Cadillac. He lived and breathed individualism. He luxuriated in nostalgia. He adored women until they fell for him – at which point he bolted. He feared emotions because he saw them as the ultimate repository of insights into the human spirit. And he used his talents to commodify this melange of memory, sentiment, fickleness and insight so as to extract from consumers monies they might have otherwise kept for themselves.

His algorithmic double Alexa may be no romantic but cloud capital monetises our emotions more effectively than Don ever could. It tailor-makes experiences that exploit our biases to drive consumption, and then it uses our responses to hone those experiences yet further. But that's only the beginning. Besides modifying our consumer behaviour in ways Don Draper would marvel at, and perhaps be appalled by, cloud capital has a far more impressive trick up its sleeve: it can command us to put work *directly* into its own reproduction, reinforcement and maintenance.

Consider what cloud capital consists of: smart software, server farms, cell towers, thousands of miles of optic fibre. And yet all of this would be worthless without 'content'. The most valuable part of the stock of cloud capital is not its physical components but rather the stories posted on Facebook, the videos uploaded to TikTok and YouTube, the photos on Instagram, the jokes and insults on Twitter, the reviews on Amazon or, simply, our movement through space, allowing our phones to alert Google Maps to the latest spot of traffic. In providing these stories, videos, photos, jokes and movements, it is we who produce and reproduce – outside any market – the stock of cloud capital.

This is unparalleled. Workers employed by General Electric, Exxon-Mobil, General Motors or any other major conglomerate collect in salaries and wages approximately 80 per cent of the company's income. This proportion grows larger in smaller firms. Big Tech's workers, in contrast, collect less than 1 per cent of their firms' revenues. The reason is that paid labour performs only a fraction of the work that Big Tech relies on. Most of the work is performed by billions of people for free.

Sure enough, most of us choose to do this, enjoy it even. Broadcasting our opinions and sharing our lives' intimate details with our digital tribes and communities seems to satisfy some perverse expressive need of ours. No doubt, under feudalism, serfs toiling away on their ancestral lands would have suffered great hardships but still found it undesirable, if not unfathomable, to have their way of life taken away from them, their shared culture and traditions. Still, the harsh reality remained: at the end of the harvest, the landlord would send the sheriff to extract the lion's share of their produce – without paying the serfs a penny for it. So it goes with the billions of us unwittingly producing cloud capital. The fact that we do so voluntarily, happily even, does not detract from the fact that we are unpaid manufacturers – cloud serfs whose daily self-directed toil enriches a tiny band of multibillionaires residing mostly in California or Shanghai.

This is the crux. The digital revolution may be turning waged workers into cloud proles, who live increasingly precarious, stressful lives under the invisible thumb of algorithmic bosses. And it may have replaced Don Draper with extraordinary behaviour modification algorithms, hidden behind elegant tabletop appliances like Alexa. But that's not the most significant fact about cloud capital. Cloud capital's singular achievement, a feat far superior to either of these, is the way it has revolutionised *its own reproduction*. The true revolution cloud capital has inflicted on humanity is the conversion of billions of us into willing cloud serfs volunteering to labour for nothing to reproduce cloud capital for the benefit of its owners.

WITHER MARKETS, HELLO CLOUD FIEFS

'Enter amazon.com and you have exited capitalism. Despite all the buying and the selling that goes on there, you have entered a realm which can't be thought of as a market, not even a digital one.' When I say this to people, which I frequently do in lectures and debates, they look at me as they would a madman. But once I start explaining what I mean, their fear for my sanity soon turns into fear for us all.

Imagine the following scene straight out of the science-fiction storybook. You are beamed into a town full of people going about their business, trading in gadgets, clothes, shoes, books, songs, games and movies. At first, everything looks normal. Until you begin to notice something odd. It turns out that all the shops, indeed every building, belong to a chap called Jeff. He may not own the factories that produce the stuff sold in his shops but he owns an algorithm that takes a cut for each sale and he gets to decide what can be sold and what cannot.

If that were all, the scene would evoke an old Western in which a lonesome cowboy rides into town to discover that a podgy strongman owns the saloon bar, the grocery store, the post office, the railway, the bank and, naturally, the sheriff. Except that isn't all. Jeff owns more than the shops and the public buildings. He also owns the dirt you walk on, the bench you sit on, even the air you breathe. In fact, in this weird town everything you see (and don't see) is regulated by Jeff's algorithm: you and I may be walking next to each other, our eyes trained in the same direction, but the view provided to us by the algorithm is entirely bespoke, carefully curated according to Jeff's priorities. Everyone navigating their way around amazon.com – except Jeff – is wandering in algorithmically constructed isolation.

This is no market town. It is not even some form of hyper-capitalist digital market. Even the ugliest of markets are meeting places where people can interact and exchange information reasonably freely. In fact, it's even worse than a totally monopolised market – there, at least, the buyers can talk to each other, form associations, perhaps organise a consumer boycott to force the monopolist to reduce a price or to improve a quality. Not so in Jeff's realm, where everything and everyone is intermediated not by the disinterested invisible hand of the market but by an algorithm that works for Jeff's bottom line and dances exclusively to his tune.

If this is not scary enough, recall that it is the same algorithm which, via Alexa, has trained us to train it to manufacture our desires. The mind rebels at the enormity of the hubris. The same algorithm that we help train in real time to know us inside out, both modifies our preferences and administers the selection and delivery of commodities that will satisfy these preferences. It is as if Don Draper could not only implant in us desires for specific products but had attained the superpower instantly to deliver said products to our doorstep, bypassing any potential competitor, all in the interest of bolstering the wealth and power of a chap called Jeff.

Such concentrated power should scare the living daylights out of the liberally minded. Anyone committed to the idea of the market (not to mention the autonomous self) should recognise that cloud capital is its death knell. It should also shake market sceptics, socialists in particular, out of the complacent assumption that amazon.com is bad because it is a capitalist market gone berserk. Actually, it's something worse than that.

'If it ain't a capitalist market, what in the sweet Lord's name are we stepping into when we enter amazon.com?' a student at the University of Texas asked me a few years ago.

'A type of digital fief,' I replied instinctively. 'A post-capitalist one, whose historical roots remain in feudal Europe but whose integrity is maintained today by a futuristic, dystopian type of cloud-based capital.' Since then, I have come to believe that it was a reasonably accurate answer to a hard question.

Under feudalism, the overlord would grant so-called fiefs to subordinates called vassals. These fiefs gave the vassals the formal right to exploit economically a part of the overlord's realm – to plant crops on it, for example, or graze cattle – in exchange for a portion of the produce. The overlord would then unleash his sheriff to police the fief's execution and collect what he was owed. Jeff's relationship with the vendors on amazon.com is not too dissimilar. He grants them cloud-based digital fiefs, for a fee, and then leaves his algo-sheriff to police and collect.

Amazon was just the start. Alibaba applied the same techniques to create a similar cloud fief in China. Copycat ecommerce platforms, offering variations on the Amazon theme, are springing up everywhere, in the Global South as well as the Global North. More significantly, other industrial sectors are turning into cloud fiefs too. Take for example Tesla, Elon Musk's successful electric car company. One reason financiers value it so much higher than Ford or Toyota is that its cars' every circuit is wired into cloud capital. Besides giving Tesla the power to switch off one of its cars remotely, if for instance the driver fails to service it as the company wishes, merely by driving around Tesla owners are uploading in real time information (including what music they are listening to!) that enriches the company's cloud capital. They may not think of themselves as cloud serfs but, alas, that's precisely what the proud owners of new, wonderfully aerodynamically gleaming Teslas are.

It took mind-bending scientific breakthroughs, fantastical-sounding neural networks and imagination-defying AI programs to accomplish what? To turn workers toiling in warehouses, driving cabs and delivering food into cloud proles. To create a world where markets are increasingly replaced by cloud fiefs. To force businesses into the role of vassals. And to turn all of us into cloud serfs, glued to our smartphones and tablets, eagerly producing the cloud capital that keeps our new overlords on cloud nine.

BACK TO YOUR QUESTION

If I had to name one thing I learned from you, it would be the ability to relish contradictions.

You worshipped iron, but were moved to tears by Hesiod's tirades against the Iron Age. You threw your lot in with the communists, knowing full well that, if your side won, you would end up in the gulag. You fell in love with every furnace, pipe, conveyor belt and crane in the steel factory where you worked, but remained horrified by their tendency to mechanise, alienate and dehumanise the workers appended to them.

It is why I wanted to talk to you about cloud capital. Because you would know how to admire and detest it at once. And because, through this contradiction, you would recognise that cloud capital is the key to answering your question about the internet's impact on capitalism.

Capitalism surfaced when owners of capital goods (steam engines, machine tools, spinning jennies, telegraph poles, etc.) acquired the power to command people and nations – powers that far exceeded, for the first time, those of landowners. It was a Great Transformation made possible by the prior privatisation of common lands. Same with cloud capital. To acquire its even greater powers to command, it too required the prior privatisation of another crucial commons: Internet One.

Like all capital since capitalism's inception, cloud capital can be thought of as a vast production and behaviour-modification machine: it produces marvellous devices *and* the power (for its owners) to command humans who do not own it. But that's where the similarity between terrestrial and cloud capital ends and where the difference between conventional capitalists and cloudalists begins.

Previously, to exercise capital's power to command and make other humans *work faster* and *consume more*, capitalists required two types of professionals: managers and marketeers. Especially under the auspices of the post-war technostructure, these two service professions achieved greater prominence even than bankers and insurance brokers. Gleaming new business schools were set up to initiate MBA students in the dark arts of quick-marching a workforce towards explosive labour productivity. Advertising and marketing departments nurtured a generation of Don Drapers.

Then, cloud capital arrived. At one fell swoop it automated both roles. The exercise of capital's power to command workers and consumers alike was handed over to the algos. This was a far more revolutionary step than replacing autoworkers with industrial robots. After all, industrial robots simply do what automation has been doing since before the Luddites: making proletarians redundant, or more miserable, or both. No, the truly historic disruption was to automate capital's power to command people *outside* the factory, the shop or the office – to turn all of us, cloud proles and everyone else, into cloud serfs in the direct (unremunerated) service of cloud capital, unmediated by any market.

Meanwhile, conventional capitalist manufacturers increasingly have no option but to sell their goods at the discretion of the cloudalists, paying them a fee for the privilege, developing a relationship with them no different to that of vassals vis-à-vis their feudal overlords.

So, back to your question: 'Now that computers speak to each other, will this network make capitalism impossible to overthrow? Or might it finally reveal its Achilles heel?' On the one hand, the rise of cloud capital has solidified, augmented and massively expanded capital's triumph over labour, society and, catastrophically, nature. And yet, here is the contradiction: in doing so, cloud capital has simultaneously ushered in the technofeudal system that has killed capitalism in so many realms and is in the process of replacing it everywhere else.

In your youth, you dreamed of a time when labour would shake off the yoke of the capitalist market. So did I. Alas, something more like the opposite happened: it is capital that has shaken off the yoke of the capitalist market! And while capital is taking its victory lap, capitalism itself is receding. A sophism to sweeten the pill of our defeat? Not so – as I intend to show in Chapter 5. For now, however, let us address perhaps the most surprising and compelling aspect of capitalism's demise: the story of how the cloudalists pulled off this astonishing feat and how, for them, profit, once the driving force of our capitalist economies, became . . . optional.

4
THE RISE OF THE CLOUDALISTS AND THE DEMISE OF PROFIT

The last time you left the family home in Paleo Phaliro was in the summer of 2020 when you came to visit us on the island of Aegina, as you liked to do every summer. That journey to Aegina was a joyous break from the suffocating lockdown of the pandemic's first phase. But it must have taken its toll because the following morning you didn't emerge from your room until well after eleven. You found me on the veranda, peering into news sites on my laptop. I was beside myself. As you sat down next to me, I exclaimed: 'The Age of Cloud Capital has just begun. In London!'

Half an hour or so earlier, the people of Britain had woken up to the news that the pandemic had caused the worst recession in history. Apparently, the UK's national income had fallen by a whopping 20.4 per cent, far worse than any comparable figures in America or continental Europe.[1] Wretched news it certainly was, though not of the sort that undermines one's world view. It was what followed fifteen minutes later, just before you woke up, that changed the way I saw the world. Instead of plummeting in response to the data, the London Stock Exchange jumped up by 2.3 per cent![2]

'We are witnessing something utterly at odds with any variety of capitalism,' I remember telling you with as much authority as I could muster.

'Nah, capitalism is full of paradoxes,' you replied.

'But, Dad, this is not one of capitalism's many paradoxes – it is unequivocal proof that the world of money has, finally, decoupled from the capitalist world.'

Unimpressed, you chose to stare out over the Saronic Sea towards the mountains of the Peloponnese, leaving me to reckon with what had truly gone down in London on that Wednesday morning in August 2020.

Share markets do rise in response to bad news, but only when the news, however awful, turns out at least somewhat better than anticipated. Had stockbrokers predicted, say, a 22 per cent fall in the UK's national income, markets would have had good cause to rise if the actual fall on the day was 'only' 20.4 per cent. Except that, on that Wednesday, the markets were expecting a drop of no more than 15 per cent. That's what made 12 August 2020 so bizarre: news far worse than anticipated had caused the share market to rise. Nothing like it had happened before.

So, what *had* happened? The news, it turns out, was so bad that traders in the City of London had the following realisation: 'When things are *this* dismal, the Bank of England panics. And what have panicky central banks been doing since the crash of 2008? They print money and give it to us. And what do we do with all the freshly minted dough from the central bank? We buy shares, sending their price up. And if prices are destined to go up, only a fool would miss out on the action. A wall of printed money is surely on its way to us. Time to buy!' And buy they did, causing the City of London to defy the gravitational laws of capitalism.

The trend was not confined to London. As the pandemic began to rip through our communities, authorities on both sides of the Atlantic, in Japan and elsewhere, responded by doing a lot more of what they had been doing since the American Minotaur's death in 2008: printing money to give to the financiers in the hope that it would buttress investment in business, thus generating stable jobs and preventing the economy from collapsing. It didn't. Fearing that run-of-the-mill businesses would not be able to repay them, the financiers lent the central bank money only to Big Business. And Big Business either refused to invest or invested solely in cloud capital.

Conglomerates founded on traditional terrestrial capital, like General Electric and Volkswagen, refused to invest the interest-free central bank money because, when they surveyed the ongoing carnage of the pandemic, they saw the same thing their bankers had seen: masses of little people condemned to low wages, bullshit jobs and diminished prospects – a sea of people unable to afford new, high-value products. So why invest in such stuff? Instead, they would do something riskless, profitable and stress-free: they used it to buy back their own company's shares – boosting their company's share price and, along with it, their own bonuses.

Meanwhile, Big Tech was having an even more fabulous pandemic. While the US economy shed 30 million jobs in a single month, Amazon bucked the trend, appearing to a swathe of Americans as a hybrid of the Red Cross, delivering essential parcels to confined citizens, and Roosevelt's New Deal, hiring 100,000 extra staff and paying them a couple of extra dollars an hour to boot. True, Big Tech did invest the central bank cash, and it did create new jobs – but the jobs it created were those of cloud proles and the investment was in building up its cloud capital. Even cloudalist companies that had a bad pandemic, like Uber and Airbnb whose customers were unable to use their services, took the central bank money and invested in more cloud capital as if there were no pandemic.

It was the pandemic, with the flood of state money it unleashed, that ushered in the Age of Cloud Capital. And if we want a milestone with which to mark its formal arrival, that summer's morning will do nicely. But as I have hinted already, the story of the rise of cloud capital on the back of state money actually begins earlier than this, for it was in the wake of the crash of 2008 that state money began to be printed en masse by the world's central banks and started to have its strange and counter-intuitive effect on profit.

THE SECRET OF THE NEW RULING CLASS

Your fireside stories of metalworkers, and ironsmiths in particular, accelerating history fascinated me no end, as you know. In the decades since, however, I have become more sceptical of narratives that place too much emphasis on technology and not enough on how powerful groups seize and manipulate it to achieve and maintain dominion over others. The steam engine would have been a historical footnote were it not for the capitalists who weaponised it so as to depose the then ruling class, the feudalists.

However, it is not a given that every magnificent new technological breakthrough will spawn a distinctly new form of capital to be seized upon by some new revolutionary class. The technological breakthroughs of the Second Industrial Revolution – the electricity grids, the telegraph, later the telephone, highways packed with automobiles, television networks – these expansive networks of phenomenal machinery may have spawned Big Business, Big Finance, the Great Depression, the War Economy, Bretton Woods, the post-war technostructure, the European Union and built the modern world that your generation and mine took for granted, but they gave rise to neither a new type of capital nor a new class who could challenge the capitalists for dominance.

But the technologies that spawned cloud capital have proved more revolutionary than any of their predecessors. Through them, cloud capital has developed capacities that previous types of capital goods never had. It has become at once an attention-holder, a desire-manufacturer, a driver of proletarian labour (of cloud proles), an elicitor of massive free labour (from cloud serfs) and, to boot, the creator of totally privatised digital transaction spaces (cloud fiefs like amazon.com) in which neither buyers nor sellers enjoy any of the options they would in normal markets.[3] As a result, its owners – the cloudalists – have acquired the ability to do that which the Edisons, the Westinghouses and the Fords never could: to turn themselves into a revolutionary class actively displacing the capitalists from the top of society's pecking order.

In the process, the cloudalists – some consciously, others unthinkingly – have changed everything that previous varieties of capitalism had taught us to take for granted: the idea of what constitutes a commodity, the ideal of the autonomous individual, the ownership of identity, the propagation of culture, the context of politics, the nature of the state, the texture of geopolitics. The pressing question is: how did the cloudalists finance all this?

The early industrialists funded their factories, steamships and canals with the blood and sweat of African slave labour and loot from American and South Asian lands and peoples. Later, the Edisons, the Westinghouses and the Fords used monies conjured from thin air by private bankers who morphed into Big Finance in the process. The cloudalists did something subtler and more impressive: they helped themselves to the rivers of cash that were being printed by the central banks of developed capitalist states.

It was nothing short of a coup. Imagine getting the world's richest capitalist states to print the money that allows you to build a new type of capital stock. Imagine that this new type of capital stock comes with the inbuilt superpower to get billions of people to reproduce it on your behalf for free. Imagine further that this type of capital, funded by state monies and reproduced by citizens' free labour, intensifies your power to extract surplus value from proletarians who are working for shrinking wages under worsening conditions – but also from capitalists forced to remove their wares from traditional markets and to sell them via your cloud capital. You wouldn't even need to laugh all the way to the bank since you would be much wiser to keep your stupendous gains stowed in some digital wallet within your cloud capital empire rather than in an account with some pathetic banker.

It sounds implausible. How on earth did the cloudalists convince major central banks to fund them in this way? The answer is: they didn't have to.

2008'S UNINTENDED CONSEQUENCES

In the fifteen years since capitalism's near-death experience, central bankers have been printing monies and channelling them to the financiers, entirely of their own accord. In their minds, they have been saving capitalism. In reality, they have been upending it by helping to finance the emergence of cloud capital. But that's how history arrives: on the coat-tails of unintended consequences.

The central bank money-printing bonanza began in 2008, shortly after the comprehensive implosion of the West's banking sector. Politicians and central bankers then feared that if they let the banks fail and people's savings disappear, as Herbert Hoover's administration had done in 1929, they would precipitate a second Great Depression. So at their London summit in April 2009, the G7's central bankers – along with their presidents and prime ministers – agreed to do whatever it took to refloat the banks. That was sensible.

What was preposterous was that, in addition to saving the failed banks, they bailed out the quasi-criminal bankers responsible for their failure, along with their lethal practices. And far worse, in addition to practising socialism for the bankers, they subjected workers and the middle class to vicious austerity.[4] Cutting public expenditure in the midst of a Great Recession is always a terrible idea. Doing so while also printing mountains of money for the financiers wins the prize for conspicuous stupidity. Not only was it a brazen double standard that did untold damage to a generation's faith in the political class, it did something lethal to the economy.

Austerity is not just bad for workers and people in need of state support during tough times, it also murders investment. In any economy, what we spend collectively translates automatically into what we earn collectively. The definition of a recession is when private expenditure is falling. By reducing public expenditure at precisely the same moment, the state accelerates the decline of economy-wide expenditure and thus hastens the rate at which a society's total income is falling. And if society's total income is falling, businesses are hardly going to spend money building up capacity when consumers don't have the money to buy. That's how austerity slays investment.

With investment first knocked out by the crash of 2008 and finished off soon after by austerity, throwing new money at the financiers was never going to resurrect it. Put yourself in the position of a capitalist at a time when austerity is eliminating your customers' income. Suppose I give you a billion dollars to play with for free, i.e. at a zero interest rate. Naturally you will take the free billion but as we've established you would be mad to invest it in new production lines. So what are you going to do with the free cash? You could buy real estate or art or, better still, shares in your own company. That way, the shares in your company appreciate in value and, if you are the CEO running it, your stature and share-linked bonuses rise too. No new investment, in other words, but a lot more power in the hands of the powerful.

This is exactly what happened. Seeing that the vast majority were likely to be stuck in poverty and precarity for the foreseeable future, Big Business went on history's deepest and longest investment strike, while spending large sums on things like real estate deals that gentrified neighbourhoods and deepened divides. Every Gilded Age has seen inequality rise, with the rich profiting faster than the poor. The post-2008 era was different. Inequality rose not because the poor saw their incomes rise more slowly than the rich – no, their incomes actually fell, just as the financiers and Big Business raked it in.

When an activist state makes fabulously wealthier the same bankers whose quasi-criminal activities brought misery to the majority, while they are punished with self-defeating austerity, two new calamities beckon: poisoned politics and permanent stagnation. The poisoned politics we need not elaborate on – from Greece's neo-Nazis to America's Donald Trump we have all lived through the nightmare. But permanent stagnation? Why would more wealth for the ultra-rich stagnate capitalism? And how did it lead to the funding of cloud capital?

POISONED MONEY, GILDED STAGNATION

The term 'inflation' refers to an increase across the board in the price of most things. Sometimes, when the price of bread rises it's simply because flour has suddenly become scarcer or bread more fashionable. But in the case of inflation, the price of one thing rises because the price of *everything* is going up, so *everyone* needs more dollars, yen or euros in order to buy their loaf of bread or cup of coffee or smartphone, not just the baker. That's how inflation *depletes money's exchange value*.

Capitalism famously drove a wedge between the value and the price of things. Money was no exception. Money's exchange value reflects people's readiness to hand over valuable things for given sums of cash – a value that inflation diminishes, as we have just seen. But under capitalism, money also acquired a distinct market price: the rate of interest you must pay in order to lease a pile of cash for a given period. The price of potatoes drops when there are stockpiled potatoes that no one wants to buy. In just the same way, when the demand for money (for loans, that is) lingers below the quantity of money available to be lent, its price – the interest rate – declines. Under capitalism, Big Business has the capacity to borrow most of the money that lenders, mostly rich people with large savings, are willing to lend (which is what they are doing when they invest in a bond). So it is Big Business, with its appetite for borrowing, that determines the overall demand for money. In theory, central banks are able to influence interest rates by adjusting the rate at which they lend money to other banks, allowing them to pass on the lower rate, and thereby to stimulate or discourage investment. But overall interest rates are determined, as with any market, by the overall supply of and demand for money.

After 2008, and especially during the pandemic, a strange thing happened. Money held its exchange value – that whole period, from late 2008 to early 2022, was one of very low (sometimes negative) inflation – but at the same time its price (i.e. the interest rate) tanked, even turning *negative* on many occasions.[5] This was a reflection of the fact that austerity was nullifying business investment and so business people's demand for money was pitiful. But surely, if the central banks keep reducing interest rates, there would eventually come a point where money was sufficiently cheap that borrowing and investment would pick up again? Not so.

In the case of potatoes, microchips or cars, falling prices generally cure an oversupply problem (i.e. where supply outweighs demand) in exactly this way: bargain-hunters swoop in while producers cut output, and thus the price 'correction' eliminates the excess supply. But when it comes to money, something different happens. When its price – the interest rate – drops fast, capitalists panic. Instead of rejoicing that they can now borrow more cheaply, they think: 'Sure, it is a good thing that I can borrow for next to nothing. But for the central bank to allow interest rates to drop so much, things must be looking grim! I won't invest even if they hand me the money.' That's the reason investment refused to recover, even after central bankers cut money's official price to almost zero. And that was only half of their post-2008 nightmare.

The other half was the failed bankers' stranglehold over everyone, including central banks and governments – a legacy of three decades of the American Minotaur's rule over global capitalism. Their stranglehold came in handy once their banks began sequentially to topple between 2007 and 2011. One panicky phone call was usually all it took for a banker to get the state to bail him out and give him an open-ended overdraft facility.[6] From late 2008 to early 2022, Europe's, America's and Japan's central banks pushed walls of freshly minted cash into the accounts of the financiers,[7] making the interest rate conundrum far worse than it already was. By boosting magnificently the supply of monies that Big Business refused to invest,[8] socialism for financiers pushed the interest rate deeper and deeper towards negative territory.

It was a strange new world. Negative prices make sense in the case of bads, the opposite of goods. When a factory wants to get rid of toxic waste, it charges a negative price for it: its managers pay someone to get rid of it, a costly process especially if it is done in an ecologically considerate manner.[9] But how could money become a bad to be offloaded? When central banks began to treat money like a car manufacturer treats spent sulphuric acid, or a nuclear power station its radioactive wastewater, that's when we knew there was something rotten in the kingdom of financialised capitalism.

How can money acquire a *negative* price? It was you, Dad, who helped me come to grips with the paradox of negative interest rates. By introducing me to Einstein's theory that light has two natures, you opened my mind to the twin nature of labour, capital and, yes, money. Money's first nature is that of a commodity that

we trade like any other for other commodities. But money, like
language, is also a reflection of our relationship to one another. It
echoes how we transform matter and shape the world around us.
It quantifies our 'alienated ability' to do things together, as a collective. Once we recognise money's second nature, everything
makes a lot more sense, for it was this collective ability that was
broken. Poisoned money flowed in torrents but not into serious
investments, good-quality jobs, or anything capable of re-
animating capitalism's lost animal spirits. Instead shareholders and
executives bought land, empty warehouses, art, Swiss chalets,
whole villages in Italy and even islands in Greece, the Caribbean
and the Pacific. They collected football clubs, superyachts and, at
some point, began to buy digital assets like Bitcoin or something
called NFTs that they neither understood nor knew what to do
with. This is how socialism for bankers and austerity for the rest
of us thwarted capitalism's dynamism, shoving it into a state of
gilded stagnation. As we shall now see, cloud capital was the only
pulsating, stirring force to benefit from the poisoning of money.

HOW PROFITS BECAME OPTIONAL
FOR THE CLOUDALISTS

I remember being puzzled during the late sixties when you and
Mum would sometimes diverge from your obsessive discussions
about the junta – the term Greeks used for the fascist dictatorship ruining our lives – to talk about something called 'the
right'. From what I could gather, it sounded like a cross between
the divine and the abominable. So I asked you: 'What is the
right, exactly?' After your usual journey through the mists of

history – describing how in the National Assembly spawned by the French Revolution in 1789, hardened revolutionaries wanting to topple the King and his regime sat on the left-hand side of the assembly, while the King's supporters took the seats on the right; how later, once capitalism had been established, the right came to be identified with the interests of capitalists and a fervent opposition to organised labour or state intervention – you eventually came to the gist of what it represented in our era: 'People on the right of politics believe that hard work aimed at private profit is the surest route to a wealthy and good society. People on the left don't.'

Later, I appreciated your definition better when exposed to the writings of Adam Smith, the eighteenth-century Scottish economist who is something like the patron saint of free-marketeers. Yes, factory owners driving fourteen-year-old workers into an early grave were brutish. But Smith argued that the needs of society – more and cheaper clothes, shelter, food; the stuff of prosperity – could not be met with moralisers or do-gooders. Only the capitalists' passion for profit could provide these. Why? Because to profit, it was not enough to squeeze the living daylights out of their workers. After all, their competitors did the same. No, to steal a march on the competition, capitalists had to invest – in new machines, for example, that could cut their costs and allow them to undercut their competitors' prices. It was in this manner, driven by the profit motive, that society would equip itself to manufacture sufficient quantities of life's essentials and at the lowest prices possible. According to Smith, it is *because* of the capitalists' cut-throat profit-hunger, not in spite of it, that capitalism begat wealth and progress. As he wrote in *The Wealth of Nations* (1776):

By pursuing his own interest he frequently promotes that of the society more effectually than when he really intends to promote it. I have never known much good done by those who affected to trade for the public good.

The crash of 1929 and the Great Depression took the shine off profit-driven markets. But throughout each of capitalism's subsequent metamorphoses – during the New Deal, the War Economy, the era of Bretton Woods and particularly with the rise of the technostructure and the Minotaur – profit remained its driving force. Coupled with debt, profit was the power that turned the cogs and wheels of every form of capitalism the planet had seen. Until, following the events of 2008, the Global North's central banks fell into the trap of pumping unending quantities of poisoned monies into the financial markets. Then, for the first time since capitalism had stirred two and a half centuries earlier, profit ceased to be the fuel that fired the global economy's engine, driving investment and innovation. That role, of fuelling the economy, was taken over by central bank money.

Profit remained the ambition of every capitalist, the goal of every vendor, the aspiration of people battling for a more comfortable life. But the accumulation of capital, the process that creates wealth by increasing the overall size of the pie, decoupled from profits, just as the end of Bretton Woods and the subsequent rise of the Minotaur had decoupled hard work from rising living standards. It was not the intention of central bankers to replace profits. They simply fell into a trap they had created for themselves. The panic of 2008 had killed off the demand for money to be invested, causing an oversupply of money that depressed interest rates. The more interest rates fell, the greater the investors' conviction that things were so bad it would be madness to invest. And yet, trillions of dollars of central bank money continued to pour into finance, and so the doom-loop continued, with interest rates going further and further south: to zero or below.

As conglomerates and governments became reliant on a diet of interest-free loans, with companies in developing countries borrowing more than their governments, in excess of $2 trillion by the end of the 2010s, the central bankers faced an ugly dilemma: either switch off the money taps, which would mean blowing up financialised capitalism, having printed all that money to save it; or continue to pump money into the system, hoping for a miracle to intervene but, in reality, facilitating the replacement of profit as capitalism's motivating power and lubricant. Unsurprisingly, they chose the latter.

The central banks' anguish was the cloudalists' delight. It was in this period that intrepid and talented entrepreneurs like Jeff Bezos and Elon Musk were able to build up their super-expensive, ultra-powerful cloud capital without needing to do any of the three things that capitalists traditionally had to do to expand: borrow money from some bank, sell large portions of their business to others, or generate large profits to pay for new capital stock. Why suffer any of this when central bank money was flowing freely? And so between 2010 and 2021, the paper wealth of these two men – meaning the total price of their shares – rose from less than $10,000 million to around $200,000 billion apiece.

To be clear, the free central bank money did not go directly to the cloudalists. It simply followed the path of least resistance. First, via the banks, it reached the managers of traditional conglomerates. Aghast at the poverty of the masses, they scorned real investment and used it to buy back their own shares. The sums involved were so vast that, like an undiscriminating tide, they lifted the price of every asset around them: shares, bonds, derivatives – any and every piece of paper that financiers put up for sale went up in price. No one cared whether that piece of paper would eventually turn a profit. As long as the central bank was trapped into producing new money, they knew that the trashiest piece of paper would sell for more tomorrow than it fetched yesterday.

The financial press called it an 'everything rally'. It went on for more than a decade. With shares in companies skyrocketing independently of whether the companies themselves turned a profit or not, the wealthy got immensely wealthier in their sleep. Then came the pandemic, giving the everything rally another almighty boost. The morning of 12 August 2020 in London, which you and I witnessed on the balcony at Aegina, was a case in point: fearing that lockdown would cause an irreversible slump in the economy, central banks did a lot more of what they had been doing since 2008: they cranked up their digital printing presses to breaking point.

In the ensuing cacophony, terrestrial capitalists – traditional car companies, oil corporations, steel producers and the like – were happy to sit on their growing paper wealth, transforming it into real estate or other traditional assets. By contrast, cloudalists like Jeff Bezos and Elon Musk acted quickly to turn their paper wealth, before it vanished, into a far greater value extractor: cloud capital.

Both knew that profit was irrelevant. What mattered was seizing the opportunity to establish total market dominance. In 2021 Goldman Sachs, one of Wall Street's least likeable banks, stunned the financial world by publishing a 'Non-Profitable Technology Index', which perfectly demonstrates capitalism's emancipation from profits: between 2017 and the beginning of the pandemic, loss-making cloudalist companies saw their share value rise by

200 per cent. By the middle of the pandemic, their value had exploded to 500 per cent their 2017 level. During 2020, Amazon's best year since its inception, when its pandemic-fuelled sales went through the roof, Bezos's company booked sales worth €44 billion at its global headquarters in Ireland but paid exactly zero corporate tax because it posted not a cent of profits. Similarly with Tesla: even though its profit margins hovered just above zero, Tesla's share price soared from around $90 at the beginning of 2020 to over $700 at year's end.

Using their appreciating shares as collateral, the cloudalists mopped up many of the billions sloshing around within the financial system. With them, they paid for server farms, fibre optic cables, artificial intelligence laboratories, gargantuan warehouses, software developers, top-notch engineers, promising start-ups and all the rest. In an environment where profit had become optional, the cloudalists seized upon the central bank money to build a new empire.

Meanwhile, the undermining of one of capitalism's core principles – the profit motive – had knock-on effects on the others.

PRIVATE INEQUITIES

Imagine Gillian, who works for a private care provider in England's Home Counties. At some point in mid-2010, she hears that the company had been purchased by a private equity firm. She doesn't know what private equity means and hasn't heard of the firm that now owns her employer. But she and her co-workers are reassured that they have nothing to fear – the new management is only interested in helping the company flourish.

At first, Gillian notices little difference, save the snazzier logo and some general sprucing up. However, behind the scenes, the new owners split the company into two separate companies: a care service provider, say CareCom, which employs Gillian and all the other staff who provided the care; and another company, say Prop-Com, that owns all of its property (its buildings, equipment, vans and so on), which then charges CareCom rent for its use.

Before long, PropCom increases the rents it is charging CareCom and announces further steep rent increases. CareCom's management gather together Gillian and her co-workers and, citing the increased rents, explain that unless they accept longer working hours for no extra pay, CareCom will have to be wound up. Meanwhile, using the boost in its long-term rent revenues from CareCom as collateral, PropCom takes out a large loan from a bank. Within days, the loan has become dividends in the pockets of the shareholders of the private equity firm.

Within five years, CareCom has been wound up. After five years of rapidly worsening pay and conditions, Gillian and her fellow workers have been thrown out of work while large contracts to provide care to local communities, paid for in advance by taxpayers, have been unceremoniously dishonoured. But along with all other real estate during the 'everything rally', the value of PropCom has appreciated. Once PropCom's property has been sold, the bank that lent it the money is made whole and the private equity firm keeps the rest on behalf of its investors.

This sordid exercise has a soothing, if mystifying name: 'dividend recapitalisation' — though to call it that would be akin to relabelling a bank robbery as 'asset redistribution'. The private equity firm that cost Gillian her job has practised straightforward asset-stripping, with financialisation providing the necessary smoke and mirrors. Looters, who have created no new value, have simply ransacked a pre-existing care provider. To use the language of early economists like Adam Smith, it is a classic case of feudal rent defeating capitalist profit; of wealth extraction by those who already have it triumphing over the creation of new wealth by entrepreneurs. And the key point to note is that the success of such a scheme depends on these looters being able to sell subsidiaries like PropCom at high enough prices once the original company has been destroyed.

Before 2008, when capitalism still relied on profit as its motive power, it would not have been possible for such a scheme to be generalised – if it were and too many of the various PropComs went on sale at the same time, their value would fall. This is what gave Adam Smith his optimism about capitalism: his faith that capitalist profit would continue to triumph over feudal rent. In reality, since Smith wrote his famous lines in the 1770s, rent has survived and even prospered under capitalism. Cartels, consumer gouging, the technostructure's successful manufacturing of desires for things we do not need, financialised asset-stripping – all of these practices have generated increasing rents *within* capitalism. Nevertheless, Smith's optimism was supported by the bigger picture: rent survived only parasitically on, and in the shadows of, profit. That changed after 2008. With central bank money replacing profit as the fuel of the economy and with the 'everything rally' driving the price of PropCom-like subsidiaries ever upwards, private equity could take over and successfully asset-strip as many capitalist firms as it could lay its hands on all at once. And that was not all.

Socialism for the financiers gave rise to another cluster of financial uber-lords to rival the cloudalists – three US companies with powers exceeding those of private equity and all terrestrial capitalists put together: BlackRock, Vanguard and State Street. These three firms, the Big Three as they are known in financial circles, effectively own American capitalism. No, I am not exaggerating.

Most people have not heard of them but they have heard of the companies the Big Three own, which include America's major airlines (American, Delta, United Continental), much of Wall Street (JPMorgan Chase, Wells Fargo, Bank of America, Citigroup) and car makers such as Ford and General Motors. Together, the Big Three are the largest single shareholder in almost 90 per cent of firms listed in the New York Stock Exchange, including Apple, Microsoft, ExxonMobil, General Electric and Coca-Cola. As for the dollar value of the Big Three's shares, it has too many zeros to mean much. At the time of writing, BlackRock manages nearly $10 trillion in investments, Vanguard $8 trillion and State Street $4 trillion. To make sense of these numbers: they are almost exactly the same as the US national income; or the sum of the national incomes of China and Japan; or the sum of the total income of the eurozone, the UK, Australia, Canada and Switzerland.[10]

How did that happen? The official version is that the Big Three's founders spotted a gap in the financial markets: ultra-rich people and institutions wanting to be 'passive investors'; that is, to buy shares without having to choose what they are buying, or even to choose professionals who will choose for them. To service their need for safe, mindless share purchases, the Big Three take the money of the seriously wealthy and buy literally everything – shares, to be precise, in every business listed in the New York Stock Exchange. Giving your money to the Big Three to buy shares on your behalf thus became equivalent to having bought a chunk not of individual companies but of the entire New York Stock Exchange!

This could not have happened before 2008 because until then the ultra-rich simply did not have access to enough cash with which the Big Three could buy a significant chunk of the New York Stock Exchange. After 2008, however, central bank-sponsored socialism for the ultra-rich created more than enough money.[11] Thereafter, the rise of the Big Three to such supreme financial power was almost inescapable, and now that they are there, the Big Three enjoy two insurmountable advantages: unprecedented monopoly power over entire sectors, from airlines and banking to energy and Silicon Valley;[12] and a capacity to offer the ultra-rich high returns for very low fees. These two advantages allow the Big Three to extort rents at a scale that would have made Adam Smith weep.

I can almost hear Smith's voice, which I imagine with a tinge of a Scottish accent, lamenting that after 2008, and in the name of saving capitalism, central banks snuffed out capitalism's dynamism and advantage. I can imagine his dismay that harmful, quasi-feudal rent got a chance to exact a historic revenge on fruitful capitalist profit, with profit-seeking consigned to the aspirant petty bourgeois while the truly rich gleefully whisper to one another that profit is for losers. I can picture his exasperation that the treasured guardians of capitalism, such as the Fed and the Bank of England, had funded a new form of cloud capital that is today snuffing out markets and turning consumers from sovereign agents into the playthings of algorithms that lie outside of the effective control of markets, governments and perhaps even their inventors.

BACK TO YOUR QUESTION

Time for a confession. In 1993, when you posed your killer question after I had connected you to the fledgling internet, I was not up to the challenge. It had been a couple of years since the left's greatest defeat: the collapse of what was known as really-existing socialism, from the demise of the USSR and its satellites to China's espousal of capitalist labour markets to India's dalliance with neoliberalism – developments that appended, within a year, more than 2 billion additional proletarians to the capitalist system. And looking back, I was perhaps too eager to clutch at any straw that might revive the prospect of a progressive alternative to capitalism. While not naive enough to ignore that capitalism had become unassailable, I did allow myself to dream improbable dreams.

Impressed by the early internet commons, and mesmerised by a very early 3D printer I had chanced upon at an MIT laboratory, I fantasised about groups of young designers forming cooperatives using industrial-scale 3D printers to create a variety of goods – from personalised cars to made-to-order refrigerators – at a cost that did not require mass production to stay low. Such cooperatives might, I hoped, steal an advantage over the General Motors and the General Electrics of the capitalist world – that, to use the language of economists, the economies of scale that underpin the power of General Motors and General Electric would be eradicated, activating a process that would at least deplete corporate power and might perhaps pave the way towards a decent non-capitalist future.

It was not just wishful thinking. It was a spectacular failure to foresee how a new form of capital, not a bunch of non-capitalist cooperatives, would grow out of the internet to turn the likes of General Motors and General Electric into shadows of their former selves. Taken in by the early internet and its market-free, decentralised nature, I fell headlong into a monumental diagnostic error.

Assuming, wrongly, that capitalism's only serious threat was the rise of organised labour, I missed completely the epic transformation of our times: how the privatisation of the internet commons, aided by the 2008 crisis that led central banks to open the floodgates of state money, would beget a new, super-powerful type of capital. How this cloud capital would spawn a new ruling class. How revolutionary that new ruling class would prove, leveraging its cloud capital to make almost the whole of humanity work for them, either for free or for a pittance – including many capitalists. And, crucially, what a backward step all that would prove in the grander scheme of emancipating humanity and the planet from exploitation.

Remarkably, as with all historic transformations, no one planned it. No capitalist imagined becoming a cloudalist. No central bankers aimed at funding the cloudalists. No politicians saw the damage cloud capital would inflict upon democratic politics. In the same way that capitalism came about against the will of everyone, including the kings and bishops as well as the peasants, the rise of the cloudalists happened out of sight and behind the back of the vast majority, including the most powerful of historical agents.

Knowing what we now know, two questions arise. The first concerns the sustainability of the cloudalists' dominance. As I write, war in Ukraine has turbocharged the mild inflation that came in the wake of the pandemic, thus causing central banks to cease minting new monies. If I am right that it was central bank cash that funded the cloudalists, will cloudalist power recede as the rivers of central bank monies run dry? Could the good old capitalist conglomerates, relying on terrestrial capital, make a comeback?

The second question, which I can imagine you putting to me forcefully, is more about language. Is life under the cloudalists' reign fundamentally different from living under capitalism? Are the cloudalists really so different from the capitalists that we need a newfangled term – technofeudalism – for the system we live in today? Why not just call it hyper-capitalism or platform capitalism?

These are the questions I address in the next chapter. But first, let us return for a moment to your beloved Hesiod. Besides warning us that every new age forged by some revolutionary technology yields a generation 'who never rest from labour and sorrow by day or from perishing by night', Hesiod also bequeathed us a crucial allegory: that of an aristocracy of gods dwelling above the clouds that encircle Mount Olympus, jealously holding on to their exorbitant power over us mortals. In describing such a world as if it were the natural and eternal order of things, Hesiod challenged humanity with a hard question, one that is as pertinent to us as it was to the Iron Age generation: can the cloud-dwelling aristocracy's power ever be claimed by the mortals? Would we mortals know what to do with it if we got hold of it? In other words, was Prometheus a fool to steal the fire of technology from the gods? If not, what would the task of a modern Prometheus be in the Age of Cloud Capital? This is the ultimate question that I will seek to answer in the final chapter of this book.

5
WHAT'S IN A WORD?

Set on the island of Lesbos, *Daphnis and Chloe* is the oldest surviving romantic novel. Written in the second century AD by Longus, it tells of two youngsters who fall in love but who are so innocent they do not understand what is happening or what to do about it. It is not until Chloe starts searching for the words to describe Daphnis' beauty that she even begins to fall in love with him.

'[W]hen a word is properly defined,' Simone Weil wrote in 1937, it helps 'us to grasp some concrete reality or concrete objective, or method of activity. To clarify thought, to discredit the intrinsically meaningless words, and to define the use of others by precise analysis – to do this, strange though it may appear, might be a way of saving human lives.'[1]

It is tempting to think that it does not really matter what we call the system we live in. Technofeudalism or hyper-capitalism, the system is what it is, whatever the word we use to describe it. Tempting perhaps, but quite wrong. Reserving the word 'fascist' for regimes that genuinely fall into that category and refraining from using it to describe regimes that, however nasty are not fascist, matters hugely. Calling a viral outbreak a pandemic can prove vital in mobilising against it. Similarly with the global system we live in today: the word we use to describe it can influence

profoundly whether we are more likely to perpetuate and reproduce it or whether we might challenge or even overthrow it.

Suppose we were living in the 1770s, as the first steam engines
began driving the water pumps that kept the mines dry and turning the wheels of William Blake's 'dark satanic mills'. As their
chimneys spewed thick smoke along the River Clyde, in Birming-
ham and around Manchester, we would not be wrong to speak of
an emergent 'industrial feudalism' or 'market feudalism'. Technically, we would be correct.

In the 1770s, and for at least another century, wherever one
looked one saw feudalism. Feudal lords dominated rural areas,
owned the freehold titles of most city blocks, commanded armies
and navies, and presided over parliamentary committees and government bodies. Even in the 1840s, as Marx and Engels were
writing their manifesto in response to the worldwide effects of
the capitalist class, most production was still taking place under
the auspices of the old feudalist class, the landed gentry. Land
ownership remained the main source of political authority and
rent continued to be more powerful than profit, especially in the
aftermath of the Napoleonic Wars when landlords regained the
upper hand over capitalists by banning grain imports with their
Corn Laws.[2]

And yet something critically important would have been lost if
those who forged the language of that era had been reluctant to
ditch the word feudalism, choosing to call the nascent system not
capitalism but industrial or market feudalism. By boldly calling it
capitalism, a century before capital had fully dominated our societies, they opened humanity's eyes to the great transformation
unfolding around them as it was happening.

Wherever we look today we see capitalism. Capitalists continue to own almost everything and run the military-industrial complex. They dominate parliaments, government bodies, the media, central banks and all of the powerful global institutions such as the International Monetary Fund, the World Bank, the Paris Club and the World Trade Organization. Markets continue to rule the lives and shape the minds and imaginations of billions. Profit remains the holy grail for the masses struggling to get by, as well as those wealthy individuals who believe in profit-making as an end in itself. And just as the Napoleonic Wars gave feudal power a second wind, so the war in Ukraine and its inflationary effects is reviving the fortunes of terrestrial capital, even the moribund fossil fuel industry. And yet, just as in the 1770s, to describe today's nascent system in the terms of the past – to call it hyper-capitalism, or platform capitalism, or rentier capitalism – would be not just a failure of the imagination but to miss the great transformation of *our* society that is currently taking place.

We have seen how with the enclosure of the internet commons, cloud capital arose, and how it differs from other kinds of capital in its ability to reproduce itself at no expense to its owner, turning all of us into cloud serfs. We have seen how with the shift online, Amazon now operates as a cloud fief, with traditional business paying Jeff Bezos to operate as his vassals. And we have seen how the cloudalists of Big Tech achieved all this: riding on the wave of central bank money that made profits optional. At the end of the previous chapter, we considered two immediate outcomes: the ever-rising value of the PropComs of this world has allowed private equity to asset-strip whatever they can lay their hands on, while the Big Three have established a kind of collective monopoly power over entire sectors of industry. So what, in essence, has changed? What in the simplest possible terms distinguishes this world from the previous one, demanding that we discard the word capitalism and replace it with technofeudalism? As I touched on at the end of the last chapter, it is very simply this: the triumph of rent over profit.

RENT'S REVENGE: HOW PROFIT SUCCUMBED TO CLOUD RENT

What would it take for capitalism to die? In your youth you had a definitive answer: capitalism will die, like Dr Frankenstein, indirectly of its own hand, a deserving victim of its greatest creation: the proletariat. Capitalism, you were convinced, was creating two great camps destined to clash: capitalists, who did not physically work with the revolutionary technologies they owned; and the proletarians who spent their days and nights working in, on, under or with these technological wonders, from merchant ships and railways to tractors, conveyor belts and industrial robots. The revolutionary technologies were no threat to capitalism. But revolutionary workers who knew how to work these incredible machines were.

The more capital dominated the global economic and political sphere the closer the two camps got to facing off one another in a critical battle. At its conclusion, and for the first time on a planetary scale, good would vanquish evil. The bitter bifurcation of humanity, between owners and non-owners, would thus be healed. Values would no longer be reducible to prices. And humankind would, at last, be reconciled with itself, turning technology from its master to its servant.

In practical terms, your vision meant the birth of a proper, technologically advanced, socialist democracy. Collectively owned capital and land would be pressed into producing the things society needs. Managers would be answerable to the employees that elected them, to their customers, to society as a whole. Profit would wither as a driving force because the distinction between profit and wages would no longer make sense: every employee would be an equal shareholder, their pay coming out of their enterprise's net revenues. The simultaneous death of the market for shares and of the labour market would turn banking into a staid, utility-like sector. Markets and concentrated wealth would, consequently, lose their brutish power over communities, allowing us collectively to decide how to provide health, education and protection of the environment.

Things could not have panned out more differently. Even in Western countries, like Germany and for a time Britain, where national labour unions grew strong, waged labour failed to organise effectively and eventually acquiesced to the idea of capitalism as a 'natural' system. Solidarity between the workers of the North and the South remains an entirely unfulfilled dream. Capital has simply gone from strength to strength. And in places where revolutions sworn to your vision succeeded, life ended up sooner or later resembling a cross between George Orwell's *Animal Farm* and *Nineteen Eighty-Four*. I shall never forget you confessing to me, while recounting horror stories of the years you spent in prison camps for Greek left-wingers, the feeling which overwhelmed you most: that, had our side won power, you would probably be in the same prison only with different guards. It resonated with the heartbreak of authentic left-wingers worldwide: good people, dedicated to your vision, who ended up in gulags guarded by former comrades or, even worse, in positions of the sort of power that their own ideology detested.

Nevertheless, your prognosis is holding up extremely well,

though not in ways that you would welcome. Capitalism *is* dying indirectly of its own hand, a deserving victim of its greatest creation: not the proletariat, but the cloudalists. And little by little, capitalism's two great pillars – profit and markets – are being replaced. Alas, instead of a post-capitalist system that finally heals human divisions and ends exploitation of people and planet, the one that is taking shape deepens and universalises exploitation in ways that were hitherto unimaginable, except perhaps by science-fiction writers. Thinking back, Dad, why did we ever allow ourselves to be lured into the soothing delusion that the death of something bad would necessarily deliver something better? Rosa Luxemburg's devastating question 'Socialism or barbarism?'[3] was not rhetorical. Its answer could easily be barbarism – or extinction.

What we need, then, is a new story that explains not what we wish would happen but what is actually happening, and that is the story of how rent – the defining economic trait of feudalism – staged its remarkable comeback.

Under feudalism, rent was easy enough to grasp. Courtesy of some accident of birth, or royal decree, the feudal lord obtained the deeds to a plot of land which empowered him to extract part of the harvest produced by the peasants who had been born and raised on that land. Under capitalism, grasping the meaning of rent, and distinguishing it from profit, is much harder – a difficulty I witnessed first-hand when as a university teacher I would struggle to help my students spot the difference between the two.

Arithmetically, there is no difference: both rent and profit amount to money left over once costs are paid for. The difference is subtler, qualitative, almost abstract: profit is vulnerable to market competition, rent is not. The reason is their different origins.

Rent flows from privileged access to things in fixed supply, like fertile soil or land containing fossil fuels; you cannot produce more of these resources, however much money you might invest in them. Profit, in contrast, flows into the pockets of entrepreneurial people who have invested in things that would not have otherwise existed – things like Edison's light bulb or Jobs's iPhone. It is this fact – that these commodities were invented and created and so can be invented and created again but better by someone else – that renders profit vulnerable to competition.

When Sony invented the Walkman, the first mobile and personal hi-fi, it raked in substantial profits. Then competition from imitators whittled Sony's profits away until, eventually, Apple rode in with its iPod to dominate the market. In contrast, market competition is the rentier's friend. If Jack owns a building in a neighbourhood that is being gentrified as a result of what others do, Jack's rents will increase even if he does nothing – he, literally, gets wealthier in his sleep. The more enterprising Jack's neighbours are, and the more they invest in the area, the larger his rents.

Capitalism prevailed when profit overwhelmed rent, a historic triumph coinciding with the transformation of productive work and property rights into commodities to be sold via labour and share markets respectively. It was not just an economic victory. Whereas rent reeked of vulgar exploitation, profit claimed moral superiority as a just reward to brave entrepreneurs risking everything to navigate the treacherous currents of stormy markets. Nevertheless, despite profit's triumph, rent survived capitalism's golden age in the same way that remnants of the DNA of our ancient ancestors, including long-extinct serpents and microbes, survive in human DNA.

Capitalist mega-firms, like Ford, Edison, General Electric, General Motors, ThyssenKrupp, Volkswagen, Toyota, Sony and all the others, generated the profits that outweighed rent and propelled capitalism to its dominance. However, like remora fish living parasitically in the shadow of great sharks, some rentiers not only survived but, in fact, flourished by feeding on the generous scraps left in profit's wake. Oil companies, for example, have raked in gargantuan ground rents from the right to drill on particular plots of land or ocean beds – not to mention the unearned privilege to damage the planet at no cost to themselves.

Naturally, oil companies have attempted to legitimise their loot by presenting it as capitalist profit, exaggerating the extent to which their returns are a reward to investments in smart, low-cost drilling technology without which, it is true, the extracted oil might not be competitive with oil extracted by competing oil producers. The same is true of real estate development where ground rent overshadows any profit from innovative architecture. Or with privatised electricity or water utilities whose returns are mostly due to rents the political class has allocated to them. What all these mega-rentiers have in common is a strong motive to legitimise their rents by disguising them as profits – something akin to profit-washing their rents.

After the Second World War, rent went one better than merely surviving capitalism: it staged a revival on the coat-tails of the emergent technostructure – the nexus of conglomerates with immense resources, productive capacity and market reach that grew out of the War Economy. The innovative marketeers and imaginative advertisers employed by the technostructure achieved this by creating something ingenious: brand loyalty.

Brand loyalty affords the brand owner the power to raise prices without losing customers. This price premium reflects the greater status afforded to the owner of a Mercedes-Benz or an Apple computer over the owner of, say, a cheaper equivalent produced by Ford or Sony. These premiums amount to brand rents. By the 1980s, branding had attained such rent-extracting powers that young, aspiring entrepreneurs cared less about who produced things, where or how than they did about owning the right brands.

If branding gave rent its first chance to flourish again in the 1950s, the emergence of cloud capital in the noughties was rent's opportunity to exact a stunning revenge on profit – to stage a comeback for the ages. Apple played a leading role in this. Before the iPhone, Steve Jobs's gadgets were a textbook case of high-end commodities that fetched premium prices reflecting substantial brand rents – not unlike Rolls-Royces and Prada shoes. The company survived brutal competition from Microsoft, IBM, Sony and an army of lesser competitors by selling desktops, laptops and iPods with beautiful design and famed user-friendliness that ultimately allowed Apple to charge significant amounts of brand rent. However, the breakthrough for Apple, which turned it into a trillion-dollar company, was the iPhone – not just because it was a great mobile phone but because it handed Apple the key to a whole new treasure chest: cloud rent.

The stroke of genius that unlocked cloud rent for Steve Jobs was his radical idea to invite 'third-party developers' to use free Apple software with which to produce applications for sale via the Apple Store. In one fell swoop Apple had created an army of unwaged labourers and vassal capitalists whose hard work yielded a host of capabilities available exclusively to iPhone owners in the form of thousands of desirable apps that Apple engineers could never have produced themselves in such variety or volume.

Suddenly, an iPhone was much more than a desirable phone. It was a ticket to a vast vista of pleasures and abilities that no other smartphone company could provide. Even if an Apple competitor, say Nokia, Sony or Blackberry, had managed to respond quickly by manufacturing a smarter, faster, cheaper and more beautiful phone, it would not matter: only an iPhone opened the gates to the Apple Store. Why didn't Nokia, Sony or Blackberry build their own store? Because it was too late: with so many people signed up to Apple, the thousands of third-party developers were not going to spend their time and effort developing apps for other platforms. To be competitive, Apple's unwaged third-party developers, mainly partnerships or small capitalist firms, had no choice but to operate via the Apple Store. The price? A 30 per cent ground rent, paid to Apple on all their revenues. Thus a vassal capitalist class grew from the fertile soil of the first cloud fief: the Apple Store.

Only one other conglomerate managed to persuade a significant proportion of those developers to create apps for its own store: Google. Long before the iPhone arrived, Google's search engine had become the centrepiece of a cloud empire which included Gmail and YouTube, and which would later include Google Drive, Google Maps and a host of other online services. Keen to exploit its already dominant cloud capital, Google followed a different strategy to Apple's. Instead of manufacturing a handset in competition with the iPhone, it developed Android – an operating system that could be installed for free on the smartphone of any manufacturer, including Sony, Blackberry and Nokia, who chose to use it. The idea was that if enough of Apple's competitors installed it on their phones, the pool of smartphones operating on the Android software would be large enough to lure third-party developers to produce apps not only for the Apple Store but also for a new store running on Android software. That's how Google created Google Play, the only serious alternative to the Apple Store.

Android was neither better nor worse than the operating system Sony, Blackberry, Nokia and others had – or could have – produced on their own. But it came with a superpower: Google's abundant cloud capital, which acted as a magnet to the third-party developers Sony, Blackberry, Nokia could never have attracted on their own. How could they resist? However reluctantly, they were forced to accept the role of vassal capitalist phone manufacturers, subsisting on scraps of profit from selling their hardware, while Google raked in the cloud rent produced by that other crowd of vassal privateers and capitalists: the third-party developers now producing apps for sale on Google Play.

The result was a global smartphone industry with two dominant cloudalist corporations, Apple and Google, with the bulk of their wealth being produced by unwaged third-party developers, from whose sales they extracted a fixed cut. This is not profit. It is cloud rent, the digital equivalent of ground rent.

During this same decade, Amazon perfected its own formula for selling physical goods via a global supply chain through its own cloud fief – amazon.com – whose dynamics we have already examined. Thanks to Amazon's algorithmically driven ecommerce formula, cloud rent was no longer confined to the digital world.

Funded by central bank money, bolstered by private equity, these cloudalists extended their cloud fiefs across the globe, extracting gargantuan cloud rents from vassal capitalists and cloud serfs alike. In a paradoxical twist, the number of capitalists relying on good old-fashioned profit *grew* even while their profit margins and power declined. Likewise, these vassal capitalists have continued to enjoy the power to command labour from the majority who are reliant on wages, and they continue to own at least some of their means of production: their computers, their cars and vans, perhaps an office, warehouse or factory. Indeed, not all vassal capitalists are small-scale artisans, some are large capitalist manufacturers. But large or small, powerful or otherwise, all vassal capitalists are by definition dependent to a greater or lesser extent on selling their wares via an ecommerce site, whether Amazon or eBay or Alibaba, with a sizeable portion of their net earnings being skimmed off by the cloudalists they depend on.

Meanwhile, as Amazon was snaring makers of physical products within its cloud fief, other cloudalists were focusing their attention on the precariat. Companies like Uber, Lyft, Grubhub, DoorDash and Instacart in the Global North, along with their imitators in Asia and Africa, wired into their cloud fiefs a vast array of drivers, delivery people, cleaners, restaurateurs – even dog walkers – collecting from these unwaged, piece-rate workers a fixed cut of their earnings, too. A cloud rent.

Recently, I watched the Super 8 silent home movies you left me in a carton at the Paleo Phaliro house, many of which you had filmed during your travels in the 1960s when, at the drop of a hat, the steel company you worked for would fly you to America, Japan and Europe to buy advanced machinery, or to the West's former colonies to secure a steady supply of high-quality iron ore and coking coal. One film reel I found was marked '1964 – Indonesia'. Most of the footage was of a road trip out of Jakarta. On mile after mile of crowded country road, I could not fail to notice the roadside *warungs* around which scores of locals congregated. *Warungs*, you explained, are like our kiosks in Greece, selling cheaply everything from drinks, pens and newspapers to shampoo, aspirin and telephone services.

You might be surprised to hear that Bukalapak, an Indonesian cloudalist firm, is taking over three and a half million *warungs*, digitising their services with a view not only to uploading their multifaceted local markets to the cloud but also to financialising the local communities who depend on them via usurious microcredits, expensive digital cash transfers and basic banking services. Never too slow to cotton on, Jeff Bezos dispatched Jeff Bezos Expeditions to Indonesia and in 2021 began to invest in a competitor of Bukalapak's.[4] Peter Thiel, co-founder of PayPal, early investor in Facebook, initiator of Palantir, has done the same with his Valar Ventures. So have Tencent, a leading Chinese Big Tech conglomerate.

From factory owners in America's Midwest to poets struggling to sell their latest anthology, from London Uber drivers to Indonesian street hawkers, all are now dependent on some cloud fief for access to customers. It is progress, of sorts. Gone is the time when, to collect their rent, feudal lords employed thugs to break their vassals' knees or spill their blood. The cloudalists don't need to deploy bailiffs to confiscate or to evict. Instead, every vassal capitalist knows that with the removal of a link from their cloud vassal's site they could lose access to the bulk of their customers. And with the removal of a link or two from Google's search engine or from a couple of ecommerce and social media sites, they could disappear from the online world altogether. A sanitised tech-terror is the bedrock of technofeudalism.

Looked at in totality, it becomes apparent that the world

economy is lubricated less and less with profit and increasingly with cloud rent. And so the delightful antinomy of our era comes into focus: capitalist activity is growing within the same process of energetic capital accumulation that degrades capitalist profit and gradually replaces capitalist markets with cloud fiefs. In short, capitalism is withering as a result of burgeoning capitalist activity. It is through capitalist activity that technofeudalism was born and is now sweeping to power. After all, how could it be any other way?

CAPITALISM ON STEROIDS?

'I am unconvinced,' I hear you say. 'Feudal lords never invested in anything except intrigue and violence. Your cloudalists, in contrast, invest massively in the highest of high-tech capital. They are the epitome of capitalists, pouring money into research and development in order to produce new and desirable commodities like search results, digital personal assistants and teleconferencing applications. Even if they manage to create something resembling a fiefdom, as Zuckerberg did with Facebook, a competitor emerges before long who syphons off millions of users to their own multibillion-dollar business. Look at the sudden rise of TikTok, for example!

'Your cloudalists are the polar opposite of lazy barons and earls and far closer to Thomas Edison, Henry Ford and George Westinghouse than any feudal lord. If anything, Yanis, they are capitalists on steroids – and in the final analysis, even if they feast more and more on what you call cloud rent, what they are doing is still capitalism. Call it rentier capitalism. Or cloud capitalism. Or hyper-capitalism. But technofeudalism? No, I don't see it.'

It is true, Dad, that the cloudalists are – or at least were – capitalists-on-steroids. That I would never dispute. Unlike the feudalists, who were invariably born with the power to extract rents, the cloudalists had to create it from scratch. And to do that, you're right, they invested gargantuan sums in their technology. But the question remains: what exactly did they invest in? And what came of their investments?

You say that the cloudalists invested in the creation of new commodities – but a commodity is a thing or service produced to be sold for profit. Search results are not produced to be sold. Alexa and Siri do not answer our questions for a fee. Like Facebook, Twitter, TikTok, Instagram, YouTube, WhatsApp, their purpose is entirely different: to capture and modify our attention. And even when Big Tech cloudalists make us pay a fee to gain access to artificial intelligence bots like ChatGPT or sell us physical devices such as Alexa, they aren't selling them as commodities. These gadgets are leased or sold cheaply not for the negligible (often negative) profit they make on them but to gain access to our homes and, via them, to more of our attention. It is this power over our attention that allows them to collect cloud rent from the vassal capitalists who are in the old-fashioned business of selling *their* commodities. Ultimately, the cloudalist's investment is aimed not at competing within a capitalist market but in getting us to *exit* capitalist markets altogether.

Cloudalists like Steve Jobs, Jeff Bezos, Mark Zuckerberg, Sergei Brin do, I admit, have some things in common with Edison, Ford and Westinghouse: big egos, oversized companies, and a readiness to break things, including existing markets and state institutions, in order to shore up their dominance. But those captains of early-twentieth-century Big Business were all focused squarely on achieving profit by monopolising markets and deploying the capital of factories and production lines. They would be the first to see that the cloudalists are now becoming fabulously wealthy without needing to organise the production of *any* commodity. Not only that, they are free from the pressure of a market to produce cheaper, better commodities or indeed the constant fear that a competitor might come up with a product that steals their market share altogether.

'But your cloudalists do live in such fear,' I hear you object. 'Look at how TikTok drained Facebook's users and revenues. Or at the existential threat to Netflix that is Disney Plus. Or at how Walmart's ecommerce site has been taking market share from Amazon. Isn't this exactly the market competition that Ford, Edison and Westinghouse faced?'

Well, Dad, despite the similarities, no, it's not.

Battles and rivalries like these, leading to the rise and fall of fiefs, were part and parcel of feudalism. At times, it took considerable effort to keep fiefs from falling into decline or conquest, especially after 1350 when the Black Death created acute labour shortages and serfs were able to leave one fief and migrate to another. But we should not confuse rivalry between fiefs with market-based competition.

TikTok's success at stealing the attention of users away from other social media sites is not due to the lower prices it offers or higher quality of the 'friendships' or associations it enables. TikTok created a new cloud fief for cloud serfs in search of a different online experience to migrate to. Disney Plus did not offer audiences the movies and series on Netflix at lower prices or in higher definition formats – it offered movies and series not available on

Netflix. Walmart did not undercut Amazon's prices or improve on the quality of its commodities – it used its own database to lure more users to its newly established cloud fief. As for Apple, the pioneer of cloud-fief construction, it deploys what it calls 'privacy rules' (e.g. it prevents competitors, like Facebook and Google, from gleaning iPhone owners' data) that are carefully tailored to prevent other cloudalists from modifying the behaviour of any users that they share, causing Mark Zuckerberg to accuse it of charging 'monopoly rents' and 'stifling innovation'.

Like Ford, Edison and Westinghouse, the cloudalists of Amazon, Tencent, Alibaba, Facebook, Apple and Google also invest in research and development, in politics, marketing, union-busting and cartel tactics, but again they do so not to sell commodities at maximum profit, but in order to extract maximum rents from the capitalists who do.

The Great Transformation, from feudalism to capitalism, was predicated on the usurpation of rent by profit as the driving force of our socio-economic system. That was why the word *capitalism* proved so much more useful and insightful than a term like market feudalism. It is this fundamental fact – that we have entered a socio-economic system powered not by profit but by rent – that demands we use a new term to describe it. To think of it as hyper-capitalism or rentier capitalism would be to miss this essential, defining principle. And to reflect the return of rent to its central role, I can think of no better name than technofeudalism.

More importantly, having defined and labelled it properly, I believe we are now better equipped to grasp the meaning and importance of this systemic transformation – and what is at stake for us all.

THE TECHNOFEUDAL METHOD
TO ELON MUSK'S TWITTER MADNESS

If I had to choose one person to illustrate the need for technofeudalism, both word and concept, in order to understand our collective predicament, it would be Elon Musk.

Brilliant and flawed, combining rare engineering talents with ridiculous public displays of ostentation, Musk is our era's Thomas Edison – the man who, you may recall, electrocuted an elephant in order to discredit a rival. Having revolutionised industries that are normally the graveyard of upstarts, from car manufacturing to space travel and even brain-computer interfaces, Musk proceeded to spend tens of billions of dollars on buying Twitter, risking in the process everything he had achieved as a manufacturer and engineer. Many commentators opined that Musk was just another rich brat looking for an even more impressive toy than the ones he had already. But there was a logic to his purchase of Twitter: a technofeudal logic that elucidates much more than Musk's mindset.

We should not be surprised if Musk was indeed feeling unfulfilled. For all his success as manufacturer, and despite attaining richest-man-in-the-world status, neither his achievements nor his wealth granted him entry into the new ruling class. His Tesla car company uses the cloud cleverly to turn its cars into nodes on a digital network that generates Big Data and ties drivers to Musk's systems. His SpaceX rocket company, and the flock of satellites it pollutes our planet's low orbit periphery with, contributes significantly to the development of other moguls' cloud capital. But Musk? Frustratingly for the business world's *enfant terrible*, he has lacked a gateway to the gigantic rents that cloud capital can furnish. Twitter could be that missing gateway.

Immediately after taking over Twitter, Musk spoke of his commitment to safeguarding Twitter as the 'public square' where we debate anything and everything. It was a bit of propaganda which successfully diverted the public's attention towards an endless global debate about whether the world should trust its foremost short-form debating forum to a mogul with a history of playing fast and loose with the truth on that same forum. While the liberal commentariat was fretting over Donald Trump's reinstatement, decent people admonished the terrible treatment of Twitter's employees, and the left agonised over the rise of a tech-savvy version of Rupert Murdoch, Musk was keeping his eye on the ball. In a revealing tweet, he admitted his ambition to turn Twitter into an 'everything app'.

What did he mean by an 'everything app'? He meant nothing less than a gateway to technofeudalism, one that would allow him to attract users' attention, modify their consumer behaviour, extract free labour from them as cloud serfs and, last but not least, charge vendors cloud rent for selling them their wares. Unlike the owners of Amazon, Google, Alibaba, Facebook, TikTok and Tencent, Musk did not own anything capable of evolving into an 'everything app' and had no way of creating one from scratch. Only one such interface belonged to no other mogul or hypercorporation and was, therefore, available for purchase: Twitter.

As a private fief, Twitter could never be the world's public square. The pertinent question is whether Musk can use it to build a prominent cloud fief and, thus, gain membership of the new technofeudal ruling class: the cloudalists. That will depend on whether he can successfully enhance Twitter's cloud capital, perhaps by hooking it up to his existing Big Data network that is constantly being enriched by his cars and satellites. Succeed or fail, Musk's Twitter escapade shows how technofeudalism and the perspective it affords help us better to understand what is actually going on in our world.

That is one particular example, whose outcome will be relatively limited. But technofeudalism also unlocks a more pervasive and pressing problem, in which we are all implicated.

THE TECHNOFEUDAL UNDERPINNINGS OF THE GREAT INFLATION

Every great transformation brings with it a new type of crisis. When we invented agriculture, we amassed plants and animals within our communities and, unwittingly, bred noxious germs that caused hideous epidemics. The arrival of capitalism begat economic crises such as the Great Depression. Today, technofeudalism is deepening pre-existing sources of instability and turning them into new existential threats. Specifically, the Great Inflation and cost-of-living crisis that have followed the recent pandemic cannot be properly understood outside the context of technofeudalism.

In the last chapter, I recounted how for twelve long years after the crash of 2008, central banks printed trillions to replace the bankers' losses. We saw how socialism for bankers and austerity for the rest of us dampened investment, blunted Western capitalism's dynamic and pushed it into a state of gilded stagnation. The only serious investment of the central banks' poisoned money during this time went into the accumulation of cloud capital. By 2020, cloud rents accruing to cloud capital accounted for much of the developed world's aggregate net income. That in brief is how cloud rent gained the upper hand and profit retreated.

One does not need to be left-leaning to know that rent's stunning comeback could only mean deeper and more toxic stagnation.[5] Wages get spent by the many struggling to make ends meet. Profits get invested in capital goods to maintain the capitalists' capacity to profit. But rent is stashed away in property (mansions, yachts, art, cryptocurrencies, etc.) and stubbornly refuses to enter circulation, stimulate investment into useful things, and revive flaccid capitalist societies. And so a vicious cycle begins: deeper stagnation ensues, causing central banks to print more money, enabling more extraction and less investment, and so on.

The pandemic exacerbated the same trend. The only significant difference from the pre-pandemic period was that, this time, and for the first time since 2008, some of the fresh trillions printed by central banks were spent by governments on the population, to keep their citizens alive while locked down. Nonetheless, most of the new monies ended up bolstering the share price of Big Tech corporations. This explains the report of Swiss bank UBS, published in October 2020, which found that billionaires had increased their wealth by more than a quarter (27.5 per cent) between April and July of that year, just as millions of people around the world lost their jobs or were struggling to get by on government schemes.[6]

Meanwhile, lockdowns closed ports, roads and airports, throttling the supply of goods in economies where, for many years, underinvestment had already depleted the capacity to produce locally. What happens when supply suddenly dies? Especially during times when the locked-down masses get some income support from the central banks' money tree? The price of groceries, exercise bikes, bread makers, natural gas, petrol, housing and a host of other goods goes through the roof and, following a dozen years of subdued prices, a Great Inflation sets in.

Many hoped that the inflation resulting from blockages in the supply chain would be mild. The expectation that inflation would be 'transitory' had a logic to it: workers' bargaining power in the 2020s was a shadow of its former self, when in the 1970s mighty trades unions could push for wage rises above the inflation rate. It followed that with only limp wage rises to support them once government furlough schemes and income support came to an end, the purchasing power of the masses would simply be depleted by rising prices, demand for goods would ebb and prices would fall. It hasn't panned out that way.

Inflation is never just a monetary phenomenon – just as money is never just a token of exchange value. When, for whatever reason, prices surge across the board, a social power game is afoot in which everyone attempts to suss out their bargaining power. Business managers try to work out how far they can raise prices – if not to profit then, at least, to recoup their own rising costs. Rentiers, both traditional and cloudalist, test the water with rent hikes. Workers assess the extent to which they can push for a pay rise – at least to compensate for the higher bills they must meet. Governments play the game too: do they intervene by using the greater income and VAT tax receipts flowing from the rising prices to assist weaker citizens being crushed by inflation? Or do they subsidise Big Business as it is squeezed by high energy prices? Or do they do nothing much? Until these questions get answered, inflation continues to roll.

In a power game like this, it is power that matters above all. If capital dominates labour, inflation ends when workers accept a permanent reduction in their wage share of total income. If government dominates capital, as for example in China, inflation dissipates when capitalists and rentiers acquiesce to a chunk of their loot being used to pay off a portion of the state's deficits, debts or expenditures. The question, for us, then becomes: what happens in societies where cloud capital dominates terrestrial capital and labour is at the bottom of the pecking order?

Two things happen – one obvious and one far less so. On the surface, supermarkets, energy companies and any other conglomerate that is able to inflate prices above its costs will rake in superprofits.[7] However, the less obvious but more interesting repercussion of the Great Inflation, in a world going through its early technofeudalist phase, is subtler and woven into society's productive fabric: traditional capital is further displaced by new cloud capital, hastening and strengthening technofeudalism's super-arching reach. Here are two examples of how it goes.

THE CASE OF GERMAN CARS
AND GREEN ENERGY

German car makers were dealt a double blow by the Great Inflation: rising fuel prices not only put their customers off but elevated the energy cost of making cars. The German press went so far as to agonise over the country's possible de-industrialisation. While their angst was justified, their analysis missed the point.

German car makers will probably continue to produce as many cars in the future as they did in the past for the simple reason that they have been relatively swift to invest in the transition from manufacturing the petrol-powered automobiles of the past to the electric vehicles of our future. You might think, then, that the hastening of the shift to electric cars, caused by energy price inflation, would work in their favour. Not so much.

The kernel of German capital's power and success is high-precision mechanical and electrical engineering. German car makers, in particular, have profited by building high-quality internal combustion engines and all the parts that are necessary to convey motion from such engines to a car's wheels: the gearboxes, axles, differentials and so on. Electric vehicles are mechanically much simpler to engineer. Most of their surplus value – and the profit they afford – derives from the software that runs them and connects the car to the cloud and the data that derives in turn from that. The Great Inflation, in other words, is forcing German industry to produce goods that rely a lot more on cloud capital than traditional capital.

The problem, then, is this: compared to their American and Chinese counterparts, German capitalists failed to realise soon enough the benefits of investing in cloud capital – of becoming cloudalists – and lag far behind in this new game. In practical terms, they are manufacturing themselves out of a competitive position. Unable to collect sufficient cloud rents, German surpluses will suffer and so will the economy of a European Union – and its citizenry – reliant on German surpluses.

A similar story can be told about the energy sector. Once the pandemic receded and energy prices surged, Big Oil and Gas made a fortune. The fossil fuel industry has had a second wind, similar to that enjoyed by landowners during the Napoleonic Wars, due to the disruption of corn imports into Britain. But second winds do not last long. Just as capitalist profit overcame the short-term revival of feudal lords' fortunes as the memory of the Napoleonic Wars receded, so the Great Inflation is already expanding cloud capital's reach into the energy sector.

The fossil fuel industry is an unholy alliance of feudal-style contracts and terrestrial capital: it relies on licences to drill on particular patches of land or ocean bed, for which governments and private landlords receive old-fashioned ground rent. It also relies on old-fashioned capital goods, including oil rigs, tankers and pipelines, to feed fossil fuels into large, highly concentrated, vertically integrated power stations which, both aesthetically and economically, are not so dissimilar from a 'dark satanic mill' of the nineteenth century.

Renewables, in contrast, are best deployed in a decentralised fashion, with solar panels, wind turbines, heat pumps, geothermal units and wave-powered devices all horizontally integrated as part of a network. With little need for licences that incur ground rent, their productivity depends instead on digital infrastructure running on sophisticated software utilising artificial intelligence. In short, green energy is cloud-capital-intensive, much like the electric car industry.

The need to switch from fossil fuels to green energy could not be more urgent. The rise in energy costs that is an integral part of the Great Inflation would seem to have taken us away from that goal, offering a windfall to the fossil fuel industry. But this will not last long. Advances in green energy are pushing down fast the costs of green electricity generation. Even though the life cycle of fossil fuels has been extended, ruinously for the planet, cloud-based green energy is growing – and, with it, so is the relative power of cloudalists.

Technofeudalism has an inbuilt tendency to dampen price inflation, as it is in its nature to squeeze wages, prices and profits. But how exactly the Great Inflation will unfold in the short term is impossible to predict accurately because, as we have seen already, inflation is always a symptom of a flare-up of the ongoing class war; its trajectory will be determined primarily by politics and power. And what is certain is that by enhancing the scope of cloud capital, the Great Inflation will ultimately be bad for labour's political power, as it turns more of us into cloud proles.

Still, a large question mark hangs over the future of techno-feudalism: now that the Great Inflation has forced central banks to stop their money-printing, causing the cloudalists' share prices to tank and tens of thousands of Big Tech employees to lose their jobs; and now that oil companies and supermarkets are enjoying some fabulous profits, won't the technofeudal bubble burst? Has it not burst already?

BACK TO YOUR QUESTION: IS CAPITALISM NOT BACK ON TRACK?

Your original question was whether the internet would make capitalism invincible or prove its undoing – and by now you know my answer. But given the economic tumult in the post-pandemic years, it would be reasonable to wonder whether the trends and principles I have identified still hold. Hasn't the Great Inflation revived capitalism?

Mainstream economic commentators found the Great Inflation rather unmysterious, and certainly not the sign of some underlying historic transformation – technofeudalist or otherwise. To them, inflation was the natural consequence of central bankers printing too much money, and of governments over-spending it during the pandemic. As red-faced central bankers were forced to raise interest rates throughout 2022 in order to choke off demand and put a lid on rising prices, normally solemn commentators were hardly able to contain their pleasure at the

WHAT'S IN A WORD?

apparent admission of their mistake.[8] The Great Inflation of 2022 was to them what the Stuart Restoration of 1660 had been to British royalists: a return to agreeably familiar patterns of authority.

Not only that, with money becoming more expensive to borrow and to hold, the mad years when money's price languished around zero had ended. Sanity had been restored. There was a price to pay, of course; the familiar hangover after the party ended. With interest rates rising, financiers relying on borrowed money to play the stock exchanges were forced to exit the market and, unsurprisingly, share prices declined even faster than interest rates had risen. And since the higher the rise the harder the fall, it was the cloudalist conglomerates – whose stock exchange value had taken off during the pandemic – that fell the most under the Great Inflation. During 2022, the total share value of US Big Tech cloudalist companies shrank by a remarkable $4 trillion – though more remarkable still, perhaps, was the fact that their stock exchange valuation remained, on average, above its pre-pandemic level. Meanwhile, lockdown winners like Peloton, Zoom and Carvana all plummeted. So did 'meme stocks' like AMC and GameStop, so-called SPACs and NFTs – not to mention Bitcoin, Dogecoin, and other crypto false promises. The commentariat was almost relieved: technofeudalism, even if it had been taking hold for a brief period, was just another burst bubble.

From their point of view, our focus for concern as we navigate persistent inflation should be the connection between energy and food prices and the war in Ukraine, US sanctions on various countries, relocalisation of production due to the prospects of a New Cold War between America and China, ageing populations, stricter immigration controls. In other words, it's back to business as usual. And many left-wingers have found similar solace in the Great Inflation. They may abhor the hardships that inflation inflicts on the poor but welcome the feeling that the world makes sense to them again. With the price of money rising well above zero once more, and the market value of companies like Meta, Tesla and Amazon crashing down to Earth, the old capitalist order they know well how to despise is back. I sense that you too, Dad, might be harbouring similar thoughts.

Well, I'm sorry to say, there will be no return to the good old bad old days.

First, those torrents of central bank money have already built cloud capital up to critical mass. It is here to stay – and to dominate – because its immense structural power, to extract vast cloud rents from every society on Earth, remains completely undiminished. This would not be the first time a bubble has built up capital that endures after the bubble's bursting. America owes its railways to precisely this pattern: that bubble burst in the nineteenth century but not before tracks were laid down that are still in place, from Boston and New York to Los Angeles and San Diego. More recently, when the dot.com bubble burst in 2001, bankrupting early internet-based companies whose stock market valuations had reached ridiculous levels, it left behind the network of fibre optic cables and servers which provided the infrastructure underpinning Internet Two and Big Tech.

Second, the central bank money has not actually run dry. It is still flowing, albeit at a slower pace which nonetheless suffices to keep technofeudalism buoyant. Central banks can't afford to stem their flow completely, even if this is what they must do to defeat the Great Inflation. Recent bank failures in California and Switzerland reminded America's and Europe's central banks that, if they dare withdraw the trillions they have pumped

into the North Atlantic economies, a vortex of volatility is
ready to hit the $24 trillion market for the United States' public
debt – the very bedrock of international banking and finance.[9]
The European Central Bank knows that it risks pushing every
German bank plus the state of Italy into a deep bankruptcy, and
in so doing blowing up the euro. The Bank of Japan, the first
central bank to practise energetic money-printing back in the
1990s, refuses even to imagine ending the practice. As for the
Bank of England, on 28 September 2022, after formally
announcing the end of its pound-printing, it had to beat an
ignominious retreat, printing an extra £65 billion to pacify the
market for the UK's public debt.[10] In short, central bank money
is here to stay and will continue to play the systemic role once
held by capitalist profits.

Third, cloud capital is now so well entrenched that it is bolstered and augmented not just by central bank money and its
own capacity to amass cloud rent but from every new development as it arises: from the need for more renewables and
self-driving cars to the demands for cheap online degree
programmes for youngsters who can't afford more student debt,
cloud capital expands its domain exponentially. Paradoxically, as
we have seen in the case of electric cars and green energy, this
even includes the Great Inflation itself, which is doing much of
the heavy lifting in the great rebalancing of power away from
terrestrial capital and towards cloud capital – in a word, from
capitalism to technofeudalism.

My aim in this chapter has been to convince you that the
word technofeudalism can, in the words of Simone Weil, 'help
us to grasp some concrete reality or concrete objective, or method of activity' in a way that no variant on capitalism can.

Technofeudalism, I claimed, is qualitatively distinct from capitalism and, thus, as a word, it illuminates crucial aspects of the real world in ways that rentier capitalism or platform capitalism or hyper-capitalism cannot. It is time now to unleash its explanatory power further, for I believe it helps us understand not only our socio-economic condition but also the titanic power struggle that may well define this century: the New Cold War between the United States and China.

6
TECHNOFEUDALISM'S GLOBAL IMPACT: THE NEW COLD WAR

On 15 May 2019, President Donald Trump issued a decree which, in effect, banned Google from allowing use of its Android operating system on smartphones made by Huawei, the Chinese telecommunications conglomerate. Trump was effectively evicting Huawei from Google's global cloud fief. Washington also told European governments to suspend their plan to involve Huawei in the roll-out of 5G mobile networks across Europe. It was much more than Trumpist folly. When Joe Biden moved into the White House, the New Cold War with China that Trump had kick-started moved up a gear – especially in October 2022 when, according to the *New York Times*, 'The White House issued sweeping restrictions on selling semiconductors and chip-making equipment to China, an attempt to curb the country's access to critical technologies.' In essence, Biden told Beijing: the United States will crush your dreams of building a technologically advanced economy.[1]

What happened there? To explain their decisions, both Trump and Biden cited national security concerns and played up long-standing tensions with China over Taiwan and the South China

Sea. But neither China's communist regime nor its stance on Taiwan were new, urgent or unexpected. Moreover, where were these 'concerns' when Apple, and many other American conglomerates, were setting up camp across communist China's coastline from the mid-2000s onwards? Or when Washington was moving heaven and earth to let China into the World Trade Organization in the 1990s? Or after 2008, when Beijing boosted investment from around 30 per cent of national income to more than 50 per cent, creating global demand for Europe's and America's products and thus helping to save US-dominated financialised capitalism from itself? Why did these 'concerns' suddenly, and well before the war in Ukraine, yield a New Cold War?

To solve the puzzle, we must briefly return to the parable of the Minotaur.

Recall how until the Nixon Shock of 1971, any non-American with large quantities of dollars could exchange them at will for gold owned by the US government at a fixed price of $35 per ounce. For as long as America sold more stuff to Europe and Asia than it imported from them, as it did between the war's end and 1965, this trade surplus meant that every time America sold a jet or refrigerator in France or Japan, the foreign-held dollars that paid for them would be repatriated and America's gold reserves would remain untouched. However, by the mid-sixties the United States had turned into a deficit country, buying goods of greater dollar value from foreigners than it sold to them. This led to a torrent of dollars leaving America for Europe and Asia and not coming back. And the larger the US trade deficit, the more claims foreigners had over America's gold. In time, they grew anxious that the US government did not have enough gold to match their dollars and there was a run on America's gold. To prevent losing it all, on 15 August 1971, Nixon told the world that they would no longer exchange foreign-held dollars for gold at that fixed price. In other words: no more gold for you from our vaults. Our dollars are now your problem.

Non-American central banks suddenly had no alternative than to use dollars instead of gold as reserves to back the value of their currency. The dollar began to resemble an . . . IOU. After the so-called Nixon Shock, the global financial system was, effectively, backed by IOUs issued by a hegemon who could decide what the foreign IOU-holders could do with their IOUs – and what they were not allowed to do with them. America was now a deficit country but was nothing like any other deficit country. 'Normal' deficit countries, such as France, Greece or India, had to borrow dollars to shore up their currency and to raise interest rates domestically to stop money outflows. America did not need to do any of that. It had, in other words, found the magic formula every empire had hitherto only dreamed of: how to persuade wealthy foreigners, and foreign central banks, voluntarily to finance simultaneously its government and its imports!

This is how the Minotaur arose. Rather than sell the world goods, America offered it an alternative use for their dollars: invest them in Wall Street. They had created a mechanism that could recycle Asian and European surpluses (mainly Chinese and German) into productive investments for the USA. With these tributes to the Minotaur, peace and prosperity for all continued – until of course it all collapsed in 2008.

So how does this relate to the New Cold War between America and China? From 1971 onwards, any non-American capitalist with massive dollar wealth faced the same problem: what to do with dollars in a country where they could not spend dollars? The only option was to take them back to America to invest them there. However, foreign capitalists soon discovered that the US government was not like other governments. In Britain, Greece or Spain, rich foreigners could buy whatever they pleased. In no uncertain terms, Washington made it clear to German, Japanese, and (later) Chinese capitalists: in our country, the United States of America, you can buy real estate. You can buy our government debt. You can buy small, insignificant companies, bankrupted factories in our rust belts and, of course, Wall Street's labyrinthine derivatives. But keep your grubby hands off our Boeing, our General Electric, our Big Tech, our Big Pharma and, of course, our banks.

Which brings us back to Trump's ban on Huawei and Biden's declaration of economic war on Chinese tech companies. The underlying logic of these prohibitions was a straightforward extension of the same thinking, adapted to the circumstances of a post-2008 technofeudal world: with cloud capital dominating terrestrial capital, the maintenance of US hegemony requires more than preventing foreign capitalists from buying up US capitalist conglomerates, like Boeing and General Electric. In a world where cloud capital is borderless, global, capable of siphoning cloud rents from anywhere, the maintenance of US hegemony demands a direct confrontation with the only cloudalist class to have emerged as a threat to their own: China's.

TECHNOFEUDALISM WITH
CHINESE CHARACTERISTICS

True hegemons prevail not by force but by offering hard-to-resist Faustian bargains. One such was the Dark Deal, as a Chinese official once described it to me, that underlay US–China economic relations prior to the New Cold War. At its heart was an implicit offer by America's ruling class to China's ruling class – an offer directly equivalent to that of the Minotaur: we shall keep demand for your products high using our trade deficit. We shall also shift our industrial production to your factories. In return, you will voluntarily invest your profits in our finance, insurance and real estate sectors – known affectionately as FIRE.

It was a tried and tested recipe. Ever since the Nixon Shock turned the dollar into a glorified IOU, Americans had been buying more or less everything that Japan's factories could produce, paying in dollars that Japanese capitalists had no alternative but to invest in American FIRE. Following Nixon's famous visit to Beijing in 1972, signalling America's strategy to push a wedge between China and the USSR by establishing relations with the People's Republic, following decades of non-communication and even war, America's smart money envisioned China as a Japan-writ-large – a vision that Deng Xiaoping eventually indulged by opening up China to the West.

Japanese electronics, Chinese clothes and Korean television sets flooded Walmart while the profits netted by Japan's, China's and Korea's capitalists bought them US Treasuries, golf courses, skyscrapers and Wall Street's derivatives. From the 1970s onwards, globalised capitalism was founded on this fascinating recycling of, mainly, Asian manufacturing profits into American rents, which in turn sustained the American imports that provided Asian factories with sufficient demand.

Why call it a Dark Deal? Because in the small print of this pact between America's and East Asia's ruling classes was written misery for workers on both sides of the Pacific. American workers faced the exploitation and immiseration that resulted from underinvestment and its industrial heartlands being hollowed out by manufacturing in Asia and the underdeveloped Global South. Meanwhile, in China's fast-industrialising coastal cities, workers suffered the frenzied exploitation associated with overinvestment – it was as if parts of the Global North, fattened by overinvestment, were migrating into Chinese urban centres where local workers struggled to survive on Global South wages and social benefits. Different miseries, same global recycling process.[2]

That was the East-meets-West aspect of globalisation. Then there was, of course, the Global South – deficit countries in Asia, Africa and Latin America with weak economies constantly agonising over a shortage of dollars which they had to borrow from Wall Street to import medicines, energy and the raw materials necessary to produce their own exports, which they needed to earn the requisite dollars to repay Wall Street. Inevitably, every now and then, they ran out. At that point, the West would send in the bailiffs – the International Monetary Fund – which would lend the missing dollars on condition that the debtor government handed over the country's water, land, ports, airports, electricity and telephone networks, even its schools and hospitals, to the local and international oligarchs who would, once in control of these companies and assets, have no alternative but to channel their earnings into Wall Street. That was the neocolonial aspect of the same global recycling mechanism which secured US hegemony or, to use my favoured analogy, the Minotaur's reign.

Then came the crash of 2008. This had two main effects that, together, underpin today's New Cold War: it strengthened China's position in the global surplus recycling mechanism, and it turbocharged the build-up of cloud capital both in the United States and in China. To see how this caused the world to divide into two new blocks or, to be more precise, two super cloud fiefs, it helps to delve a little deeper into China's hyper-evolution in the aftermath of 2008.

As mentioned at the start of the chapter, when the bottom fell out of Wall Street, China stabilised global capitalism by cranking up domestic investment to more than half of China's national income. It worked, in that Chinese investment took up much of the global slack caused by Western commitment to austerity.[3] China's international stature rose, and its accumulating dollar surpluses allowed Beijing, in addition to feeding Wall Street, to become a major investor in Africa, Asia, even in Europe through its famed Belt and Road Initiative. (There was a price, of course, for this sparkling new role: to elevate investment to such heights, Chinese workers' share of the pie had to decline while Chinese rentiers, operating within China's own FIRE sector, got seriously richer. Specifically, investment rose on the back of loans using as collateral land that China's local authorities made available to developers. Thus, the post-2008 investment drive went hand in hand with the inflation of house and land prices across China.)

In the same way that cloud capital rose in the US on the back of central bank monies from the Fed, so the same occurred in China on the back of Beijing's investment drive. Silicon Valley's Big Tech soon discovered a mighty competitor: China's Big Tech. Westerners underestimate it. We think of Baidu as a Chinese Google knock-off. Of Alibaba as an Amazon imitator. They are much more than that. Indeed, to grasp the enormity and nature of China's Big Five cloudalist conglomerates – Alibaba, Tencent, Baidu, Ping An and JD.com – consider the following thought experiment.

Imagine if, in the West, we were to roll into one Google, Facebook, Twitter, Instagram and the version of Chinese-owned

TikTok still available to American users. Then include the applications that play the role that telephone companies used to: Skype, WhatsApp, Viber, Snapchat. Add to the mix ecommerce cloudalists like Amazon, Spotify, Netflix, Disney Plus, Airbnb, Uber and Orbitz. Lastly, throw in PayPal, Charles Schwab and every other Wall Street bank's own app. Now we are getting close. Except there is more . . .

Unlike Silicon Valley's Big Tech, China's is directly bound into government agencies that make all-pervading use of this cloudalist agglomeration: to regulate urban life, to promote financial services to unbanked citizens, to link its people with state health care facilities, to conduct surveillance of them using facial recognition, to guide autonomous vehicles through the streets – and, outside of its borders, to connect Africans and Asians participating in China's Belt and Road Initiative to its super cloud fief.

The key here is the seamless integration of communication, entertainment, ecommerce, foreign investments and much else with online financial services: the portal to cloud rent. As I write this sentence,[4] WeChat, the mobile messaging app belonging to Tencent, has transmitted 38 billion messages in a single day. Its users did not have to exit the WeChat app to make a payment. While streaming music, scrolling social media, messaging their families, they are able to use the same app to send money to anyone in China, as well as to any of the millions outside of China who have downloaded WeChat and opened a yuan account with any number of China's banks.

With this great leap into financial services, China's cloudalists acquired a 360-degree view of their users' social and financial life. If cloud capital is a produced means of behaviour modification, Chinese cloudalists have accumulated cloud capital beyond the wildest dreams of their Silicon Valley competitors who, by comparison, enjoy far less power per capita to accumulate cloud rent. American Big Tech has been doing what it can to catch up.[5] But it is becoming worryingly apparent to America's rulers that China's cloudalists have already acquired a power that US cloudalists are struggling to emulate: the power stemming from a successful merger of cloud capital and finance – or *cloud finance.*

This is technofeudalism-with-Chinese-characteristics. Since its emergence, it was only ever going to be a matter of time before the geopolitical struggle for hegemony between the US and China would divide the world into two, conflicting, super cloud fiefs.

TECHNOFEUDAL GEOPOLITICS: THE EMERGING 'THREAT' OF CHINA'S CLOUD FINANCE

People often ask when the dollar's reign will end – and whether it might even be replaced by the Chinese yuan as the world's reserve currency. But this question neglects a crucial fact: the dollar's reign has suited most countries, including China, just fine.

It has allowed countries with large trade surpluses, like China and Germany, to convert their excess production – their net exports – into property and rents in the United States: real estate, US government bonds, and any companies that Washington allowed them to own. Without the dollar's global role, Chinese, Japanese, Korean or German capitalists would never have been able to extract such colossal surplus value from their workers and then stash it away somewhere safe. Michael Pettis, an economist who has been working and teaching in Beijing for many years, put it brilliantly:

While the US dollar may create an exorbitant privilege for certain American constituencies, this status creates an exorbitant burden for the US economy overall, especially for the vast majority of Americans who must pay for the corresponding trade deficits either with higher unemployment, more household debt, or greater fiscal deficits.[6]

It is a fallacy, therefore, to think that the dollar's only defender is the US. Anyone who tried to end the dollar's reign would be equally resisted by German industrialists, Saudi sheikhs and European bankers. The last thing French and Dutch exporters would want to see is the elevation of the euro to the dollar's throne. The only governments who have ever truly desired the dollar's demise are those directly threatened by Washington's attempts at regime change.[7] As for the people, the one population who stand to gain the most from the abolition of the dollar's global role are working- and middle-class Americans.

The fact that the Dark Deal between the US and China relied entirely on the dollar's ongoing status meant that Washington had no reason to feel threatened by China's rise. If anything, American officials saw it as functional to US hegemony. As long as Chinese capitalists needed the dollar in order to extract surplus value from Chinese workers, even the Chinese Communist Party was considered an ally, albeit an unsafe one. However, the rise of cloud capital changed everything.

Compare a ton of aluminium shipped from Shanghai to Los Angeles with the targeted advertisements shown to Americans on the Chinese-owned social medium TikTok. Both yield dollars for a Chinese company. The difference is that the first bundle of dollars depends on a lump of metal produced in China physically migrating to America whereas the dollars earned by TikTok on US soil require no such physical migration. Let's see why that's the case and how in this difference lies the crux of cloud capital's geostrategic significance.

To produce an additional ton of Chinese aluminium for export to America, Chinese capitalists need an American customer to be willing to pay a sum of dollars that will cover the cost of the necessary energy and bauxite plus a profit. Given the limited sales of US goods to China, that American customer would not be forthcoming if the US did not have a trade deficit with China. Additionally, America would not be able to maintain this trade deficit without the dollar's global dominance. In short, for the said ton of aluminium to ship from China to some port on America's west coast, two things are necessary: the dollar's exorbitant privilege and the red ink all over America's trade balance with China.

TikTok, in contrast, has no need for additional dollars from American customers in order to produce new products for its US market. With its servers, algorithms and fibre optic cables already in place, produced and maintained by domestic Chinese monies, throwing one more viral video to its American customer base comes at zero additional (or marginal) cost. This is crucial: TikTok can, therefore, syphon cloud rents from the US market into China without relying on either America's trade deficit or the dollar's supremacy. Without a need for dollars to create its cloud capital, TikTok uses it to rake in its dollar-denominated cloud rents directly, seamlessly and at the speed of light. Power, thus, is shifting in a way that reduces the value of the Dark Deal to America's ruling class and state.

As Chinese cloud capital grows in relation to terrestrial capital,

China's rich and powerful find themselves less and less subject to the US authorities' power to regulate Chinese goods passing through their ports. So it was only a matter of time before Washington would attempt to restore the Dark Deal's waning benefits for US business and government. The Trump administration crossed the Rubicon with its almost total ban on technology companies Huawei and ZTE as well as a move effectively to Americanise TikTok by banning its availability for further download from US app stores.[8] Its motivation was only very thinly disguised with the usual invocation of 'national security' concerns. Scratch the surface and the real motivation emerges: a serious – and not illogical – concern for the threat to Wall Street and Silicon Valley posed by the rise of Chinese cloud finance, which tilts the comparative advantages of the Dark Deal away from America's and towards China's ruling class. Compared to the original Cold War, the New Cold War has little politics behind it. Just naked technofeudal class interests.

Still, the Dark Deal was not in immediate peril as long as the dollar remained the world's indispensable IOU allowing wealthy non-Americans access to US property and rents. After all, what else could the Chinese cloudalists do with all the dollars they reaped in cloud rent from the United States, Europe and across the world? Their dependence on access to US markets gave the Trump administration confidence that the Chinese would accept, without much pushback, restrictions on their cloud capital's power and reach.

In a way, Trump was trying to do to China what Reagan had done to Japan in 1985 under the so-called Plaza Accord, which forced it to devalue the yen massively and, thus, to limit the capacity of Japanese exporters to profit from American sales and, more broadly, from the US trade deficit. The Japanese government's acquiescence had been swift and silent, leading Japanese capitalism into a permanent slump from which it never truly recovered.[9] Would China react differently?

TECHNOFEUDAL GEOPOLITICS: HOW UKRAINE HELPED DIVIDE THE WORLD INTO TWO SUPER CLOUD FIEFS

As Trump was to find out, China was no Japan. Being outside of America's defence umbrella, its soil free of giant US army bases like the one in Okinawa, Beijing felt none of the need to defer to Washington that Tokyo revealed in 1985. Crucially, China also had its own Big Tech to bolster its position, especially its impressive cloud finance capabilities. Unsurprisingly, faced with Trump's aggressive move, China held its own within the Dark Deal and continued to recycle Chinese profits into American assets. Not only did Beijing not succumb to pressure to revalue the yuan (as Japan had ruinously agreed to do with the yen), its Big Tech conglomerates, like Huawei and ZTE, licked their significant wounds and set about creating their own operating system and platform software. Despite the great costs involved, China's rulers understood that their future relied on not handing over their cloud capital, and of course their cloud finance, to America. And so, well into Biden's first year in the White House, the Dark Deal between Chinese capitalists and American rentiers limped on.

Then Vladimir Putin invaded Ukraine and in response America did something that changed the whole equation. In retaliation to Putin's aggression, the Federal Reserve froze hundreds of billions of dollars that belonged to Russia's central bank but kept within the dollar-payment circuit that the US controls fully. It was the first time in capitalist history that a major central bank's money had been, effectively, confiscated by another central bank.[10] Even during the Crimean War of the 1850s, as Russian and British soldiers were slaughtering each other, the Bank of England continued to honour financial commitments to the Czar's central bank and Russian debtors kept paying their loan instalments to English bankers.

Try putting yourself in the shoes of Chinese capitalists, or China's finance minister, whose savings are in the form of dollar assets worth trillions: US Treasury Bills (i.e. loans to the American government), real estate in California, shares and derivatives in the New York money markets. Everyone knew that the US government could confiscate the lot at any time, but no one believed Washington would ever dare to, because such a move would deter anyone from ever stashing their wealth within the US-controlled dollar payments system again. Then the inconceivable happened: four days after Putin's troops invaded Ukraine, Washington seized more than $300 billion belonging to Russia's central bank and evicted anyone transacting through Russia's central bank from all international payment systems.[11] Would you still be comfortable with trillions of dollars' worth of your assets in US hands? But what could you do?

If you are Russia, or Germany for that matter, there is nothing much you can do if Washington decides to grab your stash and evict you from all international payment systems. How about selling your exports in your own currency, emulating Putin who demanded to be paid for Russia's oil and gas in roubles? It may sound like a solution, except it is not. Who will want to sell their computers or cars to Russians in roubles, other than the very few foreign capitalists who have an eye on some Russian asset (e.g. a dacha, a factory or a local bank)? Even German exporters, who earn massive amounts of euros from selling in Spain or France or Italy, have a problem finding euro-denominated assets that they want to own.

What if you are China? Again, even though your economy's size and depth mean that many foreign capitalists will crave some of your assets enough to accept yuan, you still have a problem: if you are a Chinese capitalist cut off from the dollar, you will not be able to benefit from America's trade deficit; to use it as a vacuum cleaner that sucks into the American markets your aluminium, cement, electric vehicles and snazzy clothes. However, recall that this is a problem for Chinese capitalists but not so much for Chinese cloudalists (like TikTok) who had already built cloud finance up into an alternative global payment system. With it in hand, what is a serious problem for Chinese capitalists – i.e. the possible end of the dollar's reign – poses no threat to Chinese cloudalists.

China's cloudalists were not the only people in the country eroding the Dark Deal. On 14 August 2020, a revolution took place inside the walls of the People's Bank of China. Following six years of painstaking research, Beijing's central bank rolled out a digital yuan – in experimental form but with serious intent. For the first time, anywhere, a state had issued a fully digital currency. 'So what?' I hear you say. 'We all use digital money all the time.' Well, yes, but this was something altogether different.

When you pay for your coffee or train ticket using a smartphone app or a microchip-equipped debit card, these conventional digital payments go through the infrastructure of private banks. What China had created was digital money issued directly by a central bank, cutting out these middlemen, the private bankers. To see the global significance of this, consider Jürgen, a Hamburg-based factory owner using raw materials supplied by Xiu's factory in Guangzhou to manufacture ship propellers, which Jürgen then sells to a shipyard owned by Ai near Shanghai.

To wire payment for his raw materials to Xiu, Jürgen visits his German bank's website, fills out the necessary digital form and presses Enter. The specified number of euros leaves his bank for the Bundesbank, Germany's central bank, before passing through to the European Central Bank in Frankfurt. The European Central Bank then converts Jürgen's euros to US dollars which it subsequently channels to the People's Bank of China via a US-controlled international circuit. Once at the People's Bank of China, its functionaries convert the money into yuan and wire it to Xiu's bank. Finally, Xiu's bank credits his account.

Exactly the same clunky process is activated, in reverse, when Ai pays Jürgen for the propellers his shipyard buys from him. Is there a reason why such an unwieldy process has survived the wonders of the digital age? Of course there is: its clunkiness and mind-boggling inefficiency is a source of rent as each private banker and go-between involved in such transfers takes a small cut. Taken together, these small cuts amount to a fortune.

Compare this with what would happen if Jürgen, Xiu and Ai were to obtain the new digital wallets now on offer by the People's Bank of China: Jürgen would pick up his smartphone, open the digital yuan app, send a sum of digital yuan to Xiu who would receive it instantaneously and at zero cost. End of story! Think of all the middlemen the digital yuan cuts out: Jürgen's German bank, the Bundesbank, the European Central Bank and, crucially, the international money transfer conduit which is fully under the thumb of US authorities. It is nothing less than Washington's, and the private bankers', worst nightmare.[12]

Before 2022, Chinese cloud finance and the digital yuan resembled a brand-new road with little traffic. Why would the ultra-wealthy of the world direct their money through a yuan-paved road, policed by the People's Bank of China, when they could use the existing, albeit bumpy, dollar-built superhighway? A good reason appeared soon after the first explosions over Kyiv, Kharkiv and Mariupol: the aforementioned seizure by America of hundreds of billions of dollars belonging to Russia's central bank.

Blocked from the dollar superhighway, Russian money began to use the under-utilised, glistening Chinese alternative. And it was not just Russian money that chose this new route. Many wealthy non-Russians, too, felt reluctant to continue letting their money race down the dollar freeway. They began to question the wisdom of relying entirely on the kindness of Washington's dollar-traffic rangers, who could pull them over any time. Little by little, they began diversifying, like trucking companies redirecting some of their trucks from an older highway through a new one. In this way, Chinese cloud finance began little by little to establish itself as a viable alternative to the dollar-based international payments system.

Smart people in and around the Biden administration saw the writing on the wall. For the first time since 1971, the Dark Deal looked shaky. The dollar's supremacy could no longer be taken for granted either by the world's wealthy or by American policy-makers. Many in Washington felt that, if they failed to clip the wings of China's Big Tech quickly, before its cloud finance and digital state money achieved critical mass, the exorbitant power of American rentier capitalists was in jeopardy.

And so it was that on 7 October 2022, under the guise of

national security concerns over China's development of sophisticated weaponry, President Biden declared a total export ban on anything that might help China develop top-notch microchips. Since microchips are the building blocks of any advanced economy, and the ban on selling chips to China extended to non-American companies that wanted to do business with American ones, Biden's ban amounted to total economic war.

The intent was crystal clear: a shock-and-awe assault aimed at Chinese cloud finance, hoping to wound it critically before it could grow into a fully-fledged beast able to withstand, even to defeat, the combined forces of Silicon Valley and Wall Street. Will it work? Biden's microchip ban will, in the short term, slow down China's technological progress and impinge on the accumulation of Chinese cloud capital. However, it also has two unintended consequences, both working in the opposite direction to bolster Chinese cloud capital in the long term.

The first unintended consequence of Biden's ban was to motivate Chinese officials fully to bank on China's cloud finance – something they had previously been reluctant to do. Why were they reluctant? Because they were invested in China's export-led growth, which relied on the profits that Chinese capitalists drew from the American trade deficit as part of the Dark Deal. Anything that threatened those profits, including domestic cloud rent, was looked at askance. Until, of course, Biden unceremoniously confronted Beijing with a stark choice: ditch the Dark Deal or stay in the technological Dark Ages. It was a no-brainer: they would ditch the Dark Deal, if they had to, and shift their allegiance from China's capitalists, who depend on the Dark Deal, to China's cloudalists, who can rake in cloud rents without it.

The second unintended consequence of Biden's ban was to inspire capitalists and rentiers from across the world, including Western Europe, to flock to China's cloud finance. Consider again Jürgen, our friend from Hamburg whose business is inextricably linked with the Chinese markets. He may be a loyal citizen of the Federal Republic, proud of Berlin's alliance with Washington, and a committed free-market liberal with no sympathy for the Chinese Communist Party or the People's Bank of China. Nonetheless, every time he reads in the newspapers about Washington's sanctions and overall hardening stance towards China, he is motivated to acquire a digital yuan account to overcome future obstacles in making and receiving the payments that are crucial to his propeller export business.

It is not the first time that war has sped up, but also skewed, historic transformations. The Second World War paved the way to the dollar taking over from the British pound the dominant role in international payments (Arab oil, for example, was swiftly re-denominated from pounds to dollars). The war in Ukraine prompted the United States to make moves which diverted considerable money flows from the dollar-based payments system to a yuan-based system run by Chinese cloud capital. As we speak, Chinese cloud rents accumulate, further overshadow Chinese capitalist profits, accelerate China's transition to technofeudalism and, crucially, weaken the Dark Deal between the world's two superpowers.

The repercussions of all this for war and peace, international tensions and cooperation, cannot be underestimated. Focusing out of our present circumstances for a moment, so as to grasp the larger picture, it is worth recalling how, soon after it was born, and despite its youth and vibrancy, capitalism demonstrated an inherent inability to generate domestic markets sizeable enough to absorb all of the goods that local capitalist industries were producing.[13] The result was aggressive expansion overseas – a new type of imperialism motivated not so much by an urge to plunder faraway lands but to secure and corner faraway markets for the commodities produced domestically. As several capitalist nations competed for the same turf, in Africa, Asia and the Americas, these neocolonialist conflicts led to the repulsive blood-letting of the late nineteenth-century in Europe and ultimately, in the first half of the twentieth, to two world wars. Capitalism's rise, in short, inspired industrial-scale carnage at a planetary scale.

What should we expect, today, during technofeudalism's early phases? We already have hints of what is to come. Under the spell of the war in Ukraine and the Great Inflation, which are enhancing poverty, climate change and an atmosphere of fear, the world is dividing into two, mutually antagonistic, super cloud fiefs – one American, the other Chinese. Little that is good and worthy will come of this bifurcation.

THE SPECTRE OF TECHNOFEUDALISM OVER EUROPE, THE GLOBAL SOUTH, THE PLANET

Remember how, in 1971, President Nixon told his European counterparts 'Our dollar is now your problem'? History could not have backed him more resoundingly.

After 1971, American capitalism generated successive crises: the oil crises of 1973 and 1979, the global debt crisis after Fed chairman Paul Volcker pushed US interest rates above 20 per cent in 1981, the 1991 crisis following the bursting of several bubbles in

US financial networks, the 2001 dot.com debacle and, last but not least, the crash of 2008.[14] It was in the nature of the beast – the Minotaur, that is – which was diverting to America more than 70 per cent of European and Asian capitalists' profits. Every such crisis left Europe weaker, more divided, more reactionary.

It was not for lack of trying. In reaction to each shockwave crossing the Atlantic, European leaders did their utmost to shield Europe from the next one. Their approach was to expand and consolidate Europe's institutions and resources, leading ultimately to the establishment of a single shared currency.[15] Why did these various projects – all aimed at liberating Europe from its vulnerability to America's rentier economy – end up failing? The answer is not particularly complicated: the reason is the European Union's total dependence on its own Dark Deal with America. It is the same reason why the smartest of the most powerful of Europeans – German, Dutch and French exporters – have no interest in seeing the euro knock the dollar off its reserve currency throne. It is why Europe's monetary union remains incomplete-by-design.[16] Simply, while they may wish to protect themselves from its shifts and shocks, they have no actual desire to be free of their pact with the US, which allows European capitalists to profit from the demand generated by America's trade deficit and to turn these profits into US assets.

Could anything worse afflict a Europe dependent on the Dark Deal than the Dark Deal's demise? Yes, there is something even worse: the gradual, worldwide shift of money and power from the capitalist to the cloudalist sphere. If my hypothesis is right, that cloud capital is overpowering terrestrial capital, sucking cloud rent increasingly out of the global value chain, then Europe is in deep trouble. Because Europe is not China. It lacks a single Big

Tech company that can compete with those of Silicon Valley and its financial systems are wholly reliant on Wall Street. Europe's lack of cloud capital means that the New Cold War, along with the energy shock[17] that the war in Ukraine inflicted upon its manufacturers, has already rendered Europe geostrategically irrelevant.[18]

At least Europe is still rich and, in theory, able to look after its weaker citizens. The same cannot be said for Sri Lanka, Lebanon, Pakistan, India, most of Asia and the whole of Africa and Latin America. The rising price of food and fuel caused by the Great Inflation has pushed the Global South into a debt crisis as gruesome as that of the 1970s and 80s. Having been encouraged for decades to borrow dollars to import raw materials in order to produce goods for export (and also to facilitate the conversion of their oligarchs' domestic profits into US assets), the governments of the Global South are now being bankrupted by the vastly increased cost of servicing their dollar debts.[19]

The Global South faces an appalling choice. Default on their dollar debts, which means they won't be able to buy the energy, food and raw materials they need to feed their people, run their factories and plough their fields. Or get another dollar loan from, say, the International Monetary Fund with which they can pretend to repay their existing dollar loans under two inhuman conditions: first, by handing over control of their essential sectors, such as water, electricity, to oligarchs masquerading as 'investors'; second, by pushing domestic fuel and food prices up so high that their people will go hungry. Either way, these so-called developing countries are being forced to surrender to the dynamic of underdevelopment.

But this is not the only dreadful choice that Global South governments must make. With the world dividing into two super cloud fiefs, one dollar-based and another yuan-based, they are being forced to choose which feudal lord to submit to. Gone are the days when their oligarchs could borrow from China, or collect profits from selling grain in Shanghai, and use the money to buy properties in California or derivatives in Wall Street. Their new debt crisis is forcing the Global South's ruling classes to pick a side. To which cloud fief will they commit future earnings from the selling of their rare earths and other raw materials? Will they still rely on Wall Street? Or will they channel their profits and rents through China's cloud finance? Either way, the Global South is being divided, escalating the New Cold War further.

This is much more than neocolonial business-as-usual. Chinese and American capital have been at loggerheads for years. Except that, now, it is no longer a competition based on the prices of commodities or the comparative desirability of different vendor financing offers.[20] This is a titanic battle over as yet virgin technofeudal territory on which two systems of cloud-rent extraction wish to establish themselves as overlords. It will take a miracle for this recently evolved species of imperialism not to result in more wars and more failed states.

Speaking of miracles: given capitalism's inherent tendency to deplete the commons, it was always going to take an enormous one for our species to escape climate catastrophe. Technofeudalism's advance makes this miracle even more improbable. The Age of Cloud Capital erects two obstacles in the path of climate change amelioration. One obstacle operates at the level of politics and is obvious. A grand deal between the United States, the European Union, China (not to mention Brazil, Russia, India and South Africa) is a prerequisite for limiting climate warming to levels consistent with our species' survival. In the shadow of this New Cold War, the best we can now hope for are two separate green transitions, one in each super cloud fief – a bifurcation of the global green agenda which, I fear, will play into the hands of fossil fuel conglomerates who will find ways to play one off against the other, allowing them to keep drilling.

The less obvious obstacle technofeudalism throws in the path of any green transition are the so-called electricity 'markets'. I say 'so-called' because they are not, and can never be, actual markets. Think about it: only one electricity cable enters your home or business. It is *the* definition of a natural monopoly. Naturally, if governments were to advocate that such a monopoly be sold to a privateer, who would then have monopoly power over everyone, people would rise up. So, following Margaret Thatcher's lead, governments intent on privatisation promised magically to create competitive electricity markets around the single grid and the lone cable coming out of your wall: a handful of energy providers, the promise went, would compete in some auction house daily to provide you with the cheapest possible electricity. These pretend auction markets, in which a handful of firms collude to fleece consumers and lesser capitalists, are a rentier capitalist's delight. (Exhibit A: their immense profits during the energy crisis following the pandemic and Putin's invasion of Ukraine.) But that's not all. The rentiers that now own the privatised power generation stations gamble their future revenues in a global casino, borrowing against future revenues in order to hedge against future losses.[21] In plainer terms, our energy systems have been surrendered to oligarchs with a vested interest to entangle energy in the web of financialisation. As this web becomes increasingly fused into cloud finance, we forfeit what is left of our capacity as a demos (a community, a society, a species) to choose the energy practices that might avert climate disaster.

It is why I am anxious to convey, especially to the young, the disturbing news that the greater the power of the cloudalist class, and the faster the march of technofeudalism, the less we, the demos, can do to avert climate catastrophe. The young, who are at the forefront of 'striking for the future', must recognise that preventing our planet's overheating goes hand in hand with resisting technofeudalism.

BACK TO YOUR QUESTION: WHO WINS AND WHO LOSES?

As a young man, you had hoped organised labour would vanquish capitalism at a planetary scale. As an older man, you witnessed exactly the opposite: capitalism's unhindered globalisation.

After 1991, two things globalised: financial capital, which could jump continents at the push of a button, and production lines, or chains, which made it possible for American iPhones, engineered by Indian developers in San Francisco, and built by a Taiwanese company in Zhengzhou, to be sold in Philadelphia. Around two and a half billion labourers, mainly from China, India and the formerly communist countries, joined this international value chain, lifting many of them out of poverty. But the headline-generating rises in measurable incomes were often bought at the price of sheer grief.[22] Chinese migrant labourers, working sixteen-hour shifts in abominable sweatshops to produce iPhones, saw their incomes quadruple but became almost as suicidal as Indian farmers whose livelihoods were destroyed when their crops became dependent on Bayer-Monsanto's genetically engineered seeds.[23] Even in America, the greatest beneficiary of globalisation, millions succumbed to deaths of despair.[24] These contradictions were the direct consequence of the Dark Deal. By mobilising America's trade deficit to turn China into a capitalist powerhouse, enriching capitalists and rentiers worldwide, underinvestment-induced misery migrated to the Global North while overinvestment-induced wealth migrated to the Global South.

Two years after the collapse of the Soviet Union, as globalisation was gathering pace, you asked the question that motivated this book, betraying your stubborn hope that capitalism might not last forever. Some thirty years later, as I have argued, your wish has been granted – the internet has indeed proved capitalism's undoing – though not in the way you might have expected. If I am right, the question now becomes: who are the winners and who the losers from this transformation of capitalist globalisation into a worldwide technofeudalism?

Throughout the capitalist era, nothing good has happened when rentiers have succeeded in creaming off increasing portions of capitalists' profits. Profit's conversion into rent has always hindered capitalism's dynamic, created bubbles that burst, and plunged weaker people and states into toxic debt. The rise of technofeudalism has taken this crisis-producing process to new heights – to a state of *poly-crisis*, to borrow the neologism economic historian Adam Tooze concocted out of two Greek words.

Think of those billions of cloud serfs who are, at this very moment, putting so much time and energy into building up someone else's cloud capital. Their unpaid labour produces extractive power and cloud rent for very few cloudalists, money that will never re-enter the wider circulation of income, while earning them no income themselves. Allow me to describe this as the *shrinking of the global value base*. Add to this the wage squeeze that cloud capital also imposes on waged workers, as it increasingly turns them into cloud proles. The result is a substantial reduction in the incomes that the masses can mobilise to buy commodities. This secular drop in effective, or aggregate, demand means more and deeper economic crises. To use an ecological metaphor, capitalists and workers are experiencing something akin to the shrinking of their habitat, pushing endangered species into greater peril, while suffering more frequent extreme weather events.

That was the state of play before the war in Ukraine. Since Washington's decision to wage war on Chinese Big Tech, and its cloud finance, in a manner that puts paid to the Dark Deal and divides the world into a dollar-based cloud fief and a yuan-based cloud fief, Chinese and American workers are certain to suffer but American rentiers and Chinese capitalists have much to lose as well. If Chinese surplus value no longer migrates at the same rate to the United States, America's rentiers will be in trouble. Their misfortune will then ricochet back to hurt Chinese capitalists who are so very dependent on America's net imports which are, in turn, maintained by dollar-denominated rents. As for American cloudalists, they can't know what to expect: while they gain relative power over capitalists, and the rest of American society, the effect of the Dark Deal's demise on their bottom line is the great unknowable.

Companies like Apple and Tesla, which straddle terrestrial capital and cloud capital, will be surely hurt. Unlike, say, Google, Apple has invested billions in physical capital in China where it manufactures the iPhone and iPad. This is not an investment that it can repatriate easily into the United States. Apple is not manufacturing in China because of cheap, skilled labour but because, since 2007, it has built an entire ecosystem of manufacturing processes which blend human, terrestrial and cloud capital in ways that cannot be emulated on American soil. For companies that are more cloud-capital-intensive, like Amazon and Google, it will all depend on how the shrinking global value base, and the disruption of the flow of Chinese profits and rents into the dollar super cloud fief, will affect their sales.

One thing we know for certain. Technological advancement will help cloud capital go from strength to strength. Once combined with large-scale, versatile, advanced 3D printing and AI-driven industrial robotics, cloud capital will undermine the whole point of traditional capitalist conglomerates, whose competitive advantage is based on economies of scale. Meanwhile, the de-globalisation of physical capital, triggered by Washington's decision to wage economic war against China, will accelerate. And so will the antagonisms between the two super cloud fiefs over the plundering of raw materials – rare earths, lithium and, of course, our data – from around the world.

The peak of globalisation, between 2005 and 2020, saw large fault lines develop within the world's major trading blocks. One such fault line increasingly divided the European Union's deficit countries in its south from its surplus countries in the north. Another fault line split America's coastal economies from the rust belts in its middle. China's booming coastal regions were divided from the interior of the mainland by an economic Berlin Wall. Are these fault lines subsiding now that globalisation is on the wane? Quite the opposite. Previous fault lines remain while new ones emerge, between the East and West of Europe, for example, and between Americans connected to cloudalist power and the rest. And as a consequence of the broader technofeudal bifurcation, the world is dividing into continental superstates, not unlike those clashing permanently in George Orwell's *Nineteen Eighty-Four*.[25]

Peace is the obvious victim of this process but not the only one: given the magnitude and the nature of the power wielded by the very small band of cloudalists on both sides of the Pacific, anything resembling actual democracy seems increasingly far-fetched. Indeed, the great irony, from a Western perspective, is that the only political force that can do anything to keep the cloudalists in check and thus the hope of democracy alive is the Chinese Communist Party. It was President Xi who placed strict limits on Chinese cloudalists, like Jack Ma, in an explicit bid to keep China's cloud finance within what the party considers to be acceptable bounds – its own.[26]

The great challenge for Xi, however, is that the party's authority relies on economic growth, which has for so long been generated by the enrichment of its capitalists via the Dark Deal. In theory, and in a very roundabout way, Xi has declared a class war in the name of Chinese workers, not only on the cloudalists but on Chinese capitalists, too. In August 2021, he announced curbs on 'excessive incomes' and, crucially, a new policy to shrink aggregate investment from 50 per cent of Chinese national income to 30 per cent – something that can only happen if Chinese capitalist profits from net exports to the United States are reduced massively while domestic wages rise. But is this a real campaign or merely a propaganda drive, a form of populism with Chinese characteristics? Is China's political class capable and willing to commit to a sustained clash with both cloudalists and capitalists? It is impossible to say. Indeed, even if Xi means what he says and succeeds in boosting working-class incomes, we have no way of knowing whether any rise in the majority's incomes will reinvigorate the power of China's demos. Nonetheless, it remains endlessly intriguing that the only glimmer of hope for any demos around the world shines in the midst of a society under totalitarianism.

Liberals once feared people like you and me – leftists craving a socialist transformation. When the left was defeated, liberals were relieved but continued to rail against the power of the state: in their eyes, powerful states, even bourgeois liberal ones, are what pave the road to serfdom. Is it not delectably shocking how, in the end, a global superhighway to serfdom has been constructed not because Western states were too powerful but because they were too weak? Too weak, that is, to prevent the cloud capital they birthed from taking over, disestablishing capitalism and facilitating technofeudalism.

7

ESCAPE FROM TECHNOFEUDALISM

It felt like hours before the artist finally appeared. Awaiting him onstage was a shiny, oversized, robotic-looking metal exoskeleton suspended by a long cable from the high ceiling of the art space – a converted former power station just outside of Sydney. I was among the audience in the dimly lit turbine room, increasingly captivated by the wafting soundtrack and mesmerised by the elegantly glistening machine. The calendar read 19 August 2000 – a good four years before Mark Zuckerberg launched Facebook, six years before the first tweet, and only a year since the first search on Google. The internet was still in its Age of Innocence, and the dream of it as an open digital forum for, and governed by, sovereign participants was still alive.

At last Stelarc, the artist, emerged.[1] Once inside the exoskeleton, Stelarc would continue to be free to move his legs as he wished, but his arms would be controlled remotely by an anonymous crowd watching and participating via the internet. Stelarc climbed into the machine, which he had named Movatar, and the system began to boot up. Soon enough, it connected to the internet where the invisible strangers awaited. Unlike a dancer who

captivates you with the effortlessness of their movement, Movatar
was compelling for its awkwardness. Its upper body moved jerk-
ily, as if in opposition to the legs beneath. Its clumsy movements
were strangely moving, brimming with significance – but signify-
ing what exactly? I sensed a window opening onto the relationship
between humans and their technologies, and the same contradictions that had inspired Hesiod.

Afterwards, I remember thinking about your question: was the
internet capitalism's friend or foe? Was Movatar part of the
answer? And what did it mean for the human condition? Back
then, I hadn't a clue. But today, I see it clearly: Stelarc's Movatar
prophesied what was to happen to us when traditional capital
evolved into cloud capital, from a 'produced means of production'
into a produced means of *behaviour modification*. Stelarc was merely
experimenting with the idea of the post-human, but his Movatar
captured the essence of humanity's future reality. As I see it now,
Movatar was a creature at the mercy of hyper-connected,
algorithmically driven, cloud-based capital. Another name for it
would be *Homo technofeudalis*.

THE DEATH OF THE LIBERAL INDIVIDUAL

To this day, I envy the way you lived, Dad. You were the epitome
of the liberal individual. Sure, to make a living, you had reluctantly to lease yourself to your boss at the steel plant in Eleusis.
But during your lunch break you wandered blissfully in the open-
air backyard of the Eleusis Archaeological Museum, where you
luxuriated in the discovery of ancient steles full of clues that
antiquity's technologists were more advanced than previously
thought. And following your return home, at just after five every

afternoon, and a late siesta, you emerged ready to share in our family life and, on some nights, when we weren't messing about with various metals by our fireplace, to write your books and papers. Your life at the factory was, in short, neatly ring-fenced from your personal life.

It reflected a time when we thought that, if nothing else, capitalism had granted us sovereignty over our selves, albeit within certain limited parameters. However hard one had to work, you could at least fence off a portion of your life, however small, and within that fence remain autonomous, self-determining, free. Leftists, like us, knew that only the rich were truly free to choose, that the poor were mostly free to lose, and that the worst slavery was that of those who had learned to love their chains.[2] Still, even we, capitalism's harshest critics, appreciated the limited self-ownership it granted us.

For young people in today's world, even this small mercy has been taken away. Curating an identity online is not optional, and so their personal lives have become some of the most important work they do. From the moment they take their first steps online, they suffer like Movatar from two perplexingly contradictory demands: they are taught implicitly to see themselves as a brand, yet one that will be judged according to its perceived authenticity. (And that includes potential employers: 'No one will offer me a job,' a graduate told me once, 'until I have discovered my true self.') And so before posting any image, uploading any video, reviewing any movie, sharing any photograph or message, they must be mindful of who their choice will please or alienate. They must somehow work out which of their potential 'true selves' will be found most attractive, continually testing their own opinions against their notion of what the average opinion among online opinion makers might be.[3] Every experience can be captured and shared, and so they are continually consumed by the question of whether to do so. And even if no opportunity actually exists for sharing the experience, that opportunity can readily be imagined, and will be. Every choice, witnessed or otherwise, becomes an act in the curation of an identity.

One need not be a radical critic of our society to see that the right to a bit of time each day when one is not for sale has all but vanished. The irony is that the liberal individual was snuffed out neither by fascist Brownshirts nor by Stalinist guards. It was killed off when a new form of capital began to instruct youngsters to do that most liberal of things: be yourself! (And be successful at it!) Of all the behavioural modifications that cloud capital has engineered and monetised, this one is surely its overarching and crowning achievement.

Possessive individualism has always been detrimental to mental health. Technofeudalism made things infinitely worse when it demolished the fence that used to provide the liberal individual with a refuge from the market. Cloud capital has shattered the individual into fragments of data, an identity comprised of choices as expressed by clicks, which its algorithms are able to manipulate. It has produced individuals who are not so much possessive as *possessed*, or rather persons incapable of being self-possessed. It has diminished our capacity to focus by co-opting our attention. We have not become weak-willed. No, our focus has been stolen.[4] And because technofeudalism's algorithms are known to reinforce patriarchy, stereotypes and pre-existing oppressions, those who are most vulnerable – girls, the mentally ill, the marginalised and, yes, the poor – suffer the outcome most.

If fascism taught us anything, it is our susceptibility to demonising stereotypes and the ugly attraction of emotions like righteousness, fear, envy and loathing that they arouse in us. In our technofeudal world, the internet brings the feared and loathed 'other' closer, right in your face. And because online violence seems bloodless and anodyne, we are more likely to respond to this 'other' online with taunting, inhuman language and bile. Bigotry is technofeudalism's emotional compensation for the frustrations and anxieties we experience in relation to identity and focus. Comment moderators and hate-speech regulation can't stop this because it is intrinsic to cloud capital, whose algorithms optimise for cloud rents, which flow more copiously from hatred and discontent.

You once told me that finding something timelessly beautiful to focus on, as you did by choosing to lose yourself among the relics of ancient Greece, is our only defence from the demons circling our soul. I have tried to practise this over the years in my own way. But in the face of technofeudalism, acting alone, isolated, as liberal individuals will not get us very far. Cutting ourselves off from the internet, switching off our phones, using cash instead of plastic may help for a while but they are no solution. Unless we band together, we shall never civilise or socialise cloud capital, and so we shall never reclaim our own minds from its grip.

And herein lies the greatest contradiction: to rescue that foundational liberal idea – of liberty as self-ownership – will therefore require a comprehensive reconfiguration of property rights over the increasingly cloud-based instruments of production, distribution, collaboration and communication. To resuscitate the liberal individual, we need to do something that liberals detest: plan a new revolution.

THE IMPOSSIBILITY OF
SOCIAL DEMOCRACY

Why can't technofeudalism be tamed by politics in the same way capitalism was restrained, at least for a while, by social democratic governments?

Social democrats were able to make a difference during a time when power was vested in old-fashioned industrial capital. They acted as referees between organised labour and the captains of manufacturing industry, metaphorically (and occasionally literally) sitting them around a table, forcing them to compromise. The result was, on the one hand, improved wages and conditions for the workers and, on the other hand, the diversion of a chunk of industry's profits to pensions, hospitals, schools, unemployment insurance and the arts. But as power shifted from industry to finance after the death of Bretton Woods in 1971, European social democrats and American Democrats alike were lured into a Faustian bargain with the bankers of Wall Street, the City of London, Frankfurt and Paris. The bargain was crude and simple: social democrats in government freed bankers from the shackles of regulation: 'Go crazy! Regulate yourselves,' they told them. In return, financiers agreed to hand over the crumbs from their substantial table, in the form of a small portion of their gargantuan gains from rabid financialisation, to fund the welfare state.[5]

In Homeric terms, the social democrats had become the era's lotus eaters. As they gorged themselves on financialisation, they became intellectually soft and morally complicit in its practices. Its honeyed juice lulled them into the belief that what had once been risky was now riskless, that this magic goose would always lay golden eggs, and if those eggs could be used to finance the welfare state, then whatever else the goose did could be justified. And so, when in 2008 financial capital came crashing down, they lacked both the mental tools and the moral values to tell the bankers: 'Enough! We may save the banks but not you.' Hence, the lethal combination of socialism-for-bankers and austerity-for-almost-everyone-else, described in Chapter 4, that stagnated our economies while funding the rise of the cloudalists.

In the old days, social democrats had a degree of power over the industrialists because they had the backing of the trades unions and could threaten painful regulation. Today, cloudalists do not fear powerful unions because cloud proles are too weak to form them and cloud serfs do not even consider themselves producers. As for regulation, that has worked by putting a lid on prices or by breaking up cartels. In the Age of Cloud Capital, cloudalists feel safe in the thought that neither makes any sense. Price regulation is irrelevant when the services that consumers need to be protected from are either free or the cheapest on the market already.[6] As for breaking them up, as President Theodore Roosevelt did to Rockefeller when he broke up Standard Oil and other cartels, that was only possible in the old days of terrestrial capital. Standard Oil comprised petrol stations, refineries and fuel transport systems strewn all over North America. Breaking it up into regional oil companies, and encouraging these to compete with one another, was politically hard but technically dead easy. But how does one break up Amazon, Facebook, PayPal or, indeed, Tesla today?

Cloudalists know they can destroy any third-party developer (i.e. vassal capitalist), eking out a living on their cloud fief, who dares to contact one of their users (i.e. cloud serfs) without first paying a cloud rent.[7] They know they can treat their users however they like – when did anyone last decline the terms and conditions of a software update? – because of the hostages they are holding: our contacts, friends, chat histories, photos, music, videos, all of which we lose if we switch to a competing cloud fief. And they know that there is little that government can do to stop them. Unlike national phone companies, which our national governments forced to charge the same rates when calling customers of competing companies, how can they force Twitter to share the backlog of all your tweets, photos and videos with, say, Mastodon?[8]

Even worse, they see that the ideological tide favours them. When you were still a young man, the political left maintained a belief in objective truth and a commitment to constructing new institutions in the service of redistributing incomes, wealth and power for the higher purpose of improving the human condition. Marxists, like yourself, went even further, arguing for revolution because they were convinced by the righteousness of their ethical code, the scientific foundation of their social theory, not to mention the belief that they were working towards a desirable end of history – a luxurious liberal communism in which all systemic exploitation and conflict has vanished. Even though the social democrats increasingly distanced themselves from, and denigrated, the Marxist perspective, much of what they accomplished drew strength from those Marxist convictions. The social democratic agenda was presented as a way to achieve the same things the Marxists advocated – such as universal health care and free education – but without ditching markets, capitalism and, importantly, without the drabness of Soviet communism, the secret police, the gulag.

From today's vantage point, it is fascinating to recall that to counter the left's conviction it was the political right back then which embraced a form of relativism, cautioning against the moral certainties of social democrats, anti-Vietnam War demonstrators, civil rights campaigners, feminists, and arguing that things are more complicated, less black and white, than the unwashed hippies and their older communistic fellow travellers assumed. But once the red flag was lowered over the Kremlin in 1991, signalling the defeat of the global left, the tables turned entirely. Suddenly, it was the right that embraced unalloyed truths and non-negotiable virtues: the same reactionaries who had questioned that all peoples had a universal right to statehood or democracy became converts to their imposition (albeit selectively) at gunpoint.[9] The right presented its own new take on the 'end of history': not socialism, ushering in shared property and radical equality, but liberal democracy, free markets and possessive individualism. Meanwhile, the left obliged the right by abandoning all certainty and embracing the relativism that the right had just shed: the principle that we all have the right to be free from the extractive power of others transmuted into the principle that no one perspective is worth more than any other.

Underlying this transformation of the left was, of course, the West's de-industrialisation, which fragmented the labouring classes, a process that technofeudalism continues to this day. When the working class was still relatively homogenous, a relatively solid class consciousness allowed it to put at least a degree of pressure on social democratic governments. Today, class struggle has been replaced by so-called 'identity politics'. Tragically, the drive to protect racial, sexual, ethnic and religious minorities and for reparative justice suits just fine people in power who like to appear socially liberal. They enthusiastically embed those causes in their language as long as they only pay lip service to them and do little of substance to protect minorities from the systemic causes of their oppression. Moreover, this discursive espousal of identity politics allows people in authority to do nothing about the economic and political extractive power that is increasingly intertwined with cloud capital. As for the alt-right, nothing could have pleased them more. They recognise in identity politics a golden opportunity to capitalise on the in-group, defensive, tribal and racist feelings it arouses in white voters.

On this new political stage, social democracy is impossible. We no longer have capital on the one side and labour on the other, allowing a social democratic government to play referee and force the two sides into a compromise. Instead we have a centre and an alt-right both in thrall to a new ruling class, the cloudalists, whose rise to power they have enabled, while the left is preoccupied with a civil war on the definition of 'woman', on the hierarchy of oppressions and all the rest. Meanwhile, no one speaks for the cloud proles, the cloud serfs, the vassal capitalists, what is left of the traditional proletariat-precariat, the victims of climate change, the masses that technofeudalism stifles and imprisons in its cloud fiefs.

To revive the original idea of social democracy, and indeed of the liberal individual, two things are essential. First, we must discard the myth that the old left–right distinction is obsolete. As long as we live in an Empire of Capital that rules over, and ruthlessly exploits, humans and the planet, there can be no democratic politics that is not rooted in a leftist agenda of overthrowing it. Second, we must fundamentally reconfigure what that means and how it can be achieved in the world of technofeudalism, where that empire is built on cloud capital, with all of the new, fiendishly complex class structures and conflicts that it engenders.

If this sounds hard and complicated, let me offer a simpler formulation. After the war, Marxism confidently offered a threatening Truth, the angst-ridden right went relativist, and social democracy got its chance. Following Marxism's great defeat in 1991, Marxist Truth perished, Liberal Truth made a comeback, and social democracy died. After capitalism's 2008 Waterloo and the rise of technofeudalism, liberals, social democrats and the alt-right are fighting over whatever scraps of power the cloudalists will let them have. Today, our future depends on recovering the confidence to unveil a Truth consistent with our technofeudal condition. It will not be sufficient. But it is necessary.

CRYPTO'S FALSE PROMISE

Thomas More wrote *Utopia* in the sixteenth century as a thought experiment in how to cure the evils of the feudal order (in which, it must be said, he played a prominent part). Half a century later, Tommaso Campanella published his own Utopia, *The City of the Sun*, as a polemic against the prominent Aristotelian view that anyone doing manual labour should be denied full citizenship. He counterargued that it was the artisans and the builders, not the parasitic feudal classes, who ought to have political power. Today's evangelical advocates of crypto technologies – with their faith that Wall Street, cloudalists, governments, the deep state, the entire technofeudal order can be brought down by smart computer code and unhackable proof-of-work algorithms – are today's economic utopians, and crypto is as much a reaction to technofeudalism as the original Utopia was a reaction to feudalism.

Truth be told, when I first encountered the original paper heralding crypto's arrival, a 2008 blogpost signed by the now infamous and elusive Satoshi Nakamoto,[10] I was mesmerised. It began with the sentence: 'Commerce on the Internet has come to rely almost exclusively on financial institutions serving as trusted third parties to process electronic payments.' It then proceeded to present an algorithm that would allow us to transact with one another online bypassing every financial institution ever created. It was not hard to see the enormity of the claim and the potential emancipation it offered from the parasites of the financial sector – private and state-owned.

To appreciate crypto's attraction, consider what happens when you use your debit card to buy a train ticket from London to Brighton using a service like trainline.com that charges you a small cloud rent, say 75p.[11] Where does it go? From the trainline app, your 75p is uploaded to another company, Trainline Holdings Limited, which owns the trainline app. But this company is owned by another which is owned by another, and another, and another. As your 75p shifts from one shell company to another, it travels from London to Jersey to Luxembourg, it is validated by a number of central banks, until it reaches some balmy tax haven. Eventually, it joins a global torrent of dollarised financial capital that no government, no parliament, no demos, no human mind can track, let alone regulate.

Now, compare this to a crypto transaction of the kind Nakamoto's paper heralded. You sit in front of your computer. You need no bank account, no plastic card, no social security number to identify yourself with, not even an email account. You just need a private key in the form of a sequence of seemingly random characters that you generated earlier through a few simple automated cryptographic steps. This private key is all you need to make a payment, send money to a good cause, even vote on an online survey or referendum.[12] In essence, your private key is an address, a bank account and a social security number all rolled up in one string of characters that lives only on your computer and is known exclusively to you. However, the moment you use it to transact, it is transmitted to a global network of computers belonging to people like yourself. For a transaction to work, it needs to be verified and recorded, in the same way your bank verifies that you have the cash and that, once you have spent, you cannot spend it again. The difference is that, instead of entrusting the verification of your transaction to a bank or to some other parasitic capitalist institution, the verification is performed automatically by computers, like yours, comprising that common network.

These machines work together to verify your transaction. They do this by competing with each other to solve arbitrary mathematical puzzles, whose purpose is to offer incentives to owners of the fastest computers to help verify your transaction. The machine that wins this contest wins the privilege of adding, or recording, your transaction as a 'block' on a long record – known as a blockchain – of every transaction made within this network. In return for that privilege, the winning machine – and its owner – is rewarded with a proof-of-work token, a small payment that can be used on the network for future transactions.[13]

You can see the lure of crypto: in contrast to the madness that begins the moment you pay for anything using a bank-issued card, the blockchain-based transaction seems like democracy-in-action. No one takes a cut. No bank or corporation is involved. No state monitors your transaction. No cloudalist retains a record of what you bought, when and from whom. No crazy path is taken via dozens of intermediaries, contributing at each stage to the accumulation of capital among financiers. Moreover, no one owns the network of machines that helped complete your transaction and, therefore, no investors are watching, checking that the pie is growing and their cut of the cloud rents along with it, ready to pull their support the moment confidence in the enterprise begins to wane – not least because this cloud-based network generates *no* cloud rents.

Crypto's birth in 2008 could not have been timed better. In the year that capitalist finance almost died of its own hubris, Bitcoin inspired a wide spectrum of people seeking alternatives: sworn libertarians, the anarchists and socialists who made up the Occupy Wall Street movement, the so-called cypherpunks – a medley of cryptographers and coders who had been worrying about privacy since the 1980s. But soon cracks began to appear, and it was the libertarian faction of the crypto movement who ultimately gained the upper hand. For them, enemy number one had always been the central banks, which they portrayed as a sort of Catholic Church, insisting on acting as intermediary between humans and their sacred profits, with themselves in the role of a latter-day Martin Luther pushing for a Protestant Reformation. Thus, the crypto movement which had also initially attracted anarchists and socialists, became a supremely volatile currency market, in which anyone sufficiently expert in the new blockchain technology issued their own 'coins' whose dollar value they tried to boost before cashing in. Their ideological contempt for fiat, or state-created, money turned out to be a ruse for issuing their own fiat money. By the time, in 2017, one Bitcoin traded for more than $20,000, the early emancipatory promise of crypto had vanished.

Using similar blockchain methods, model Kate Moss sold a digital photo of herself in the form of a Bitcoin-like string of characters for more than $17,000. Jack Dorsey, then Twitter's chief, raised the stakes by selling code linked to an image of the first ever tweet for $2.9 million. To top the madness, Mike Winkelmann, an artist known as Beeple, managed to sell at a Christie's auction in New York a string of characters linked to a photographic collage of his earlier works for a stunning $69.3 million. Mocking them all, a Brooklyn film director received $85 for a string of characters attached to an audio file of him flatulating, hopefully in the face of this crypto folly.

It could not have been otherwise. Betrayal of its early emancipatory promise was hard-wired into the nature of cryptocurrencies. Nakamoto's ambition had been that Bitcoin should take off as a parallel currency. To succeed, people would need to want to use Bitcoin to buy train tickets, drinks and even houses. But to engineer the scarcity that he believed was necessary to give Bitcoin value, Nakamoto built into the Bitcoin code a fixed upper limit in the total number of Bitcoins – 21 million to be precise. Its limited supply meant that as soon as the demand for Bitcoin rose, so would its exchange rate with dollars. At some point, when the dollar value of Bitcoin rises above some threshold, it makes sense to keep your Bitcoin and use dollars to buy train tickets, drinks and houses, as well as more Bitcoin in the hope that its value will rise further. It was inevitable that the moment a cryptocurrency began to succeed as a currency it would stop working like a currency and would turn instead into a pyramid scheme, with its early adopters growing richer as more and more people bought into it.

Besides this crypto aristocracy, the only true beneficiaries of crypto technologies have been the very institutions that crypto evangelists supposedly aimed to overthrow: Wall Street and the Big Tech conglomerates. For example, J.P. Morgan and Microsoft recently joined forces to run a 'consortium blockchain', based on

Microsoft data centres, to improve their joint power to dominate financial services. Similar blockchain projects have been announced by Goldman Sachs and the Hong Kong central bank, by the World Bank, indeed by Mastercard and Visa themselves![14] Rather than inching towards Utopia, crypto has become another tool of cloud finance and engine for the accumulation of cloud capital.

Blockchain is, no doubt, a fascinating tool. When I first encountered it, I wrote that it was a brilliant answer to a question we have not discovered yet. But if the question is how to fix capitalism or dethrone technofeudalism, this is not it. Both are encompassing and exploitative systems that by nature have the power to co-opt technical innovations to their own ends. Under capitalism, crypto serves financial capital. Under technofeudalism, it aids and abets the logic of cloud-capital accumulation. This does not mean that crypto tech will not, at some point, prove useful to progressives. If and when we manage to socialise cloud capital and democratise our economies, blockchain technologies will come in handy.[15] But before any of this becomes remotely possible, we need to answer the most pressing of questions: what is the alternative to technofeudalism? And if social democracy is impossible and crypto a false promise, how will we build it?

IMAGINING ANOTHER NOW

One reason that we, the left, are wallowing in perpetual defeat is our failure to answer the killer question once put to me in a pub by a self-described 'cockney Tory' who had heard that a socialist was in the house: 'If you don't like what we have, what would you replace it with? How would it work? I am all ears. Convince me!' I didn't even try. Not just because of the din in the crowded pub, which meant I could barely hear myself think, but primarily because I lacked a convincing answer.

My consolation was that I was in excellent company. Karl Marx, not exactly a man lacking self-confidence or imagination, refused to go beyond vague references to the socialism or communism which he predicted and wanted to replace the Empire of Capital. Why? Marx's own excuse for offering no socialist blueprint was smart: it is beyond the capacities of middle-class intellectuals working in the British Library reading room or chatting in their posh living rooms. Rather, it is the proletariat who, in pursuing their collective interests, should and will create socialism as they go along – or so Marx said. Today, we know from both the Soviet and the Western European experience with social democracy that this was wishful thinking: a bottom-up socialist blueprint has simply not transpired, anywhere. But what was my excuse? Trying to conjure up the blueprint for a realistic utopia is damned hard, not to mention risky. Nevertheless, without a convincing answer to that killer question, the prospect of recruiting people to the cause of reclaiming our minds, bodies and environment will remain hopeless.

A few weeks after that pub encounter, I came across a review of a book I had written, the one addressed to your granddaughter, about how capitalism works.[16] It was by a political opponent, Ireland's finance minister at the time. He surprised me with some kind words for the book but, predictably, was scathing towards my call for systemic change: 'An exhortation for the creation of an "authentic democracy" and the collective ownership of technology and the means of production,' he wrote, 'sits very poorly alongside his appreciation of entrepreneurship and individual initiative.' Oops, I thought, the man is right. The time had come to stop hiding behind my little finger and to flesh out a blueprint for a convincing alternative system – one that combines collective ownership of the means of production, personal freedom, room for innovative thinking and technological progress and, yes, authentic democracy.

The task was clear and daunting: I had to explain how production, distribution, innovation, land use, housing, money, prices and a host of other stuff would work in a society that has socialised land and capital, including its algorithmic, AI-powered, cloud-based variety. I would have to explain how international trade and money flows would work. What democracy would mean and how it would function. Between you and me, nothing short of panic describes my state of mind as I sat down to write a book that seemed like a duty bordering on purgatory.

It took me a day or two to hit the wall. Every idea I had for how companies would be run, or how money would be issued, immediately crashed on the shoals of my own objections. Progress was impossible. Then, I had an epiphany. What does an author do if he disagrees with everything he writes? My answer was to write a novel populated with characters that each represented one of the various perspectives that were jostling for influence in my mind.

Eventually, I managed to boil it down to three characters: Eva, a former Wall Street banker, would keep a check on my blueprint from a liberal, technocratic standpoint (one that the aforementioned Irish finance minister ought to appreciate). Iris, a retired anthropologist, would bring to the novel the Marxist-feminist perspective that you would love. And Costa, a brilliant technologist disillusioned by his experiences working within Big Tech, would shed light on the role of cloud capital. But one more issue still needed resolving.

The guy at the pub wanted to know how his life would differ under my system in the here and now, with the technologies currently at hand, with our existing human stock, warts and all. I was not allowed, in other words, to project into a technologically more advanced future. Nor to populate my alternative system with people better, smarter or nicer than the ones we meet down the pub or in front of our bathroom mirror. In short, my blueprint had to be written as if it had been implemented already. However, since history matters, and everything we do is path-dependent, it would be daft to describe my system as if it existed in 2020 – the year the book would be published – without explaining how it had come about. In other words, I needed a believable alternative history of a political and social revolution that had occurred at some point in the past. To this end, I chose the year 2008 as the point when this alternative history diverged from our own. In my story, I imagined what might have happened if the protests and rebellions that had sprung up in the wake of the crash – gatherings like Occupy Wall Street, Spain's *indignados*, and the protests in Athens at Syntagma Square – had actually succeeded.

And yet it seemed important to me that my three characters somehow keep one foot in the reader's side of history – our messed-up technofeudal reality – from which to assess and critique the alternative system I was conjuring up. How could this possibly work? Minds uninfected by science fiction might find this preposterous, but having misspent – as you well know – part of my youth immersed in science fiction, where parallel universes and wormholes are commonplace, the die was cast: I would imagine two parallel realities. One our own, in which the reader, myself, Eva, Iris and Costa live. And another in which alternative versions of

ourselves inhabit a world where technofeudalism has been replaced
by a technologically based socialism. (In the book, it is referred to
as anarcho-syndicalism – but a simpler term would simply be tech-
nodemocracy.) The drama would be precipitated when an invention
of Costa's would open up a portal for written exchanges between
the two, allowing the characters to offer one another descriptions
of their alternative worlds.

My answer to the guy in the pub, to the Irish finance minister,
to anyone who wants to know what the alternative to technofeudalism is that I am proposing, can be found in the pages of the
book that resulted: *Another Now: Dispatches from an alternative present.*[17] What follows is the gist of it, without the various perspectives,
objections and debates of my three characters, but packaged simply in brief glimpses of my alternative to technofeudalism. Ready
to imagine Another Now?

DEMOCRATISED COMPANIES

Imagine a corporation in which every employee has a single share
that they receive when hired, the way a student collects a library
card upon enrolling at university. This share, which cannot be
sold or leased, grants each employee a single vote. All decisions –
hiring, promotion, research, product development, pricing,
strategy – are taken collectively, with each employee exercising
their vote via the company's intranet, which thus functions as a
permanent shareholders' assembly. Equal ownership does not,
however, mean equal pay.

Pay is determined by a democratic process that divides the
company's post-tax revenues into four slices: one to cover the
firm's fixed costs (such as equipment, licences, utility bills, rent

and interest payments), another set aside for R&D, a slice from which basic pay to staff is made and, lastly, a slice for bonuses. Again, the distribution between these four slices is decided collectively, on a one-person-one-vote basis.

Any proposal to increase one slice must be accompanied by a proposal to reduce expenditure on one or more of the other slices. Competing proposals are put to a vote where employee-shareholders rank each proposal in order of preference via an electronic ballot form. If no plan wins an absolute majority of first preferences, a process of elimination takes place. The plan with the fewest first preferences is knocked out and its first-preference votes are reallocated to the voter's second preference. This simple algorithmic process is repeated until one business plan has acquired more than half the votes cast.

Having determined the amount of money the company will spend on the various slices, the basic pay slice is then divided equally among all staff – from persons recently employed as secretaries or cleaners to the firm's star designers or engineers. Which leaves one important question unanswered: how do they decide the distribution of the bonus slice between staff? The answer is via a variant of the voting scheme made famous by the Eurovision Song Contest, in which each participating country is given a set number of points that it can allocate to the songs of every other country. In this spirit, once a year, employees are each given one hundred digital tokens to distribute among their colleagues. The idea is simple: you allot these tokens to those colleagues whom you believe to have contributed most during the previous year. Once the tokens have been distributed, the total bonus slice is allocated in proportion to the number of tokens each employee has received from their colleagues.

The impact of legislating such a corporate governance system would be the equivalent of a large comet crashing into technofeudalism's bedrock. On the most superficial level, it would liberate employees from the tyranny of self-serving managers, but on a structural level it would do so much more. First, it would eliminate the distinction between wages and profits; thus we have collective ownership and we have eliminated the fundamental class divide between those who own and collect profits or rents and those who lease their time for a wage. We have also abolished the market for shares – only an employee can own a share in a company, and only one share that can't be sold or leased – thus cutting the umbilical cord that links finance and share market speculation. In a stroke, we have ended financialisation and destroyed private equity. We have also, most probably, done away with the need for regulators whose job is to break up large corporations before they establish monopolies. As collective decision-making becomes unwieldy in companies beyond a certain size – say, five hundred people – it seems wholly likely that the employee-shareholders would not form them and, in the case of already formed conglomerates, would vote to break them up in smaller companies.

Most people I know, including generations of students I have taught, assume that capitalism equals markets. That socialism must mean the end of prices as signals to producers and consumers. Nothing could be further from the truth. Capitalist firms are market-free zones within which a non-market process extracts surplus value from employees which then takes the form of rent, profit and interest. The larger the firm, and the more cloud capital it employs, the greater the rents it extracts from a society whose markets malfunction as a result.

In contrast, the democratised companies I propose here, and

in *Another Now*, are more consistent with well-functioning, compet-itive markets in which prices – free from the scourge of rent and concentrated market power – are formed. Put differently, doing away with capitalist firms, through terminating labour and share markets, paves the ground for truly competitive product markets and a process of price formation that powers up the great engine of entrepreneurship and innovation which conventional thinking, wrongly, associates with capitalism.[18]

What would all this mean for the cloudalists? The various Bezoses, Zuckerbergs and Musks would wake up to find they owned a single share in 'their' company granting them a single vote. On every single item of the continuous-time agenda of the Amazon, Facebook, Twitter or Tesla decision-making process, they would have to sway a majority of their fellow, equally empow-ered, employee-shareholders. Control over the firm's cloud capital, including the almighty algorithms at their centre, would be democratised, at least within the bounds of the company. Even so, cloud capital's potency would be no less great – its nature as a produced means of behavioural modification would remain unchanged – and so the good society would need additional pro-tections from it.

One such protection would be a Social Accountability Act stipulating that every corporation be graded according to an index of social worthiness, to be compiled by panels of randomly selected citizens, the equivalent of juries, chosen from a diverse pool of stakeholders: the company's customers, members of the communities it affects, and so on. If a company's rating falls con-sistently below a certain threshold, a public inquiry may result in the company's deregistration. A second, even more pertinent, social protection is afforded by the termination of 'free' services.

We have learned the hard way what happens when services are funded by selling users' attention to third parties. It turns the users into cloud serfs, whose labour enhances and reproduces cloud capital, further tightening its grip on our minds and behaviour. To replace the illusion of free services, our alternative reality features a micropayment platform, let's call it 'Penny For Your Thought'. This works a bit like Netflix's subscription model but combined with the British National Health Service's principle of universal provision. App developers needing our data have to pay to get it from consenting users, who are protected by a Bill of Digital Rights that guarantees us all the right to choose which of our data to sell and to whom. The combination of the micropayment platform and the Bill of Digital Rights terminates, in practice, the current attention-grabbing market model. At the same time, anyone using an app pays the developer for access to it. The sums involved are small for the individual but for an app with a large pool of users they add up. Would that not prevent some people from being able to afford digital services they need? No, because of the way money works in this alternative system.

DEMOCRATISED MONEY

Imagine that the central bank provided everyone with a free digital wallet, effectively a free bank account. To attract people to use it, a stipend (or basic dividend) is credited monthly to each account making universal basic income a reality. Taking one step further, the central bank pays interest to those who shift monies from their savings at commercial banks to their new digital wallet. In time, a mass if not total exodus would follow as people moved their savings from the private banks to this new public digital payments and savings system. Would this not require the central bank to mint vast amounts of money?

Yes, the stipends will have to be minted anew, though not at a rate that exceeds the quantities central banks have been minting since 2008 to bolster permanently unstable private banks.[19] As for the rest of the money, it has already been minted by the private banks. All that happens here is that it migrates from the private banks' unsafe ledger to the safe ledger of the central bank. As people and companies begin paying one another using this system, all money stays on the central bank ledger, moving from one part of it to another with every transaction, rather than being available to bankers and their shareholders to gamble with.

This turns central banks from pliant servants of private bankers to something like a monetary commons. To oversee its operations, including the quantity of money in the system and the privacy of each person's transactions, the central bank is answerable to, and monitored by, a Monetary Supervision Jury comprising randomly selected citizens and experts drawn from a wide range of professions.

What about investment? In this system you can lend your savings to a start-up or to a mature firm but you can't buy a chunk of any firm – since shares are distributed solely on the one-employee-one-share basis. Rather, you can lend your savings directly, either using your central bank digital wallet or via an intermediary – but with this crucial stipulation: that intermediary cannot create money out of thin air, as banks do today whenever they issue a loan, but must trade in already-existing funds from really-existing savers.

What about taxation? Recall that there are three types of income. First, the basic dividends credited to citizens' digital wallets by the

central bank. Second, earnings from working in the democratised
companies, comprising basic salary plus bonuses. Third, interest
paid to savers by the central bank or by private intermediaries. None
of these incomes are taxed. Nor are there any sales taxes, VAT or
anything of that sort. So, who finances the state? Every company
does via a fixed tax on all revenues, e.g. 5 per cent. Note that this is
a fixed portion of total revenues, not profits, preventing the infinite
scope for accounting tricks that dress up expenses as costs in order
to shrink companies' taxable income. The only other taxes fall on
commercial land and buildings, discussed further below.

When it comes to international trade and payments, a new
international financial system guarantees continual wealth
transfers to the Global South, while also restraining trade and
financial imbalances of the type that inflate bubbles and cause
financial crashes. The idea is that all trade and all money movements between different monetary jurisdictions – such as the
UK, Germany, China and the United States – are denominated
in a new digital international accounting unit, which I called the
Kosmos. If the Kosmos value of a country's imports exceed its
exports, the country is charged an *imbalance levy*, in proportion
to its trade deficit. Equally, if a country's exports exceed its
imports, it is also charged the same levy in proportion to its
trade surplus. This terminates the mercantilist motive for one
country persistently to extract value from another country by
selling to it goods of greater value than those it imports from it,
and, subsequently, lending them the money to continue buying
from it – a form of vendor finance that places the weaker country in permanent debt bondage.

Meanwhile, a second *surge levy* is charged to a country's Kosmos account whenever too much money moves too quickly out of,

or into, the country. For decades, developing countries were undermined whenever the 'smart' money, detecting future economic growth (e.g. South Korean, Thailand, some African countries), rushed in to buy land and companies before their price went up. As the money inflows surged, the prices of land and companies skyrocketed and false expectations regarding the level of growth set in, thus inflating bubbles. The moment the bubbles burst, as they inevitably do, the 'smart' money rushed out of the country faster than it had rushed in, leaving nothing but ruined lives and economies behind. The purpose, therefore, of the *surge levy* is to tax these speculative money movements to stop unnecessary damage to the weakest of countries.[20] Proceeds from these two levies are then used to fund direct green investments in the Global South.

The one-employee-one-share-one-vote system has revolutionary effects: it brings to an end share and labour markets and the Empire of Capital, it democratises workplaces and it organically diminishes the size of conglomerates. The reconfiguration of the central bank's ledger as a common payment and savings systems has similarly revolutionary effects: without actually banning private banks, it pulls the rug from under their feet by liberating us all from our dependence on them to make payments or to store our savings. Moreover, the basic dividend provision revolutionises our way of thinking about work, time and value, liberating us from the oppressive moral equation of paid drudgery and virtue. Finally, the Kosmos system balances the international ebb and flow of goods and money, preventing the exploitation of weaker economies by the more powerful ones while funding green investments in the parts of the world they are most needed.

These are the fundamental building blocks of an economy liberated from the tyranny of capital and, thus, denying
technofeudalism the foothold it needs to take us over. The question now arises: how exactly do we free our societies from the
tyranny of rent – the ancient ground-rent variety, which survived
capitalism's defeat of feudalism, and the cloud rents on which
technofeudalism relies?

THE CLOUD AND THE
LAND AS A COMMONS

The coffee is almost ready. Your laptop is booting up. Before long,
coffee mug in hand, you are perusing the morning's newsfeed
from a media site run from your neighbourhood library. The first
item on the news concerns an upcoming local referendum, the
second is beamed in from Brazil on the struggle to compensate its
indigenous peoples for decades of illegal logging, the third relates
a debate within the current membership of the Monetary Supervision Jury on whether the central bank should lower the interest
rate savers receive or, alternatively, increase everyone's basic dividend. It is a little dry for your taste so, careful to avoid the sports
pages, you click on your favourite section devoted to archaeology,
which is constantly updated by researchers from all over the world.
Ah yes, now this gets your pulse racing!

Your newsfeed and its accompanying sections are compiled by
an algorithm calibrated and maintained by the local public media
centre which is, in turn, owned by your municipality but controlled
by local people selected through a combination of lotteries and
elections. Sometimes you get bored with their newsfeed and turn

to a digital world map full of dots, each one representing other local public media centres whose newsfeeds you can access at a click.

Every time you visit a media centre outside your area, a tiny payment leaves your central bank account and helps fund the good people who offer you a window to their world. No ads, no behavioural modification algorithms. As for these tiny payments, they are insignificant in comparison to the basic dividend paid to you by the central bank monthly. Besides, paying them makes you feel good. They buy you – and everyone else – civilisation. They offer you a bay window onto the world, to cooperative media centres strewn all over the planet trying their hardest to provide 'good, diverse, exciting information, knowledge and a touch of wisdom' – as your local media outlet advertises its wares.

Your coffee mug empty, it is time to go to work. You tap on your phone's travel app, also provided by your municipality, and then tap again on 'work'. A list appears of fares offered by various driver cooperatives, alongside information on where and when you can catch the nearest bus or train. You recall with a brief shudder the days of Uber and Lyft, those cloud fiefs that exploited drivers' labour, turning them into cloud proles, and passengers' data, turning you into a cloud serf. The bad memory dissipates when you remind yourself that, these days, the driver-owners and the public transport staff control the algorithms – not the other way round. And you set off with a spring in your step now that you are no longer employed by a capitalist firm, owned by opaque shell companies, that treated you like a cross between a robot and human fodder. Life is still a minefield of worries, especially as we may have wrecked the climate irreparably, but at least work is not systematically soul-destroying.

At work, you have an app on your phone that gives you access to all sorts of shareholder-employee ballots, some of which you vote in and some of which you choose to skip. If you have an idea for a new way of doing things or a new product, you post it on the company's Ideas Board and wait to see who, among your colleagues, wants to work with you to develop it. If no one does, you can still go ahead and re-post the idea once it is better developed. Things are not perfect. Human nature always finds ways of messing up even the best of systems. Your colleagues, if they summon a majority, can vote to have you fired. But the atmosphere at work is now one of shared responsibility which reduces stress and creates an environment in which mutual respect has a better chance to flourish.

On your way home, as your cab exits the commercial zone, you cast your mind back to the *sad ages* when, to have somewhere to live, people had to choose between mortgage debt bondage and renting; between life in thrall to either the banker or the landlord; between predatory mortgage rates and rapacious rents. Now, every region is run by a County Association that oversees the division of land between commercial and social zones, so that rents collected from the former fund the provision of social housing in the latter. As is the norm, the people who officiate at the County Association are selected randomly – with the help of an algorithm that guarantees fair representation of the various groups and communities within the county. Home is no longer a constant source of anxiety but somewhere you feel able to put down roots for the long term.

I'll leave you to imagine the rest of your life in this alternative present, while I explain a bit more about this most crucial aspect of it: the ownership of land and property, that oldest of foundations of both the feudal and capitalist systems, and the sharing of power.

The key to the rent charging system in the commercial zone is a Permanent Auction Subletting Scheme (PASS), a mechanism designed to ensure that communities can extract maximum rents from their commercial zones with which to invest in their social zones. PASS works a little like the famous trick for fairly distributing a cake between two people: one person cuts, the other chooses. In the same spirit, PASS creates a permanent auction that pits current occupiers of a commercial space against prospective occupiers.

Once a year, as a current occupier in the commercial zone, you must visit PASS and submit your valuation of your property based on two rules. First, PASS will compute your monthly rent as a fixed portion of your self-declared market value – with no audits, no red tape, no haggling, no estate agents. Great, right? But here comes the second rule: anyone can, at any point in the future, visit PASS and offer a higher valuation, in which case you are out and they are in within six months. This second rule guarantees that you have an incentive to declare your valuation as truthfully and accurately as you can. If you overstate your true valuation, you will end up paying a rent higher than it's worth. And if you understate it, you increase the chances of regretting your valuation – the moment someone offers a higher value, one closer to its true valuation, and in so doing boots you out.

The beauty of PASS is that the County Association does not have to set rents in the commercial zone. In the first instance, their job is simply to decide which land and buildings to assign to the commercial zones and which to the social zones. If they set aside too much land for social zones, they will have less money to invest in them. Conversely, expanding the commercial zones leaves less room for social housing and social enterprises. Once the County Association has decided how to resolve the trade-off, their second, harder task awaits: defining the criteria according to which social housing – especially the more desirable homes – are distributed. This is the toughest nut to crack. So who sits on the County Association is crucial.

An elected County Association would replace the tyranny of land ownership with the tyranny of electoral systems, which have an inherent propensity to beget powerful hierarchies. Knowing this, ancient Athenian democrats opposed elections and replaced them with lotteries – the idea in which the Western jury system has its roots. If anything can recreate a land commons in a technologically advanced society, your County Association, comprised of randomly selected locals, is surely it.

The same principle extends beyond the regions and the counties to the governance of your nation as a whole, which takes place with the help of a nationwide Citizens' Assembly. Comprising randomly selected citizens from all over the land, this functions as a test bed of ideas, policies and legislation. Deliberation by its juror members helps shape the bills that Parliament later debates and passes.[21] The demos, at long last, has been put back into democracy.

A CLOUD REBELLION TO OVERTHROW TECHNOFEUDALISM

Over the course of this book, I have outlined the system that I have come to believe is replacing, and in many contexts has already replaced, capitalism: the system I call technofeudalism. Whenever I have presented this argument in the past, it has invariably been met with consternation and even anger among those on the left. Understandably so: anyone who finds solace, as you did, Dad, in the faith that capitalism is bound to be replaced by socialism, as Marx predicted it would be, is bound to feel disheartened and dismayed that post-capitalism has arrived but socialism has not – indeed, that the system that has replaced it is even worse. But there is another, more troubling reason for their reaction.

A Marxist activist once put it to me splendidly: 'Yanis, if you are right that exploitation takes place beyond the confines of the capitalist firm,' he said with disarming honesty, 'then organising the proletariat is never going to be enough!' This is precisely my point. I am not suggesting that organising factory workers, train drivers, teachers and nurses is no longer necessary. What I am saying is that it is far from sufficient. In a world increasingly dominated by cloud capital, which is produced largely by the free labour of unwaged cloud serfs, organising the proletariat – and indeed the precariat – is not going to cut it. To stand any chance of overthrowing technofeudalism and putting the demos back into democracy, we need to gather together not just the traditional proletariat and the cloud proles but also the cloud serfs and, indeed, at least some of the vassal capitalists. Nothing less than such a grand coalition that includes them all can undermine technofeudalism sufficiently.

It may sound like a tall order – and it is. But resistance to capital's exorbitant power was always a tall order. When I think of what it took to organise a trade union in the nineteenth century, I shudder. Workers, miners, dockers, shearers, seamstresses faced beatings by mounted police and violence from thugs in the capitalists' employ. Above all, they faced losing their jobs at a time when forgoing a day's wages meant hunger for their families. Even when they managed to stage a successful strike, whatever wage rise they secured was shared by the non-strikers, adding to a calculus that already weighed heavily against mobilisation. And yet they mobilised. They did so against the odds, expecting certain massive personal losses in exchange for small and uncertain shared benefits.

Technofeudalism erects a great new barrier to mobilisation against it. But it also bestows a great new power upon those who dare dream of a coalition to topple it. The great new barrier is the physical isolation of cloud serfs and cloud proles from one another. We interact with and are subject to cloud capital via our individual screens, via our personal mobile phones, via the digital devices that monitor and manage Amazon warehouse workers. Collective action is made harder when people have fewer opportunities to come together. But herein lies the great power that cloud capital presents to its potential rebels: a capacity to build coalitions, organise and take action via the cloud.

In its early days, this was one of the promises of Twitter, of course: that it could enable the mobilisation of the masses. From the Arab Spring to Black Lives Matter, we have seen how far that promise has been realised and how far it has not. But I am talking not just about a mobilisation *via* the cloud but about actions that could actually take place using the systems and technologies *of* the cloud. In *Another Now* I imagined global action targeting one cloudalist company at a time – starting with Amazon. Imagine an international coalition of trades unions calling upon Amazon warehouse workers worldwide to stay away for one day.[22] On its own, such action is feeble. But not so if a broader campaign persuaded enough of its users and customers globally not to visit the Amazon website just for that one day, to resist their status as serfs or vassals for that brief window. The personal inconvenience involved would be trivial but its cumulative effect remarkable. Even if it were only mildly successful, causing say a 10 per cent drop in Amazon's usual revenues, while Amazon's warehouse strike disrupted deliveries for twenty-four hours, such action might prove enough to push Amazon's share price down in ways that no traditional labour action could achieve. This is how cloud proles and cloud serfs can unite effectively. It's what I call *cloud mobilisation*.

The beauty of cloud mobilisation is that it stands on its head the conventional calculus of collective action. Instead of maximal personal sacrifice for minimal collective gain, we now have the opposite: minimal personal sacrifice delivering large collective and personal gains.[23] This reversal has the potential to pave the way towards a coalition of cloud serfs and cloud proles that is large enough to disrupt cloudalists' control over billions of people.

Naturally, actions of this sort against one or even several major cloudalist enterprises won't be enough. The cloud rebellion I envision will need to recruit to its cause many diverse constituencies – including, for example, anyone who loses sleep when their water and energy bills arrive. Smartly calculated, targeted payment strikes could be used to cause an equivalent drop in the private utility companies' share and derivatives prices. Timed well, these peaceful guerrilla strikes could do a lot of damage to the political and economic clout of conglomerates whose fates are increasingly fused with that of cloud finance. The rebellion could gather international support as well if it used, say, a consumer boycott in the Unites States specifically to target a company for its squeezing of workers in Nigeria or the destruction of natural reserves in the Congo.

Another campaign could involve inviting nominations from all over the world for companies with the worst record of zero-hours contracts or low pay, big carbon footprints or poor working conditions, or those that are in the habit of 'downsizing' to boost share prices – and then organising a mass withholding of pension contributions to the pension funds that own shares in those companies. Merely announcing the targeting of a pension fund would be enough to send its shares crashing and to cause an exodus of worried investors from equity funds related to it.

Inspired by Wikileaks, I imagined in *Another Now* a group of rebels writing and uploading digital viruses whose purpose would simply be transparency: to trace and reveal to the world the hidden digital connections between cloudalists, government agencies and bad actors like fossil fuel companies. How and whether this is possible, I do not know, but I am convinced that if by whatever means these institutions knew that they had billions of eyes trained on their actions, they would be paralysed – and as the scales fell from those billions of eyes, the coalition would summon further allies and support.

None of this is either easy or inevitable. But is it harder or less likely than what the miners, the seamstresses and the dockworkers envisioned and sacrificed their very lives to achieve in the nineteenth century? The cloud takes – but the cloud also gives to those who want to reclaim freedom and democracy. It is up to them, to us, to decide, and to prove, which is greater.

BACK TO YOUR QUESTION,
ONE LAST TIME

Your younger self was on to something. Private capital, you surmised back in the 1940s, can only be owned by the very few. As long as it is privately owned, it's in its nature to concentrate. But concentrated capital means concentrated power. Which means that, unless society takes capital over, it's all futile: freedom, autonomy, social democracy, liberal democracy – every single one an empty word in the business of embellishing and prettifying an inevitable Tyranny of Capital.

When in 1981 the socialists won the Greek general election by a landslide, you were glad we no longer had to fear the secret police. Nevertheless, as everyone around you was getting drunk on the spirit of the moment, you remained defiantly pessimistic. Without democratising work, you insisted, social democracy is impossible no matter how well meaning or smart the social democrats in government. History came down on your side, but not in a way that pleased you.

Our greatest defeat was, of course, not the failure of social democracy in Greece or anywhere else. It was the failure of the Soviet experiment, the only large-scale attempt to take capital under society's control. It produced significant innovations, in both science and technology. But the Soviet central planning system failed to press these into society's service. Soviet scientists invented cybernetics with the potential, decades before Google or Amazon, to coordinate people's preferences and efforts automatically. Except that the Soviet top-down system could not exploit these for the benefit of the society it was meant to serve. And so appalling authoritarianism and daily drudgery led to total defeat in 1991.

Subsequently, private capital was free to go on a global rampage that culminated in the crash of 2008 and the rise of its most formidable mutation – a cloud-based capital with a monstrous power to usurp minds and markets. Thanks to the endless funds of central banks with which the cloudalists have built their empires, we are all now, like Stelarc's Movatar, wired into the circuits of technofeudalism.

So, there you have it, Dad, the answer to your question is in. It bears good and bad news. The bad news is that the internet bred a form of capital which killed capitalism but replaced it with something far worse. The good news is that we now have at our disposal tools that neither the Soviets nor the reforming social democrats ever had and with which we might re-establish a new commons. In short, we live under a new form of serfdom but we hold in our hands a hitherto non-existent golden opportunity to realise your dream of a leisured, freedom-maximising, bottom-up communism.

How likely is it that we take advantage of it? I am damned if I know. But, then again, could people like us in, say, 1776 realistically have imagined universal suffrage or the abolition of slavery? What I do know is that which you and Hesiod taught me: our remarkable knack for technological revolutions does not let us stay put. It pushes us violently into contradictions – and the choices that go with them. We are fast approaching a fork in the road where our path will lead either to a world resembling *Star Trek*, where machines help us improve ourselves, or to a dystopia like *The Matrix*, in which humans are merely the fuel that powers an empire of machines.

To most people, I am sure, barbarism, climate Armageddon, *The Matrix* seem much more likely than any good outcome. Then again, whenever people thought good outcomes were guaranteed – I am thinking of your comrades in the prison camp who believed that a redemptive communism was just around the corner – the result was either a new type of tyranny or defeat. You, on the other hand, bore the hardships of that prison camp despite harbouring deep doubts in place of your comrades' certainties. Today, we must do the same. As long as there is even the remotest chance of a successful cloud rebellion, then our only chance of achieving a good life – of the *eudaimonia*, or flourishing, which Aristotle believed to be our ultimate aim – is to hope and to act without the slightest of guarantees. At the very least, we do not have fewer reasons to persevere than you did in that prison-camp hellhole.

Marx famously described our condition under capitalism as one of 'alienation', owing to our having no ownership of the products of our labour, to our having no say in how things get done. Under technofeudalism, we no longer own our minds. Every proletarian is turning into a cloud prole during working hours and into a cloud serf the rest of the time. Every self-employed striver mutates into a cloud vassal, while every self-employed struggler becomes a cloud serf. While privatisation and private equity asset-strip all physical wealth around us, cloud capital goes about the business of asset-stripping our brains. To own our minds individually, we must own cloud capital collectively. It's the only way we can turn our cloud-based artefacts from a produced means of behaviour modification to a produced means of human collaboration and emancipation.

Cloud serfs, cloud proles and cloud vassals of the world, unite! We have nothing to lose but our mind-chains!

Appendix 1
The Political Economy of Technofeudalism

Under feudalism, the power of the ruling class grew out of owning land that the majority could not own, but were bonded to. Under capitalism, power stemmed from owning capital that the majority did not own, but had to work with to make a living. Under technofeudalism, a new ruling class draws power from owning cloud capital whose tentacles entangle everyone. In this Appendix, after summarising how capitalism generated value, surplus and power, I'll sketch out the generation and distribution of surplus and power in our technofeudal societies.

DISCLAIMER: My theoretical take is not objective science. It could not be because no economist can claim to be objective or scientific (especially those who claim to be). Unlike Physics Nobel Laureates, who always respect (even if they do not like) each other, two winners of the equivalent economics honour (the Bank of Sweden's Prize for Economics in the Memory of Alfred Nobel) often consider each other to be charlatans. That's because economics is more like a philosophy (or religion) embellished with complex equations and voluminous statistics offering those who speak its language huge power over the rest who do not. Economics is best seen as a contested terrain on which armies of politically motivated ideas (some favouring the ruling class, others the exploited classes) clash mercilessly to win over our hearts and minds. For the record, the analysis that follows is in the tradition of the classical economists, e.g. Adam Smith, David Ricardo, Karl Marx – with splashes of John Maynard Keynes, John Kenneth Galbraith and Hyman Minsky.[1]

CAPITALISM

Key to understanding how capitalism produces wealth and distributes it is by virtue of value, labour and capital, each possessing a dual nature. The duality in their natures was the source of the great surpluses from which capitalist profits sprang. These profits, along with debt, funded the formation of capital whose accumulation shaped the modern world.

1. COMMODITY PRODUCTION

Commodities are goods or services produced exclusively to be sold, rather than to be experienced or gifted by their producers. Under capitalism (but also under all pre-capitalist systems), buying and selling was confined to markets.

> 1.0 Markets – A market is any decentralised trading site where buyers and sellers meet freely and spontaneously.

Note: They can be less or more competitive, oligopolistic (few sellers, many buyers) or oligopsonistic (many sellers, few buyers); tending at its limit to monopoly (a single seller and many buyers) or monopsony. Markets wither when the number of buyers and the number of sellers both shrink, tending to one on each side (in which case we have a case of one-on-one bargaining, or bilateral monopoly/psony).

Note: Under technofeudalism, trading is centralised and takes place not in markets but in cloud fiefs (e.g. Big Tech platforms) created and run by the algorithms of cloud capital which match buyers and sellers – see 11.2.3.

> 1.1. Value's two natures
>> 1.1.1. Experiential Value
>> 1.1.2. Exchange (or Commodity) Value

Experiential Value flows out of any experience humans value; from drinking a glass of cold water when thirsty, to enjoying a beautiful sunset, to solving an equation or humming a song, to shopping, to feeling appreciated. Experiential value is, thus, an intangible, unquantifiable, subjective, quicksilver value.[2] It always existed, and always will as long as humans are sentient, independently of how we organise production.

Exchange Value is the quantifiable value of a commodity under capitalism. More precisely, the exchange value of a unit of some commodity is measured by how many units of other commodities it can be exchanged with. It is reflected in (but is not reducible to – see note below) the price of a good or service which has been produced for sale, not to be experienced or gifted by those who produced it (i.e. a commodity is aimed at end buyers prepared to pay for the experiential value they will derive from it).

Note: The greater the competition between several sellers, the closer the price of a commodity reflects its exchange value which, in turn, is determined by (or reflects) the total experiential labour (see 1.2.1 below) expended in its production by every human involved, directly or indirectly, in producing it.

1.2. Labour's two natures
1.2.1. Experiential Labour
1.2.2. Commodity Labour

Experiential Labour is the elusive, unquantifiable, quicksilver and occasionally magical aspect of human work that, during the production process, breathes into a thing or a service the capacity to impart experiential value (see 1.1.1) to whomever gets to experience or consume the final product or service.[3] Focusing on commodities (that have been produced for sale), experiential labour is the human input that infuses them with exchange value during the process of production (see 1.1.2).

Commodity Labour is the bundle of labour time and skills a worker leases to an employer. The exchange value of commodity labour equals the sum of the experiential labour that other workers have put into the commodities that a waged worker's wage can buy. In the same way that price is the (seldom perfect) reflection of a commodity's exchange value, the wage is the (seldom perfect) reflection of commodity labour's exchange value.

1.3. Capital's two natures
1.3.1. A produced means of commodity production
1.3.2. A social relation that affords its owners extractive power over non-owners

A produced means of commodity production takes the familiar form of physical capital, e.g. machines, factory or office buildings, tractors, etc. Because they are commodities (or, as they often called, capital goods) produced exclusively to assist in the production of other commodities, they can be thought of as physical artefacts purchased as labour productivity enhancers. More abstractly, they can also be thought of as previously expended, or 'dead', experiential labour now crystallised in physical means of production.

A social relation that affords capital's owners extractive power over non-owners – besides its physical presence and function, capital provides its owners with the social power necessary to extract surplus value (see 1.4) from workers who do not own capital.

Note: There is nothing mystical or puzzling about the physical nature and function of fishing rods, tractors or industrial robots (i.e. of capital goods). However, capital's nature as a provider of extractive power is less obvious. The extractive power it affords derives from the social relations between people with property rights over (and, therefore, autonomous access to) means of production (capitalists, landlords) and the rest. The asymmetry in capital ownership leaves those who do not own capital no alternative but to sell to capitalists their commodity labour (see 1.2.2), for a wage, and, in the process, to generate surplus value (see 1.4) for the capitalists. To illustrate, recall how (Chapter 3, pp. 60–61) Mr Peel lost his extractive power over the English workers he had transported to Western Australia once they gained autonomous access to means of production (i.e. to plentiful land in the surrounding areas) independently of Mr Peel. Capital's second nature, its *extractive power*, originates from such asymmetrical access to produced means of commodity production.

> 1.4 Surplus Value is the difference that an employer retains after producing and selling a unit of commodity X. More precisely, it is the difference between (a) the value infused into a unit of X by the *experiential labour* necessary to produce it and (b) the value of the amount of *commodity labour* that the employer had to buy to produce that same unit of X.[4]

2. DISTRIBUTION

Revenues from the production and sale of commodities turn into four main types of income: Wages, Interest, Rents and Profit.

2.1 Wages

In the same way that prices reflect (but are not reducible to) the value of commodities, wages reflect (but are not reducible to) the exchange value of commodity labour (1.2.2).

Note: The greater the competition between several employers, the closer the wage reflects the exchange value of the worker's commodity labour. Thus, in labour markets dominated by one or few employers, the wage falls short of the exchange value of the worker's commodity labour – which translates into a type of monopsony rent (see 2.3.3 below) retained by the employer.[5]

2.2 Interest

Capitalists must borrow (occasionally from themselves, i.e. from their accumulated profits) to purchase labour, land and capital goods before production begins. To break even, their revenues must cover – in addition to all their other costs – the interest financiers charge them (or which they would have earned from saving that money had they not entered into production).

2.3 Rents

Rent is any price paid by a buyer above the price which most closely reflects the exchange value of the commodity (1.1.2). An equivalent definition of rent is as monies paid for a commodity in excess of the minimum price necessary for that commodity to have been produced. Four types of rent are prevalent under capitalism:

2.3.1 Financial Rent
2.3.2 Ground Rent
2.3.3 Monopoly Rent
2.3.4 Brand Rent

Financial Rent refers to payments to financiers (e.g., bankers) in excess of the minimum interest necessary to motivate them to provide the loan. Financial rent also includes returns from speculating in share, real estate and derivative markets, in private equity, etc.

Ground Rent predates capitalism and comes close to (though it does not coincide with) the everyday use of the word 'rent': any payment for leasing land over and above the minimum (which may tend to zero) that would be necessary to motivate its owner to lease it.

Monopoly Rent obtains due to low or non-existent competition (oligopoly or monopoly) which allows a seller to extract from consumers payment in excess of the commodity's exchange value. In common parlance, the monetary equivalent of monopoly rent is known as a 'mark-up' (or 'price-cost margin') that the seller can charge the customer over and above a commodity's exchange value.[6]

Brand Rent is a form of monopoly rent which the seller can extract from consumers who are motivated to pay for a branded item or service more than its exchange value, e.g. in pursuit of status signalling or ownership of positional goods (i.e. goods desired not so much for themselves but, rather, for the fact that others cannot own them, e.g. a limited-run print or an antique vase).

2.4 Profit

Profit is the portion of the revenue capitalists retain after they have paid wages to workers, ground rent to landlords, interest and financial rent to financiers plus fees to professionals (e.g. marketers, advertisers), helping them build up brand rents.

3. MONEY and CIRCULATION

The exchange values that capitalism produces (see Figure 1) are transformed into prices, wages, interest and profits within various markets where commodities are exchanged for money.

For production to begin, private monies (comprising previous profit and new bank loans) are spent by firms on inputs such as commodity labour (see 1.2.2), physical capital (see 1.3.2), buildings and land, and other commodities needed as raw materials.

Within the firms, due to the twin natures of labour and capital, surplus value is generated which the firm's owners retain (i.e. capital's nature as an extractive power enables the firm to extract – unpaid for – experiential labour that infuses its output with exchange value greater than that of its inputs).

Once commodity output is sold, the firms (courtesy of the surplus value generated during the production process) end up with more money than they started this cycle with. These monies then turn into incomes (wages, taxes and the different types of rents – see 2.2). The augmented private incomes (net of taxes and all spending on repaying financiers or landowners), plus public expenditures and new consumer debt, return to markets in the form of consumer and government (private and public) consumption. Lastly, unspent capitalist profit, plus new corporate debt, funds the new cycle of the production process. And so on.

The two linchpins holding capitalism's circulation process together (see Figure 2) are:

3.1 Profit and Private Debt as capitalism's main fuel

3.2 Markets as value's decentralised distribution mechanism

Profit fuels capital accumulation, motivates capitalists, and lubricates capitalisms' cogs and wheels,[7] while Private Debt (created by financiers from thin air)[8] allows capitalists to finance the large fixed costs involved in building up new plants and networks of physical capital.[9]

Markets are the *decentralised price-formation mechanisms* in which exchange values are realised in the form of money prices, wages, nominal interest rates, rental rates, etc. – see also Figure 1.

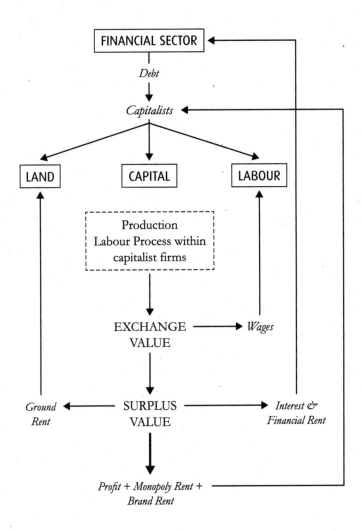

Figure 1: *The Production and Distribution of Value Under Capitalism*

4. CAPITAL ACCUMULATION

Capital goods – like all commodities – are produced within capitalist firms utilising waged labour and previously produced capital goods. Capital accumulation thus occurs at the micro level (i.e. the level of the firm, enterprise, corporation or conglomerate – see 4.1 below). However, the rate at which capital accumulates within firms depends on macro forces that are irreducible to the micro level (see 4.2 below).

4.1 Micro (internal to the firm) determinants of capital accumulation

These determinants include the level of investment (financed by past profits and new debt), R&D investment, innovative designs, managerial strategies, etc.

4.2 Macro (external to the firm) determinants of capital accumulation

A capitalist's motivation to accumulate capital depends on the anticipated level of demand for her or his output which, in turn, is largely determined by the level of aggregate (or economy-wide) demand. The latter depends on:

- the expected investment expenditure by all other capitalists (since the higher the capitalist class's overall investment the higher the economy-wide incomes that are spent on commodities) – which, in turn, depends on the capitalist class's *animal spirits*,[10] *and*
- the government's spending (i.e. fiscal policy).

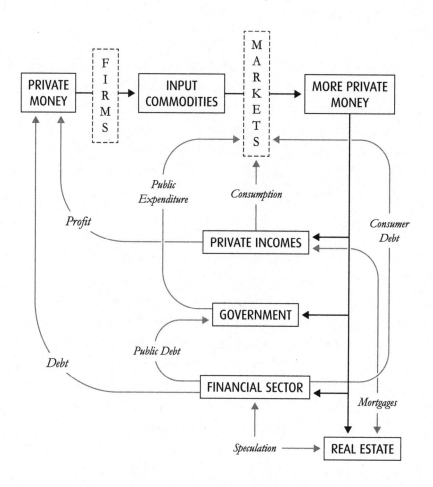

Figure 2: *Money and Circulation*

5. CRISES

Two main forces cause capitalism to enter into crises.

5.1 Falling rate of profit

Falling profits depress the capacity of firms to invest in new capital, consequently limiting future surplus value. At some point, the weakest firms go bankrupt. The workers fired as a result reduce their consumption which, subsequently, depresses further the profit of firms that just managed to hang on – some of which also go bankrupt thus precipitating a doom-loop, a domino effect of bankruptcies causing, and being amplified by, related financial and real estate sector slumps.[11]

5.2 Debt crises

During the good times, the financiers' rents rise geometrically – if not exponentially. Caught up in a gold-fever-like mentality, they lend burgeoning sums to capitalists – which they borrow from the future. At some point the present cannot produce enough value to repay the future, the bubble bursts, and the psychological pendulum swings the opposite way, causing financiers to go on a credit strike. The result is a domino effect of collapsing corporate, FIRE (finance, insurance and real estate) and, often, public debt.[12]

Note: Recessions are often self-correcting, e.g. wages and input prices fall so much during a slump that surviving firms (which now face less competition, courtesy of so many of their competitors having shut down) see their profit rate rise again. However, when the crisis is deep enough to cull banks and to depress capitalists' animal spirits, only state intervention can save capitalism – via stimulus (fiscal policy), loose monetary policy and bank/corporate bailouts.

6. SOCIAL CLASSES

6.1 Class – A group of persons in a community identified by their location within a system of social production in which some class (or
classes) succeed in appropriating part of the product of the experiential labour of members of another class (or classes).

6.2 Class system – The collective social expression of the way in which
exploitation is embodied in a social structure.

6.3 Class society – Any society built around a class system is a class
society. It is in the nature of every class society that one or more of
the numerically smaller classes, by owning and controlling the
dominant factor of production, manage to extract value from the
other classes; and, thus, to accumulate wealth and power.

6.4 Capitalism's class system – A capitalist class system comprises capitalists and proletarians (waged labourers), plus a middle class
(shopkeepers, salaried skilled workers, etc.) that is squeezed with
every capitalist crisis or technological revolution.

Note: Under feudalism, land was the dominant factor of production and ground rent (paid to landlords by peasants and vassals)
was the main income stream on which political and social power
was built. Feudal class societies contained a variety of subservient
classes (artisans, peasants, vassals, etc.) but only one dominant
factor of production (land) yielding a single ruling class (landlords) and a uniquely powerful income flow (ground rent). Under
capitalism, land was replaced as the dominant factor of production by capital, the fief was replaced by the market, and ground
rent was replaced by profit.

7. TYPES OF EXTRACTIVE POWER

Prior to capitalism, every system of authority relied on three types
of extractive power.

7.1 Brute Force: the power to command by exercising (or credibly threatening) different forms of physical violence.

7.2 Political (or Agenda Setting) Power: the capacity to determine (a) who is represented in the forums where collective decisions are reached; (b) what is being debated, discussed and decided upon in these forums; and (c) what issues remain unspoken, tacit, buried across society.

7.3 Soft (or Propaganda) Power: the power to shape what others think, are prepared to tolerate, to wish for and, ultimately, to do.

Capitalism introduced a fourth type of extractive power, which helped it reshape the world:

7.4 Capitalist Power: the power vested in owners of capital (i.e. capitalists) to command those lacking capital *voluntarily* to generate surplus value for the capitalists within their firms.

Note: Capitalist Power (7.4) extended beyond the confines of the capitalist firm and infected the pre-existing three types of extractive power. E.g. the capitalist class largely controlled the state's monopoly of lethal force (7.1), society's deliberative processes (7.2) and, via the media, the education system, the machinery of propaganda, etc. (7.3).

8. HOW THE TECHNOSTRUCTURE ENHANCED CAPITAL'S SECOND NATURE

The technostructure (see Chapter 2) developed two new economic sectors whose purpose was to modify the behaviour of workers and of consumers respectively. These highly professionalised *behavioural modification sectors* significantly enhanced capital's power (its second nature more precisely).

8.1 Labour Command Service Sector – Located in and around the workplace, these professionals applied well-researched, scientific management procedures to speed up the labour process and to squeeze more experiential labour out of a given quantity of commodity labour. Their techniques included Taylorist organisation of the factory floor, sophisticated surveillance, Fordist production lines, Japanese management practices (co-opting workers to the company's ideology), etc.

8.2 Consumer Command Service Sector – Brimming with advertisers, marketers, copywriters and creative types (epitomised in Chapter 3 by the fictional Don Draper), this sector helped maximise brand rents by manufacturing consumer desires for the large firms' branded products – thus underpinning their power over both consumers and smaller competitors lacking access to this sector.

The development of these two sectors was mirrored into two brand-new markets.

- Market for Professionalised Influencers – A new type of manager began to dominate the conglomerates, pushing aside the engineers who used to rise through the company's ranks. A whole market for their services, and for training them (e.g. the cult of the MBA), extended from traditional industrial sectors to Wall Street and even to public administration.
- Market for People's Attention – The Consumer Command Service Sector was dedicated to capturing the attention of television and radio audiences before selling it on to advertisers (see Chapter 2 – Attention markets and the Soviets' revenge).

Having access to these two command service sectors and markets, the technostructure secured for itself an inordinate double privilege: an asymmetric (soft) power to manipulate, and to modify, the behaviour of both workers and consumers.

TECHNOFEUDALISM

Just as capitalism pushed aside feudalism by replacing land with capital as the dominant factor of production, so too did techno-feudalism ride in to displace capitalism on the coat-tails of cloud capital – a mutation of (standard, terrestrial) capital.

9. CLOUD CAPITAL

Cloud capital is, physically, defined as the agglomeration of networked machinery, software, AI-driven algorithms and communications' hardware criss-crossing the whole planet and performing a wide variety of tasks, new and old, such as:

- Inciting billons of non-waged people (cloud serfs) to work for free (and often unconsciously) at replenishing cloud capital's own stock (e.g. to upload photos and videos on Instagram or TikTok, or submit film, restaurant and book reviews)
- Helping us switch off the lights while recommending to us books, films and holidays, etc., so impressively in tune with our interests that we become predisposed to other goods sold on cloud fiefs or platforms (e.g. Amazon. com), which are running on exactly the same digital network that helps us switch off the lights while recommending to us books, films and holidays, etc.

- Utilising AI and Big Data to command workers' labour (cloud proles) on the factory floor while driving the energy networks, the robots, the trucks, the automated production lines and the 3D printers that bypass conventional manufacturing

By automating the technostructure's two behaviour modification sectors (see 8.1 and 8.2), cloud capital has removed them from the economy's human-driven service economy and incorporated them fully into its machine network. The jobs performed, under the technostructure, by shop-floor managers, advertisers, marketers, etc. under Technofeudalism are now assigned to AI-driven algorithms incorporated fully into cloud capital.

In terms of the analysis under 1.3, which pertained to capital's two natures (see 1.3.1 and 1.3.2), cloud capital distinguishes itself from earlier forms of capital by adding a third nature to capital's original twin nature:

1.3.3 Cloud Capital's Third Nature: A produced means of behavioural modification and individuated command

Cloud capital's third nature straddles three types of algorithmic behaviour modification. One strand commands consumers to reproduce cloud capital (i.e. turns them into cloud serfs). A second strand commands waged labour to work harder (i.e. turns proletarians and members of the precariat into cloud proles). And a third strand replaces markets with cloud fiefs. In a sense, cloud capital's third nature grants its owners (the cloudalists) a great brand-new power to extract surplus value produced in the traditional capitalist sector – as Figure 3 on p. 239 illustrates.

More analytically, cloud capital's third nature furnishes it with the three functions or forms.

9.1   Produced Means of Commanding Labour (i.e. the automation of 8.4)

    9.1.1   Cloud Proles: Cloud-based devices entered the labour process (factories, warehouses, offices, call centres, etc.) replacing the Taylorist middle managers hitherto driving output gains and surplus value extraction in the workplace. The proletariat thus becomes more precarious and is increasingly marched to a quicker pace by cloud capital.

    9.1.2   Cloud Serfs: Persons unattached to any corporation (i.e. non-workers) choose to labour long and often hard, for free, to reproduce cloud capital's stock, e.g. with posts, videos, photos, reviews and lots of clicking that makes digital platforms more attractive to others.

Note: For the first time in history, capital has been (re)produced by unwaged labourers. Cloud capital's platforms make it easy for work to move out of the labour market into an economy that is disguised with the paraphernalia of gaming, chance and lotteries when, in reality, it is all about mechanical, repetitive, Fordist work. Digital spaces that appear modern, snazzy, friendly and neutral are in fact well-designed projects of cutting much of paid labour out of the labour market, making the wage optional and even altogether replacing it with a sequence of wagers.[13]

9.2   Produced Means of Extracting Cloud Rent from Capitalists for Access to Cloud Fiefs (achieved, partly, via the automation of 8.5)

As explained in Chapter 3 (see pp. 85–88, 'Wither markets, hello cloud fiefs'), ecommerce platforms like amazon.com or alibaba.com are not markets (defined in 1.0 and 3.4). The reason they cannot be thought of as markets is that the cloudalists' algorithms succeed in isolating every buyer from every other buyer, and every seller from every other seller. As a result, the cloudalist's algorithm concentrates in itself the power to match buyers and sellers – which is the exact opposite of what a market is meant to be: decentralised. Such power vested in the cloudalist's algorithm grants its owner the capacity to charge sellers (i.e. conventional capitalists) large amounts of rent (cloud rent) for access to customers.

> 9.2.1 Cloud Fiefs are digital trading platforms on which buyers and sellers are matched by the algorithms of cloud capital. While they look like markets, their perfect centralisation (achieved by the algorithm's power to match and to determine the full information set of each buyer and each seller) renders them a form of cloud fief belonging to whoever owns the algorithm or cloud capital which (a) built the platform and (b) attracts cloud serfs to play the role of buyers (as well as contributors to its cloud capital) and vassal capitalists in the role of sellers.

> 9.2.2 Vassal Capitalists are capitalist producers who, in order to sell their commodities, must pay cloud rent for access to the cloudalists' cloud fiefs.

> 9.2.3 Cloud Rent is the payment cloudalists extract from the vassal capitalists for access to cloud fiefs.

In summary, cloud capital's greatest accomplishment was increasingly to induct into its AI-algorithmic-digital network not only the processes of modifying workers' and consumers' behaviour in the interests of cloudalists but, also, the market itself – turning whole segments of the capitalist class into its vassals.

10. DISTRIBUTION UNDER TECHNOFEUDALISM

Figure 1 illustrated the distribution of exchange value under capitalism. Under technofeudalism, the capitalist sector continues (as it did under capitalism) to produce all of the economy's exchange value. However, the capitalist sector is now embedded into, and is subjugated within, the broader realm of cloud fiefs built on cloud capital. As cloud capital accumulates, due to the unpaid labour of cloud serfs and the cloud rents of the vassal capitalists, more and more of the surplus value generated in the capitalist sector is syphoned off in the form of more cloud rent to the cloudalists. Figure 3 illustrates this.

10.1 Universal Exploitation – Whereas capitalists can only exploit their employees, cloudalists benefit from universal exploitation, i.e. cloud serfs work for free to increase the stock of the cloud capital which allows cloudalists to appropriate more and more of the surplus value that the capitalists extract from employees already converted into cloud proles whose work is guided and sped up by cloud capital.

11. SUMMARY: THE MAJOR DIFFERENCES BETWEEN CAPITALISM AND TECHNOFEUDALISM

11.1 Cloud Capital – Cloud capital's third nature (see 1.3.3) made possible the full automation of the technostructure's service sectors (8.1 and 8.2) whose purpose was to modify, in the interest of capital, the behaviour of workers and consumers. The result was a new type of capital (cloud capital) which became a produced means of, on the one hand, commanding labour and, on the other, of extracting cloud rent from capitalists for access to consumers (9.1 and 9.2).

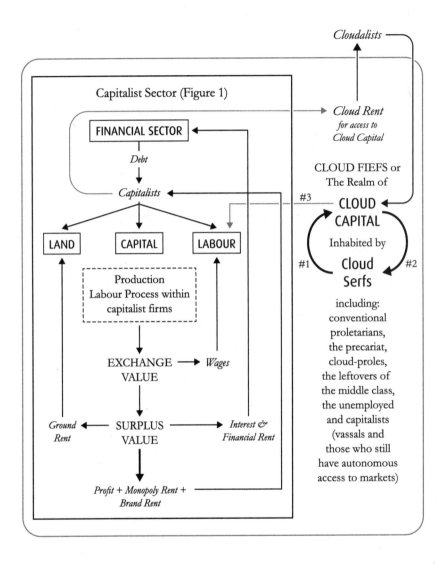

FIGURE 3: *The Production and Distribution of Value Under Technofeudalism*

#1 Cloud-serf, unpaid labour helps reproduce cloud capital.

#2 Cloud-capital modifies the desires, beliefs and propensities of cloud-serfs
    – including their consumer choices.

#3 Cloud-capital also speeds up the work rate of waged labour within the
    capitalist sector.

11.2 Profit and Markets Dethroned – Technofeudalism replaced capitalism's twin pillars – Profit (2.4 and 3.3) and Markets (1.0 and 3.4) – with its own twin pillars – Cloud Rent (9.2.3) and Cloud Fiefs (9.2.1).

11.3 Technofeudal Class System – Under technofeudalism, the cloudalists (a segment of the capitalist class who managed to accumulate considerable cloud capital) became our new ruling class, confining the rest of the capitalists (lacking sufficient access to cloud capital) to vassal class status (9.2.2). Meanwhile, waged workers are turning into increasingly precarious cloud proles (9.1.1) and almost everyone acts as a cloud serf (9.1.2) helping cloud capital accumulate and construct the cloud fiefs (9.2.1) that are replacing markets.

11.4 Capital Accumulation – Unlike standard, or terrestrial, capital which accumulated strictly within capitalist firms (4.1), albeit at rates dictated at the macroeconomic level (4.2), cloud capital accumulates at another two levels most forcefully: on the back of cloud-serf labour (9.1.2) provided by almost all of us. And, with massive funding directly from the West's main central banks – see Chapter 4.

11.5 A Fifth Type of Extractive Power – Cloud capital adds a new extractive power to the four pre-existing ones – brute (7.1), political (7.2), soft (7.3) and capitalist (7.4) – a cloudalist power vested in the owners of cloud capital with which to modify the behaviour of those who do not own or control cloud capital in a manner that permits massive surplus value produced in the capitalist sector to be directed to the cloudalists as cloud rent.

11.6 Crises – The accumulation of cloud capital amplifies the two forces that generated severe capitalist crises: the falling rate of profit (5.1) and the bursting private and public debt bubbles (5.2). Under technofeudalism, the decommodification of labour (cloud-serf labour) along with the depression of the income share of cloud proles combine to squeeze society's aggregate spending power or aggregate demand. Meanwhile, the channelling of more surplus value from the vassal capitalists to the cloudalists reduces investment in terrestrial capital; yet another negative influence on aggregate demand.

Note: Technofeudalism is synonymous with the universalisation of exploitation (see 10.1) and with the shrinking of the value base (in proportion to the rise of cloud rent's share of all incomes – see Figure 3). This dynamic accentuates the system's propensity to deeper and more frequent crises. As a result, the central banks that funded the initial accumulation of cloud capital (see Chapter 4) will be forced perpetually to print more and more monies to replace the role that profits and wages used to play under capitalism. But this only helps cloud capital accumulate further (since cloudalists will always have a greater capacity than every other class to appropriate the printed central bank money). In short, technofeudalism is condemned to exhibit a dynamic doom-loop more volatile and explosive than even that of capitalism.

Appendix 2

The Madness of Derivatives

It all began with an old, harmless idea. For decades, farmers were insuring themselves against falling prices by buying the right (or option) to sell next year's harvest at a pre-agreed, fixed price. It was nothing more than an insurance contract: the wheat farmer paid a premium to insure against a catastrophic drop in the price of wheat.

The first mutation of this idea into something more sinister was when the 'thing' that was being insured stopped being a thing (like wheat) and became a bet, a wager, a gamble. Consider Jack who is about to buy shares worth $1 million. Like the farmer who buys insurance to protect himself against a drastic fall in the price of wheat, Jack could buy from Jill a *get-me-out-of-here* option to sell his shares to Jill at, say, $800,000 (i.e. he limits his potential loss to $200,000). Like any form of insurance, if disaster does *not* strike (i.e. the shares' price does not fall more than 20 per cent, to below $800,000), Jack's insurance policy (or option) will pay him nothing. But if, say, Jack's shares shed 40 per cent of their value, Jack is covered for half of that loss. Not great but not terrible either.

These options (or derivatives) had been available under Bretton Woods. To mutate into something truly dangerous, though, Bretton Woods had to die first. Its death meant that bankers, liberated from their New Deal chains, were allowed to bet on the stock exchange first with other people's money and, later, with money they conjured up from thin air. Soon, Wall Street was going gangbusters, especially after 1982. Without even knowing why, finance's golden boys and girls began to see themselves as the invincible masters and mistresses of the universe. Under the influence of that feeling, they had an idea: instead of purchasing an *option to sell* shares (as an insurance in case the shares they were buying dropped in value), why not buy an *option to buy* even more shares? Sounds crazy? Perhaps. But the madness went unnoticed in the cacophony of all the money-making it enabled.

Here is what Jack would do: on top of spending $1 million on, say, a bundle of Microsoft shares, he would pay Jill another $100,000 for a guarantee that, in a year's time, she will sell him another such bundle of Microsoft shares for the same total price he paid today ($1 million). In their language, Jack would buy from Jill an *option to buy* more Microsoft shares in a year's time but at today's price. Why do that? Because if during the next twelve months Microsoft's shares were to rise by, say, 40 per cent, Jack would receive two gains: the $400,000 gain from the appreciation of the bundle of Microsoft shares he actually bought, plus another $400,000 from the *option to buy* a second such bundle of Microsoft shares at last year's lower price – an option that he can now sell to others for $400,000 without even having to buy that second bundle of shares himself. Jack's total net gain, considering he paid Jill $100,000 for the option, would come to $700,000: a much better return (64 per cent) to his $1.1 million expenditure than the return (40 per cent) from only buying $1 million of Microsoft shares.

In a Wall Street where the bulls dominated the bears for many consecutive years, and everything was going up, up and away, a contagion of unchecked greed (captured so well on celluloid by Oliver Stone's *Wall Street*) led the Jills and the Jacks to an even more radical idea: why buy shares at all? Why not buy only options? Here was their thinking: if Jack spent his $1.1 million only on *options to buy* Microsoft shares next year at today's share price, and the share price were to increase by 40 per cent, his net gain would be a stunning $3.3 million – an exorbitant 300 per cent rate of return! Jack, seeing this, decided to go all in: to borrow as many millions as he could to buy such options from Jill. Jill, seeing how much Jack made from the *options to buy* she had sold him, decided to copy him. Using the money she received from Jack, and a whole lot more that she borrowed, she bought similar *options to buy* from other traders.

You may well ask: were there no smart people in Wall Street to sound the alarm bells? Of course there were. But their warnings were drowned out. Month after month the Jills and the Jacks raked in gargantuan profits. Traders who spoke out against them were shunned as moaning losers. Managers who hardly understood the complexity of the derivatives that overfilled their coffers with money felt compelled to silence dissent. The dissenters had a choice: quit, which some did, or join in this *leverage* racket – a techno-euphemism for huge debt fuelling ridiculous bets. As long as the going was good, it was as if they had discovered an ATM in their living room which kept churning out unlimited cash without charging it to any bank account. All they had to do was borrow as if there were no tomorrow. Unsurprisingly, by 2007, ten times more money than humanity's total income had been placed on the roulette of, mostly, Wall Street and the City of London.

In this new Gilded Age that Nixon's Shock occasioned, the technostructure faced stiff competition for the best and brightest minds. Physics PhDs from the best schools, dazzling mathematicians, even artists and historians were flocking to Wall Street.

Power was shifting fast from the Fords, the Hiltons and the Drapers to Goldman Sachs, Bear Stearns and Lehman's. To catch up, large parts of the technostructure adapted by joining in. When auditors entered the bankrupted General Motors in 2009, after this financialisation bubble had burst, they discovered that a company famed for producing cars and trucks had been transformed into a hedge fund buying and selling options – with some car production on the side to keep up appearances.

Influences, Readings and

Acknowledgements

One influence that led me to technofeudalism – the word – came from John Kenneth Galbraith's 1967 book *The New Industrial State* (Princeton University Press). In it, Galbraith coined the term technostructure to denote the de facto merger of US government departments and corporations whose interchangeable band of professional managers, marketers, analysts, financiers and engineers stood out as a class quite distinct from capitalists and workers. While Galbraith's technostructure never threatened to undermine capitalism (indeed, it did the opposite – see Chapter 2), there are clear trajectories leading from it to our technofeudal order half a century later (see Chapters 3 and 4).

By 2018, I was already testing the waters with my technofeudal hypothesis in various papers and talks. Meanwhile, the debates on the impact of Big Tech were reinforced by the notion of surveillance capitalism made popular by Shoshana Zuboff's book *The Age of Surveillance Capitalism: The Fight for a Human Future and the New Frontier of Power* (Public Affairs). Two years later, Cédric Durand added to the excitement with his *Technoféodalisme: Critique de l'Économie Numérique* (Zones).

Both Zuboff and Durand treat Big Tech as monopoly capitalists whose digital platforms (e.g. Facebook, Amazon) function like utilities (e.g. electricity providers, water and sewage corporations, railway networks or phone companies), except that Big Tech use the cloud to harvest our data so as to boost their monopoly power over us. While sympathetic to their thesis, I was convinced that a lot more was going on than Silicon Valley capitalists merely boosting their market power over us by means of cloud-based surveillance.

One book from which I drew much courage that I was not wrong to believe that something more fundamental was in play, and that capitalism itself was in question, is McKenzie Wark's 2019 exquisite *Capital Is Dead: Is This Something Worse?* (Verso). I cannot recommend it too strongly. Many of my ideas resonated loudly with hers, except perhaps one: Wark writes of a new 'vectoralist' class in control of a vector that connects a supplier of materials to all stages of production and distribution in a manner that undermines, and usurps, capital. That's not how I saw it. What she refers to as a vector choking capital seemed to me a new mutation of capital – a cloud capital so virulent that it created a new ruling class with feudal-like powers to extract wealth.

Readers who know me even a little will not be surprised by the *Star Trek* reference I am about to make. Believe it or not, my term cloud capital harks back to the twenty-first episode of the third season (originally screened on 28 February 1969) of the original series entitled 'The Cloud Minders'. Written by Margaret Armen (based on a story by David Gerrold and Oliver Crawford), the episode unfolds on Ardana, a planet where a ruling class lives luxuriously in Stratos – a city floating motionlessly atop the planet's clouds. Meanwhile all labour is performed on the ground, and in underground tunnels, by the Troglytes whose minds are continually poisoned by a noxious gas which placates and stupefies them. The temptation to make the leap from *Star Trek*'s cloud minders to technofeudalism's cloud capital proved impossible to resist. Then, in 2022, I felt vindicated when Brett Scott published his excellent neo-Luddite book, railing against plastic and digital money, entitled *Cloudmoney: Cash, Cards, Crypto and the War for our Wallets* (The Bodley Head).

Besides McKenzie Wark, Cory Doctorow is another author whose arguments and ideas are closest to mine. I highly recommend anything he has written on his blog and in various magazines (e.g. *Wired*) plus, of course, the 2022 book he co-authored with Rebecca Giblin entitled *Chokepoint Capitalism: How Big Tech and Big Content Captured Creative Labor Markets and How We'll Win Them Back* (Beacon Press).

Last but not least I must thank my editor Will Hammond, with whom working is such an unalloyed joy, and Judith Meyer, a friend and comrade to whom I owe much of the little I know about modern algorithms, coding, cloud tech et al.

Notes

1. Hesiod's Lament

1 9:360
2 174–200
3 Karl Marx, speech at the anniversary of the *People's Paper*, 1856.
4 The Communist Manifesto 1848
5 1865
6 1844
7 1848

2. Capitalism's Metamorphoses

1 https://time.com/mad-men-history/
2 The Bretton Woods agreement was named after the town in New Hampshire where the international conference which led to the said agreement took place.
3 To be more precise, Nixon announced the rescindment of the United States' obligation (under the Bretton Woods system) to redeem any quantity of US dollars for gold at the fixed price of $35 per ounce. However, in effect, he was ending the fixed

exchange rate between the dollar and the currencies of Europe and Japan. To stunned European leaders, his Texan Treasury Secretary, John Connally, uttered the inimitable words: 'The dollar is our currency and your problem.'

4 See Appendix 2 for a full explanation of how these derivatives worked.

3. Cloud Capital

1 Karl Marx, who recounts Peel's story in *Capital*, Vol. 1, put it this way: 'Unhappy Mr. Peel who provided for everything except the export of English modes of production to Swan River!'

2 See K. Marx and F. Engels, *The Communist Manifesto*.

3 See Chapter 6 of *Talking to My Daughter: About the Economy*.

4 Neural networks were pioneered by Frank Rosenblatt at Cornell Aeronautical Laboratory. More recently, such networks have managed to synthesise antibiotics (e.g. Halicin) by crunching huge data sets connecting molecules and their potential to impede bacterial proliferation – and all that by an algorithm that knows nothing about the chemistry of the bacteria the antibiotic is meant to annihilate!

5 For a pertinent account, see https://www.theverge.com/2019/4/25/18516004/amazon-warehouse-fulfillment-centers-productivity-firing-terminations.

4. The Rise of the Cloudalists and the Demise of Profit

1   https://www.theguardian.com/business/2020/aug/12/uk-
    economy-covid-19-plunges-into-deepest-slump-in-history.

2   https://markets.ft.com/data/indices/tearsheet/historical?s=
    FTSE:FSI.

3   Interestingly, the first boisterous digital markets that emerged
    within video game communities were, in some ways, a liber-
    tarian's delight. Producers produced freely, engaged freely with
    buyers who also associated freely with each other – while the
    company stood back, promoted none of the products on sale
    and simply got a cut from every sale (the one aspect of the set-
    up that a rent-hating, purist libertarian would have detested).
    In sharp contrast, on trading sites like Amazon or Alibaba
    buyers and sellers enjoy none of these freedoms to associate, to
    even see the same things, while online – the algorithm instead
    banning buyers and sellers from autonomous communica-
    tions with one another and selecting itself what each one of
    them can, and cannot, see or do.

4   The European Union proved the most enthusiastic champion
    of austerity, followed at some distance by two different UK
    governments that also imposed self-defeating austerity – espe-
    cially that of Cameron and Osborne after 2010. Meanwhile in
    the United States, though President Obama made a big deal
    out of his stimulus programme, the reality begged to differ:
    not only was his federal stimulus too small in relation to the
    drop in demand for goods, services and labour, but, more
    pertinently, it was cancelled out by massive expenditure cuts

at the level of states whose income had collapsed (primarily because of the massive fall in real estate prices).

5 Note that it was no aberration. Between 2009 and 2022, the official interest rates stayed negative in the eurozone, Scandinavia, Switzerland, Norway and Japan. And it was not just the official rate. During that period loans amounting to more than $18 trillion (which was more the total annual income of Europe and Japan) paid lenders negative interest rates.

6 Bank bailouts do not need to be as corrupt as those following the crash of 2008. In 1992 Scandinavian banks failed and states stepped in to save them. But they did not save the bankers. Instead, they kicked them out, nationalised the banks, appointed new directors and, years later, sold them to new owners. Similarly in South Korea after the 1998 South East Asian banking crisis. In contrast, after 2008 in the United States and Europe, with the exception of Lehman Brothers, the central banks saved the bankrupt bankers, prompting me to coin the term 'bankruptocracy' – the new, post-2008, reality where a Western banker's power is analogous to the size of his bank's losses! See my *The Global Minotaur*, Zed Books, 2011.

7 How does the central bank do this in practice? You and I cannot have an account with our central bank. Only bankers can. All the central bank (like the Bank of England or the Fed) needs to do is to authorise an overdraft by typing in a sum in the account that a private bank (like Barclays or Bank of America) keeps at its central bank. Legally, for this to happen, the private bank must post collateral, in the form of monies owed to it by government (bonds) or privateers (mortgages, credit card debt, private bonds). But during times of financial

stress, when everyone owes to everyone else and no one can pay, the central bank accepts collateral not even worth the paper it was written on.

8 The nominally independent central bankers, naturally, needed to justify the banker bailouts by appealing to the public interest. So, they explained, to 'restore confidence' and 'stimulate investment' they had no choice but to send torrents of cash the bankers' way. The situation was so bad, they told the public, that the central bank was compelled to hand money to banks to pass it on to businesses to invest.

9 To give another example, during the pandemic, for a day or so, the price of oil also dropped below zero. It was strange but understandable: because most of us were locked down, demand for petrol and diesel oil buckled. Suddenly oil reservoirs overflowed and their owners, who had long-term obligations to buy certain quantities of oil every week independently of demand for oil, were forced to pay people to take that excess oil away.

10 https://www.pionline.com/money-management/blackrock-aum-recedes-10-trillion-high; https://corporate.vanguard.com/content/corporatesite/us/en/corp/who-we-are/sets-us-apart/facts-and-figures.html;   https://newsroom.statestreet.com/press-releases/press-release-details/2022/State-Street-Reports-First-Quarter-2022-Financial-Results/default.aspx. The total of $22 trillion of shares and derivatives controlled by the Big Three amounts to more than half of the aggregate value of all shares for companies listed in the New York Stock Exchange (about $38 trillion). Before long, analysts writing in the *Boston University Law Review*, predicted that the Big Three could control as much as 40 per cent of shareholder votes in the US.

11 Approximately one year's US gross national product, once the capacity of Wall Street to turbocharge actual central bank (i.e. Fed, ECB, etc.) credits is taken into account.

12 For example, Vanguard is the largest shareholder in both Ford and General Motors. How would Vanguard benefit from allowing real competition between the two?

5. What's in a Word?

1 Taken from an essay entitled 'The Power of Words', inspired by Weil's experience of the Spanish Civil War.

2 The Napoleonic Wars disrupted the importation of grains to Britain, boosting prices and benefitting the landlords who, naturally, sought to extend this windfall after the end of the wars. To do so, they enacted the Corn Laws that banned grain imports after the wartime blockades had ended.

3 Rosa Luxemburg warned us that socialism was not inevitable, and that barbarism was just as likely, in a pamphlet she wrote in her prison cell in 1915. Entitled *The Crisis in German Social Democracy*, it is better known as *The Junius Pamphlet* – a powerful critique of the pro-Great War leadership of the German Social Democratic Party.

4 https://www.cnbc.com/2021/10/31/ula-inside-jeff-bezos-first-investment-in-indonesian-e-commerce-.html.

5 David Ricardo, an early-nineteenth-century London banker and famed free-marketeer economist, was clear on this: any rise of rent as a share of all income is bound to reduce investment, lower demand for goods and stunt growth. See his *On the Principles of Political Economy and Taxation*, 1817.

6 https://www.theguardian.com/business/2020/oct/07/covid-19-crisis-boosts-the-fortunes-of-worlds-billionaires.

7 See Appendix 1.

8 In previous chapters, I too spoke of central bankers poisoning money through their practice of printing large amounts and channelling it to the financiers. However, I also made the point that it was the combination of money printing on behalf of the bankers and austerity for the many that poisoned money – not just the money printing. It fascinates me that mainstream commentators keep quiet about the austerity part (clearly because they agree with it) and concentrate their arrows at central bankers for printing money. What they neglect to tell us is what they would have done differently after 2008. Would they agree with the only alternative to what the central bankers actually did, i.e. annulling unpayable (public and private) debts, nationalising failed banks, and printing money to fund a basic income that lifts all boats at once during the Great Recession? Of course they wouldn't. Thus, their anti-central bank philippics are the epitome of hypocrisy.

9 https://www.ft.com/content/65713f3f-394c4b31-bafe-043dec3dc04d.

10 https://www.reuters.com/markets/europe/bank-england-buy-long-dated-bonds-suspends-gilt-sales-2022-09-28/. This sharp and brief crisis spelled the end of the shortest tenure of any British prime minister – that of Liz Truss, who had just announced the intention to add considerably to the UK's debt on behalf of Britain's richest. The reason the bottom fell from the UK's bond (or gilt) market, in response to Truss's announcement, was a landmine buried in the City during the years of socialism-for-the-bankers: the derivatives UK pension funds

had massively invested in, to hedge against inflation and higher
interest rates – derivatives they could not afford except by borrowing against their stock of UK government gilts. So, when
the news came in that Truss was planning to issue more gilts to
pay for large tax cuts, without frontloading austerity, the price
of gilts fell and, suddenly, pension funds had to post more cash
to cover the debt they had incurred to buy the derivatives. In a
state of panic, they sold the only liquid asset they had: gilts!
And so the doom-loop began until the Bank of England inter-
vened and Liz Truss left 10 Downing Street in disgrace.

6. Technofeudalism's Global Impact: the New Cold War

1 https://www.nytimes.com/2022/10/07/business/economy/
   biden-chip-technology.html.
2 There were also secondary ill effects on American and Chinese
   workers: as the Chinese capitalists' profits flooded American
   real estate, US house prices rose, further heightening American workers' suffering and making them more vulnerable to
   the toxic dream of an even larger mortgage that allowed them
   the fantasy that they 'own their own home'. Meanwhile, the
   higher American net imports pushed the Chinese capitalists'
   dollar profits, which were then re-exported back to the US,
   the less the total income left within the Chinese economy for
   the masses that produced it.
3 It was not just the US economy that massive Chinese investments benefitted. When the eurozone's weaker economies
   begin to topple like dominoes (first Greece, then Ireland,
   Portugal, Spain, Italy, Cyprus, etc.), German manufacturing

exports were diverted from those fallen markets to China – where demand was kept high by China's immense investment expenditures, e.g. the thousands of miles of ultra-fast railway lines that were constructed in less than three years.

4 10 January 2023, when I wrote this sentence.

5 American Big Tech is playing catch-up with its Chinese counterpart the best way it can. Because it must face an already formed mega-power in Wall Street (whose monopoly over finance it cannot directly challenge), Silicon Valley is cosying up to finance. For instance, Microsoft struck a deal with the London Stock Exchange Group, its third such alliance. Earlier, Google had invested $1 billion into a ten-year cloud computing agreement with Chicago-based CME. Not to be outdone, Amazon Web Services (AWS) went into business with New York's Nasdaq which agreed to move one of its US options exchanges on to AWS.

6 Michael Pettis, 'Will the Chinese renminbi replace the US dollar?', *Review of Keynesian Economics*, Vol. 10, No. 4, Winter 2022, pp. 499–512. See also his *Trade Wars Are Class Wars: How Rising Inequality Distorts the Global Economy and Threatens International Peace* (co-authored with Matthew C. Klein), Yale University Press, 2020.

7 E.g. Saddam Hussein, after he fell out with Washington, and Iran, Venezuela, of course Cuba and, after the war in Ukraine broke out, Russia.

8 https://www.theverge.com/2018/8/13/17686310/huawei-zte-us-government-contractor-ban-trump https://www.reuters.com/article/us-usa-tiktok-ban-q-a-idINKBN2692UO.

9 On 22 September 1985, the United States, Japan, West Germany, France and Britain signed the Plaza Accord. The

agreement's stated purpose was to devalue the US dollar in an attempt to rein in the Minotaur: to contain America's trade deficit. While the Plaza Accord did succeed in devaluing the dollar vis-à-vis the yen by more than 50% (within two years of its signing), the Accord's real purpose was subtler: the aim was, at least in part, *to prevent Japan from becoming a rentier nation* in opposition to US rentier capitalism. As the yen climbed, the Japanese economy went into a sustained slowdown. In response, Japan's central bank pumped a lot of new money into Japan's banks, causing massive bubbles to build up in real estate. When in the early 1990s the authorities tried to deflate that bubble, by increasing interest rates, house and office prices crashed. The nation's banks ended up with huge loans on their books that no one could repay. For the first time since the mid-1930s, an advanced capitalist economy had been caught in a recessionary *liquidity trap* – a precursor to what happened after 2008 across the West. Then, Japan's central bank inaugurated the policy of industrial-scale money-printing (euphemistically called 'quantitative easing') which, after 2008, was adopted by every one of the West's central banks.

10 Western central banks had, in the past, frozen the funds of central banks, e.g. Venezuela's and Afghanistan's. But, the seizure of the Russian central bank's money was the first time money belonging to a major central bank was actually confiscated.

11 Such as SWIFT, the international messaging system making the global movements of money possible. Though owned by a Belgian outfit, Washington has the final word on who is allowed to use SWIFT and who is banned.

12 The US Federal Reserve and the European Central Bank are, naturally, dead keen to create their own digital currencies to compete with China's digital yuan. But they face a steep obstacle that the People's Bank of China did not: frenzied opposition from the Wall Street and Frankfurt banks, who understandably see a digital dollar or euro as the devil incarnate (since it ends their monopoly over the payments system). China's private bankers did not like their central bank's digital yuan either. But unlike in the United States or in Europe, where the bankers dictate the law of the land to politicians and bureaucrats, in China the bankers are dictated to by the Communist Party. Once the party decided that the digital yuan was the way to go, it was game over.

13 The local population, naturally, was very keen to get their hands on the products produced domestically. The problem was they could not afford them, given the low wages that capitalists could get away with. In the language of John Maynard Keynes, it was not lack of demand but lack of effective demand.

14 See my *The Global Minotaur.*

15 E.g. the creation of the European Monetary System in the 1970s, the single market in the 1980s, the euro itself in the 1990s, the European Stability Mechanism in the 2010s, the post-pandemic Recovery Fund in the 2020s, etc. Curiously, Europe's grandest failures materialised not despite but because of these grandiose projects: for my account of this litany of grand failures, see *And the Weak Suffer What They Must?*, Nation Books, 2016, and *Adults in the Room* , Farrar, Straus & Giroux, 2018.

16 A proper monetary union requires not only a common central bank but also a common Treasury — with a capacity to issue

substantial common debt (i.e. eurobonds, the European equivalent of US Treasury bills). Indeed, if the EU were to create a common Treasury issuing proper eurobonds, then Chinese capitalists exporting to the EU would be able to invest their euro profits in eurobonds, instead of dollar-denominated assets like US Treasury Bills. That would turn the euro into a reserve currency challenging the dollar's supremacy. But then the US would find it harder to finance its trade deficit, which is the source of demand for the net exports – and capitalist profits – of European surplus economies, like Germany's and Holland's. Is it any wonder that Northern Europe's capitalists and governments oppose the completion of Europe's monetary union?

17 Europe's energy prices are not the only issue. By cutting itself off Russian natural gas, it has become reliant on liquified natural gas coming from the United States. This means that a larger chunk of European capitalist profits will have to be recycled to the United States, though not as US assets belonging to European capitalists but, instead, as US assets belonging to US companies. The Dark Deal that kept European capitalists happy has been dealt another blow by Europe's need to switch from Russian to American natural gas.

18 The European Union's strategic irrelevance can be gleaned via a question: when, eventually, peace talks over Ukraine begin, and the United States insists that the EU pays the huge sums necessary for Ukraine's reconstruction, who will represent the EU in those talks? Eastern, Baltic and Nordic EU governments do not trust Paris or Berlin to do so, believing them to be too soft on Putin. But Berlin and Paris control EU funds. The EU will, of course, do as Washington says and pay

for Ukraine. But without serious EU representation in the talks. Taxation without representation at a continental scale!

19 The difference with the 1970s and 80s was that, back then, the Global South's pain was mainly due to US interest rates rising from 4 per cent to 20 per cent. Today, US interest rates have increased far less. However, the Global South's pain is just as bad as in the 1970s and 80s because the dollar appreciated by 15 per cent. Taken together, the dollar's appreciation and the rise in US interest rates, brings the current pain to the same level as that of the 1970s and 80s.

20 Vendor financing means that the seller provides the buyer with the loan to buy what the seller is selling. For example, when Volkswagen or General Motors arranges the loan with which you can afford to buy their car. The same often applies at the national economy level, e.g. when banks in London or New York lend the government or importers of Lebanon, Egypt, Sri Lanka the money to buy Western warships, raw materials or even run-of-the-mill consumer goods.

21 Here is what they do: to reduce their losses from a fall in electricity prices tomorrow, they bet serious money that the price will fall tomorrow. But because they do not want to use money they have, they borrow money to place these bets using as collateral electricity that has not been produced yet. If prices fall, their bet wins and they are compensated for the loss of revenue now that electricity prices fell. But when in 2022 electricity prices went through the roof, the financiers against whom they bet that prices would fall demanded a lot more collateral in exchange for keeping their bets alive. So the electricity companies had to sell a lot more of their future electricity to raise more collateral. That reduced the

price of the future electricity which, in turned, pushed down their shares to such a level that they needed to post more collateral to back their bets. A vicious, demonic cycle had begun from which they could only get out with the help of a government bailout.

22 Do note, however, that the main drivers of globalisation's effect on incomes were China, South Korea and, to a lesser degree, the rest of South East Asia. If we take China and South Korea out of the statistics on the positive impact of globalisation upon world poverty, very little remains to support the hypothesis that globalisation defeated poverty. This is ironic, and a nuisance to free-marketeers (who, naturally, want to claim globalisation as proof of the superiority of free-market capitalism), since China's conversion into an economic powerhouse happened *because* Beijing resisted the neoliberals' recommendation that financial markets should be deregulated and that the Chinese state should desist from investment planning.

23 See Kathrin Hille, 'Foxconn to raise salaries 20% after suicides', *Financial Times*, 29 May 2010; and Saloni Jain and Khushboo Sukhwani, 'Farmer Suicides in India: A Case of Globalisation Compromising on Human Rights', *Defending Human Rights and Democracy in the Era of Globalization*, IGI Global, 2017.

24 See Anne Case and Angus Deaton, *Deaths of Despair and the Future of Capitalism*, Princeton University Press, 2020.

25 In *Nineteen Eighty-Four*, George Orwell imagined three super-states vying for, and failing to achieve, global domination: Oceania, Eurasia and Eastasia.

26 Jack Ma is the Chinese equivalent of Jeff Bezos, with splashes of Warren Buffett thrown in. He founded and led Alibaba, Amazon's Chinese competitor, and the Ant Group, a cloud

finance company – among many others. When President Xi wanted to signal to Chinese cloudalists that their power was about to be curtailed, he targeted Jack Ma to make a point. In 2018 Ma was 'encouraged' to step down from Alibaba, and in 2021 he was forced to relinquish control of the Ant Group. Meanwhile, the Chinese government leaked to the press that Jack Ma was not an isolated target but, instead, signalled the authorities' determination to rein in cloudalists.

7. Escape from Technofeudalism

1 Stelarc's performance, entitled *Movatar*, was part of 2000 CYBERCULTURES and took place at the Casula Power-house, Casula, Australia.

2 For more on this, see *Talking to My Daughter*.

3 John Maynard Keynes once famously used the example of a beauty contest to explain the impossibility of ever knowing the 'true' value of shares. Stock-market participants are unin-terested in judging who the prettiest contestant is. Instead, their choice is based on a prediction of who average opinion believes is the prettiest, and what average opinion thinks average opinion is – thus ending up like cats chasing after their own tails. Keynes's beauty contest sheds light on the tragedy of today's young.

4 See Johann Hari, *Stolen Focus: Why You Can't Pay Attention*, Bloomsbury, 2022.

5 A good example is Tony Blair's government under which the National Health Service saw an increase in its funding paid for by a small cut of the burgeoning profits of the City of

London – at least until the City of London crashed and burned in 2007/8, leading to huge taxpayer bailouts of banks and bankers.

6 In a world where marginal costs (i.e. the cost of providing one more unit of something, e.g. another minute of broadband, another video to stream, another ebook) are tending to zero, prices vanish and serious money can only be made by charging cloud rents (e.g. money to promote one's post on Facebook or the 35 per cent of revenues sellers are charged by Amazon to sell their stuff).

7 Cory Doctorow, author and Big Tech critic, put it well: 'Working for the platform can be like working for a boss who takes money out of every paycheck for all the rules you broke, but who won't tell you what those rules are because if he told you that, then you'd figure out how to break those rules without him noticing and docking your pay. Content moderation is the only domain where security through obscurity is considered a best practice.'

8 In the 1990s and 2000s, mobile telephone companies tried hard to prevent regulators from forcing *interoperability* upon them – to grant customers the right to phone, at no extra cost, numbers on a competing company's network; or to leave while keeping their phone number. By enforcing interoperability, regulators succeeded in creating a lot more competition between telecom companies and lowering prices. The one thing cloudalists fear is cloud interoperability, i.e. allowing their users to switch to another cloud fief without losing their own data, ebooks, chat histories, photos, music, etc. However, given the complexity of personal data users would like to transfer (as opposed to one telephone number and a contacts list), it is easy to see why cloudalists are not worried.

9 In the 1950s and 60s, the demands of Palestinians, Kurds and Western Saharans were met with conservative diatribes disputing the moral basis of their right to self-determination. Similarly, the demands for democracy by the peoples of Latin America, Egypt, South Korea, etc. were resisted on the basis of Burkean arguments that their societies had not yet developed the social conventions and institutions ready to act as democracy's pillars. After 1991, however, these conservative doubts about statehood and democracy vanished – selectively, of course, in former Yugoslavia, with the invasion of Afghanistan and Iraq performed in the name of democratising the Middle East – all with NATO troops in tow.

10 The post, which was uploaded on 31 October 2008, was entitled 'Bitcoin: A Peer-to-Peer Electronic Cash System'.

11 I have borrowed this example from Nicholas Shaxson's *The Curse of Finance: How global finance is making us all poor*, The Bodley Head, 2018.

12 Here I am referring to the Ethereum cryptocurrency which, unlike the original Bitcoin, allows participants not just to make payments but also to transmit other types of communications, e.g. votes, digital contracts, etc.

13 Here is how Nakamoto summed up the peer-to-peer verification process in his original 2008 paper: 'Nodes work all at once with little coordination. They do not need to be identified, since messages are not routed to any particular place and only need to be delivered on a best effort basis. Nodes can leave and re-join the network at will, accepting the proof-of-work chain as proof of what happened while they were gone. They vote with their CPU power, expressing their acceptance of valid blocks by working on extending them and rejecting invalid blocks by

refusing to work on them. Any needed rules and incentives can be enforced with this consensus mechanism.'

14 According to the *Financial Times*, Goldman Sachs has joined forces with the Hong Kong Monetary Authority, with the Bank for International Settlements and other financial institutions. Their joint project is entitled 'Genesis' and seeks to deploy blockchain to help green bond purchasers track the linked carbon credits over time. The World Bank is also doing something similar using a blockchain system called 'Chia'.

15 Back in 2014, preparing tools that would help a future progressive Greek government create a payments system outside the control of the European Central Bank and the systemic banks, I had put forward a design for a blockchain-based payments system of what I called fiscal money. A year later, I was Greece's finance minister and worked, under the radar, to implement that design. Unfortunately, the then prime minister vetoed its activation, surrendered to the international financial establishment and, thus, gave me no alternative other than to resign. See my *Adults in the Room*.

16 See Paschal Donohoe's review of *Talking to My Daughter*, *Irish Times*, 4 November 2017.

17 Published by The Bodley Head in 2020.

18 And here is my answer to the aforementioned Irish finance minister who assumed that my intention to end share markets and the ownership of capital by private investors is inimical to entrepreneurship initiative and innovation.

19 At the time of writing, in April 2023, even though central banks are meant to print no new monies because of their stated goal to fight the Great Inflation, a string of bank failures has forced them to print billions to support bailouts. As

explained in Chapter 5, after 2008, central bank money has replaced capitalist profits as the system's fuel.

20 Note that these two levies are in the spirit of the International Clearing Union (based on a currency called the Bancor, instead of my Kosmos) proposed by John Maynard Keynes at the 1944 Bretton Woods Conference, which established the post-war financial system – a proposal that was unceremoniously ditched by the United States's representative who, predictably, imposed the US dollar at the centre of global finance.

21 The idea of a Citizens' Assembly that works in parallel with Parliament is, of course, not mine. Ireland established such an assembly (called An Tionól Saoránach, or We the Citizens). It proved pivotal in debating abortion and formulating the referendum question that, with Parliament's approval, was put to the people of Ireland. See also *Against Elections: The Case for Democracy* (The Bodley Head, 2016) by David Van Reybrouck for a detailed account of how citizens' assemblies could be used for national governance as a whole.

22 Since *Another Now* was published, a number of people who built the Progressive International mounted precisely such an international campaign under the banner #MakeAmazonPay.

23 Or, to coin pseudo-scientific terms, moving from a maximin strategy (maximising personal sacrifice for a minimal personal gain) to a minimax strategy (minimising personal sacrifice for a maximal personal gain).

Appendix 1. The Political Economy of Technofeudalism

1 For a brief (and not too technical) introduction to the contested
  terrain that is economics, the reader may consult my 1998 book
  entitled *Foundations of Economics: A beginner's companion* (Routledge). Readers of a more masochistic disposition may enjoy a
  heftier, and more technical, volume I co-authored with Joseph
  Halevi and Nicholas Theocarakis entitled *Modern Political Economics: Making sense of the post-2008 world* (Routledge, 2011).
2 Traditionally, within the circles of political economics, experiential value was known as use value; a confusing term
  because wise people can – indeed, *should* – assign great subjective value to things that are ends in themselves, that – in
  other words – have no use or utility, e.g. great art and beauty,
  knowledge for its own sake, the thrill of climbing a mountain
  just because it is there. Thus, my term 'experiential value' – i.e.
  the value one derives from any positive, wholesome, pleasur-
  able, satisfying experience, useful or not. (NB Neoclassical
  economists refer to experiential value as utility – following
  the lead of Jeremy Bentham.)
3 In classical political economics (e.g. Adam Smith, David
  Ricardo, Karl Marx), what I call *experiential labour* is referred
  to simply as *labour*. I add the adjective *experiential* in order to
  distinguish it (labour-as-an-experiential-activity) from
  labour-as-a-commodity. See *commodity labour* – which classical economists referred to as *labour power*. In short, while
  classical political economists made the distinction between
  labour and *labour power*, I find it less confusing (and more

enlightening) to define the two natures of labour as *experiential labour* and *commodity labour.*

4 By surplus value we mean *surplus exchange value*, since experiential value is purely subjective and personal, and thus cannot be surplus to anything.

5 To be a little more precise, we should be calling this monopsony rent (since the employer is buying commodity labour as a monopsonist).

6 Sellers get away with charging mark-ups (i.e. monopoly rents) in proportion to their power to 'corner the market' (or to 'gouge' the consumer). In highly competitive markets, monopoly rent tends to zero. Put differently, the more monopolised the market for a commodity, the more its price exceeds the value equivalent of the total experiential labour infused in its production – since any commodity's exchange value (1.1.2) equals the total experiential labour (1.2.1) infused in its production.

7 Profit emerged as the main economic driver only after capitalism deposed feudalism. Under feudalism, it was ground rent that functioned as society's economic driver. Profit was, of course, always present and always welcome, except that it did not become society's main driver until capital replaced land as the main source of power. See Chapter 4 of *Talking to My Daughter* for more.

8 Bankers, and other related types of financiers, create loans from thin air by an audacious transfer of future values to the present, to be invested in capitalist endeavours that will hopefully produce enough value to repay the . . . future, with interest too!

9 Unlike feudalism, which followed the pattern production →distribution→financialisation (i.e. peasants produced grain, the landlords collected their share and, only then, was surplus sold to markets to accumulate money that was to be lent out), capitalism reversed that temporal sequence: debt (i.e. financialisation) comes first (in the sense that business must secure financing first), distribution follows (e.g. the capitalist signs wage, rental and financial contracts), and only then does production begin. See Chapter 3 of *Talking to My Daughter* for more.

10 John Maynard Keynes's phrase to capture the collective mood (or mass psychology) of the capitalists whose collective investment expenditure determines the overall level of demand.

11 Karl Marx argued that, all other things being equal, capital accumulation causes the profit rate to fall in the long term because, as production becomes more capital intensive, each unit of output contains less human experiential labour within it. Consequently, the exchange value of each unit of output follows a path of secular decline. Inevitably, the profit rate must follow suit – downwards!

12 Hyman Minsky, building on the work of John Maynard Keynes, demonstrated how financial instability can be caused by periods of financial stability (which, after a while, encourages hitherto risk-averse financiers to start taking stupid risks).

13 There is indeed a category of workers who fall into a grey zone where payment for work beneficial to cloudalists is considered an optional extra. Its origins are to be found in mass multi-player video games where systems of quasi-payments were developed before spreading to many digital platforms or cloud fiefs. Initially, gamers' own behaviour breathed

spontaneously exchange value into certain relative scarce digital artefacts within their gaming environment (e.g. a particular sword or helmet). Soon, they were rewarded by the corporation behind the game with coveted digital items – the first inklings of the NFTs that became all the rage outside the gaming communities in 2020. Later, corporations found ways to 'gamify' work that added to their cloud capital. Like Amazon preferring to refer to its workers as 'associates', these workers are not called workers but, instead, 'players', 'users', 'taskers', etc. To keep them working hard on its behalf, cloud capital (e.g. Mechanical Turk, Amazon's cloud sweatshop, where workers in 2020 made less than \$2 per hour while 90 per cent of tasks paid less than \$0.10 per task) uses a plethora of non-monetary, token-based payments and, crucially, on-screen rankings in order to motivate almost Stakhanovite levels of competition between workers.

Index

imbalance levy, 204, 269n20
imperialism, 168, 171
India, 151, 170, 171, 173–74
ancient, 8
neoliberalism, 116
indignados, 197
individualism, possessive, 182, 187
Indonesia, 130–31
Industrial Revolution, 8, 23, 69–70, 120
First, 8, 69–70
Second, 8, 99
inequality, ix, 13, 24, 41, 51, 59
post-2008, 102
inflation, 20, 34, 41, 103–6, 139–41, 144,
145–46
and the Ukraine war, 117, 121
See also Great Inflation (2022–)
influencers, professionalized, 233
innovation, 8, 34, 108, 135, 196, 201,
215
Instacart, 130
Instagram, 133
interest, 44, 224. *See also* interest rates
interest rates, 102, 104–5, 108–9,
144–45, 254n5
and the debt crisis in the Global
South, 263n19
International Clearing Union, 269n20
International Monetary Fund (IMF),
121, 154, 170
internet, x, 71–73, 181–83
capitalism and, 57–58, 92, 216
and death of the liberal individual,
181–83
as digital commons, 71–78, 92,
116–17
digital identity and, 75–78, 181–83
enclosure of (New Enclosures),
74–78, 121
Internet One, 73–74, 92, 116–17

Internet Two, 77–78, 146
Stelarc's Movatar performance (2000),
179–80
See also cloud capital
interoperability, 266n8
iPad, 175
iPhone, 125, 127–29, 135, 173, 175
iPod, 125
Ireland
Amazon headquarters, 111
citizens' assembly (An Tionól
Saoránach), 269n21
iron, 3–10
Iron Age, 7–10, 78, 92, 118
Italian lire, 40
Jameson, Fredric, 24
Japan
and Bretton Woods system, 41–43
Central Bank, 105, 147, 259–60n9
and the Dark Deal, 153
Global Minotaur and, 47, 48
and the Great Financial Crisis (2008),
105
internet in, 72
US-Japan trade and the Plaza Accord
(1985), 160–61, 259–60n9
World War II, 33–34
yen, 40, 103, 160–61, 259–60n9
Jazz Age (1930s–40s), 33
JD.com, 155
Jeff Bezos Expeditions, 131
Jobs, Steve, 127, 133
Johnson, Lyndon, 42, 51
JPMorgan Chase, 114, 193–94
The Junius Pamphlet (Luxemburg), 256n3
Justice League (2017 film), 61
Keynes, John Maynard, 18, 19–20, 219,
265n3, 269n20, 272n10
Kosmos (digital international accounting
unit), 204–5

ABOUT THE AUTHOR

Yanis Varoufakis is an economist, political leader, and the author of numerous bestselling books: *Talking to My Daughter About the Economy*, *Adults in the Room*, a memoir of his time as finance minister of Greece, and an economic history of Europe, *And The Weak Suffer What They Must?* His most recent is *Another Now: A Novel.* Born in Athens in 1961, he was for many years a professor of economics in Britain, Australia, and the USA before he entered politics. He is co-founder of the international grass-roots movement DiEM25 and a Professor of Economics at the University of Athens.